BTEC Introduction

BUSINESS

Hala Seliet

www.heinemann.co.uk
✓ Free online support
✓ Useful weblinks
✓ 24 hour online ordering

01865 888058

Heinemann

Inspiring generations

Heinemann Educational Publishers
Halley Court, Jordan Hill, Oxford OX2 8EJ
Part of Harcourt Education

Heinemann is a registered trademark of
Harcourt Education Limited

Text © Hala Seliet, 2005

First published 2005

10 09 08 07 06 05
10 9 8 7 6 5 4 3 2 1

British Library Cataloguing in Publication Data is available
from the British Library on request.

10-digit ISBN 0 435 40121 1
13-digit ISBN 978 0 435401 21 4

Typeset by Wearset Ltd
Printed by The Bath Press Ltd
Designed by Lorraine Inglis
Cover photo © Powerstock
Picture research by Ginny Stroud Lewis

Websites
Please note that the examples of websites suggested in this book were up to date at
the time of writing. We have made all links available on the Heinemann website at
www.heinemann.co.uk/hotlinks. When you access the site, the express code is
1211P.

Contents

Y077 08

Acknowledgements

The author would like to thank her daughters and her husband for their patience and support throughout the writing of this book. She would also like to thank all who have helped in the writing and production of this book. Special thanks to Anna Fabrizio, Jenni Johns, Stig Vatland and Frances Ridley.

The author and publishers are grateful to those who have given permission to reproduce material.

MBA Publishing Limited, p20; J Sainsbury plc, p55, p84, p204; Co-op Group, p119; Tesco plc, p204.

Photos
Peter Newark, p20; Getty Images, p46; Corbis, p53; Alamy Images/Thinkstock, p82; Alamy Images/Sally and Richard Greenhill, p92; Alamy Images/The Photolibrary Wales, p116; Alamy Images/Ace Stock Limited, p118; Alamy Images/The Photolibrary Wales, p157; Corbis, p175; Alamy Images/Michael Booth, p194; Getty Images/Photodisc, p198; Getty Images, p215; Alamy Images, p226; Getty Images/Photodisc, p232.

Every effort has been made to contact copyright holders of material reproduced in this book. Any omissions will be rectified in subsequent printings if notice is given to the publishers.

Introduction

This book has been written for students who are working towards the BTEC Introductory Certificate or Diploma in Business, Retail and Administration. It covers the three core units, the three personal skills units and the four option units for successful completion of this award. The core units provide an introduction to business, retail and administration; the personal skills units help you to prepare for working in the industry; and the option units offer you more insight into the working world of business, retail and administration.

The qualification

If you are working towards the Certificate you will need to successfully complete four units: Units 1 and 3, one personal skills unit and one option unit. If you are working towards the Diploma you will need to successfully complete eight units: Units 1–3, two personal skills units and three option units.

• *Assessment and grading* •

All units except the personal skills units are graded as pass, merit or distinction. Personal skills units are only graded as a pass.

For the Certificate, Unit 1 is externally assessed. For the Diploma, Units 1 and 2 are externally assessed. This means you will complete a project set by Edexcel, the awarding body of this qualification. You can complete the project over a period of time, giving you plenty of chances to have your work checked and reviewed by your tutor. You can complete the project in a variety of ways, so choose a way which best suits your working style.

The remaining units are internally assessed. This means, to pass the unit, you will complete an assignment set and marked by your tutor.

You must achieve at least a pass grade in every unit to gain the qualification. The qualification is made up of units of 30 and 60 hours of learning. It is the grades awarded for the 60-hour units that will determine your grade for the qualification. For example, if you are taking the Certificate, your grade will be decided by your best performance of the two 60-hour units. If you are taking the Diploma, your grade will be determined by your two best performances in the four 60-hour units.

The personal skills units and externally assessed units don't contribute towards your qualification grade.

Special features in the book

There are a number of features throughout the text to encourage you to think about the business, retail and administration sector. They also encourage you to find out information, undertake activities and gather evidence towards your assessment.

Glossary: Key terms are picked out and explained where they are used for the first time. You can find all of these key terms in the glossary at the back of the book.

Case studies: These are real-life (or simulated) situations involving customers and people working in the sector. The questions that follow each case study give you the opportunity to look at important issues and widen your understanding of the subject.

Give it a go: Relevant issues are raised for you to discuss or work through either with a partner, in groups or on your own.

*What if?...*These present situations which may arise and provide you with opportunities for problem solving.

Think about it: These are thought-provoking questions about issues or dilemmas that are relevant in business, retail and administration. They can be done individually or in groups.

Evidence activity: These are activities that let you show that you understand the work required in the unit. By working through these you will gain evidence to meet the grading criteria for each unit at pass, merit or distinction (pass grade only for personal skills units). All the learning outcomes for a unit are covered in the End of Unit Assignments.

I wish you the best of luck on your course as you begin your journey towards a career in business, retail and administration. I hope you find this book interesting and useful.

Hala Seliet

unit 1

Starting work in business, retail and administration

In this unit you will explore starting work in the business, retail and administration sector. This sector covers a wide range of opportunities and, to begin with, you will find out about the different kinds of job opportunities that exist, including different roles, types of job and the personal qualities needed to work in the sector.

You will also learn about the different types of organisations in business, retail and administration, for example, sole traders, partnerships and limited companies, as well as the functional areas within organisations. You will then find out the effects of an organisation's location on the business it carries out.

The unit ends with a look at how your choice of job will affect your lifestyle and also how your lifestyle could affect your choice of job, now and in the future.

To complete this unit you must:

- ▭ find out about the different types of jobs available within the business, retail and administration sectors
- ▭ explore how the type of organisation may affect your choice of job
- ▭ consider the relationship between lifestyle and job choices.

Different types of jobs

In every industry or **sector**, there are a great many kinds of jobs to choose from. There are many personal qualities and skills that are relevant to all jobs, but most jobs will also need you to have some specific skills or knowledge. It is useful to understand the different jobs available and which ones interest you most, so that you can direct your career path successfully.

Job roles

Within the business, retail and administration sectors there are many different job roles available. Some of the more common of these roles are outlined below, but there may well be other roles that would interest you.

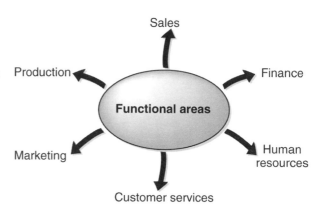

▲ **The main functional areas of a business**

• *Shop assistant* •

Sales assistants usually work behind the counter or on the shop floor in retail outlets. They offer advice and information to help people find and choose goods. In smaller shops they may also be responsible for taking payments from customers and arranging delivery of large items as well as setting up guarantees and warranties for expensive items. They may need to use a computer, an electronic till and sometimes also barcode scanners and credit or debit card processing machines.

• *Administration assistant* •

Administration assistants are responsible for a variety of duties necessary to run an office or organisation efficiently. They serve as information managers for the office where they work. They will almost always need to use a computer in their work. Some examples of the work an administration assistant might do include:

- *organising and maintaining paper and electronic files*
- *arranging meetings*
- *handling travel arrangements*
- *typing and distributing memos, letters, faxes and emails*
- *conducting research*
- *providing information by telephone, post and email.*

◀ **Administration assistants need to be calm and well organised**

● *Stock control* ●

Working in stock control may involve a combination of computer work and manual lifting and moving stock around. Computers may be used to monitor and keep track of stock. The job may involve picking items from stock and packing them for delivery as well as unloading deliveries. It may also involve placing orders for new stock.

● *Cashier* ●

Cashiers work on tills in retail outlets. They usually need to use electronic tills and barcode scanners as well as credit and debit card machines. They are responsible for taking payment from customers for their purchases. Sometimes cashiers may also need to pack customers' goods for them.

● *Clerk* ●

A clerk's work can involve:

▭ *use of computerised payroll systems and report writing tools*

▭ *calculating and issuing pay by cash, cheque or electronic transfer*

▭ *making sure tax and National Insurance payments are deducted correctly*

⊃ *processing and recording holiday, sick and maternity pay and expenses*

⊃ *calculating overtime and shift payments.*

Most clerks, these days, need to work with computers, although some businesses still use manual accounting systems.

● *Finance assistant* ●

The main duty of a finance assistant is to assist the financial controller in the production of the monthly accounts and to be responsible for the ledgers. They must also ensure that all purchase invoices are correctly coded and added to the computer system and that sales invoices are raised on a timely basis and sent to customers. Most finance assistants need to work with computers.

● *Customer service* ●

Customer service assistants can work in retail outlets at the customer service point or in businesses or other organisations on phone lines, or answering email enquiries. Their main role is to answer customers' enquiries and to deal with and resolve any complaints that customers have. Most customer service assistants will need to work with computers.

▲ **Customer service staff use various ways to communicate**

• *Receptionist* •

The duties of a receptionist will vary according to the organisation, but will usually include meeting and greeting clients when they arrive and answering the phone and directing calls. They may also deal with other administrative tasks such as handling the post, filing, distributing and managing petty cash, word processing and managing databases. Receptionists will often need to use computers and also telephone switchboards. Examples of organisations that employ receptionists include hotels, factories, hospitals, doctors' surgeries, firms of solicitors, schools and hairdressers.

• *Data processing* •

Data processors work with computers to enter data – usually into databases. The data will vary widely according to the organisation and job role, but will usually involve numeric and/or textual data. Accurate and fast typing skills are usually a requirement of the job.

• *Contact centre assistant* •

Contact centre assistants are similar to customer service assistants. However, their role is usually limited to taking note of a customer's enquiry and then finding the right member of staff to deal with that enquiry. They are not usually responsible for providing any information to customers directly. Sometimes they will redirect a caller immediately to the correct member of staff and other times they will take down the details and arrange for the member of staff to contact the customer later. Contact centre assistants usually need to work with computers and telephone switchboards.

GIVE IT A GO: job roles

1 Choose one of the job roles described above.
2 Interview someone who works in this role to find out more about what the job involves.

Type of job

We have seen that there are many different jobs roles available, each involving different tasks. There are also different types of job in the business, retail and administration sectors.

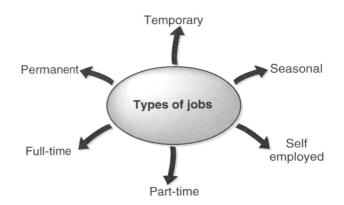

▶ **Not everyone works nine to five**

● *Part-time* ●

A part-time employee is generally someone who works less than the standard working week within the organisation. For example, a receptionist who works three days a week and a sales assistant who works five mornings a week are both part-time employees.

● *Full-time* ●

A **full-time** employee is generally someone who works the standard working hours per week within the organisation. For example, a data processor who works from 9 am to 5 pm Mondays through Fridays and a customer service assistant who works 2 pm to 10 pm Wednesdays through Sundays are both full-time employees. A full-time working week can involve working anything from 36 to 48 hours.

● *Temporary* ●

Temporary work is where someone is hired for a limited period of time. This could be just for a few days to cover for someone who is on holiday or off sick; or it could be for a month or two to fulfil a large order; or it could be for six months or longer, for example, to cover maternity leave.

● *Seasonal* ●

Many businesses and organisations need extra staff at certain times of the year to cover busy periods. For example, farmers may take on extra people to harvest the crops, retail outlets may take on extra staff at Christmas or during the January or summer sales and hotels and restaurants may take on extra staff over the summer months to cater for larger numbers of tourists.

● *Permanent* ●

A **permanent** job is one where there is no fixed time for the employment to end. An employee will work in a permanent job for an indefinite period of time, for example, until they decide to move to a different job or until the employer **restructures** the organisation and needs to make some staff **redundant**.

● *Freelance* ●

Freelancers tend to do work for a number of different organisations. They charge an hourly rate or a fixed rate for each job. Many freelancers work from home, although some may go into the organisations to do the work. Examples of types of work freelancers do include consultancy, book-keeping, editing, programming and graphic design.

GLOSSARY

Full-time means working a full week (e.g. 9–5, Monday–Friday).

Temporary work is short-term work (e.g. over the summer holidays or for six months to cover maternity leave).

Permanent means there is no fixed time to end (e.g. permanent job).

Restructuring is when the structure or organisation is changed (e.g. having fewer managers and more operatives).

Redundancy happens when a company needs to cut down on staff (it often comes with a lump sum to make up for losing the job).

Freelance work is done by a self-employed person, who does jobs for a number of different individuals or organisations (e.g. photographers, illustrators, web designers).

● *Skilled work* ●

Skilled work usually requires some level of off-the-job training as well as use of judgement. Examples of skilled work could include book-keeping, computer programming, teaching and nursing. There are varying levels of skilled work – some only require a few hours or days of training, while others may require a number of years at university.

● *Unskilled work* ●

Unskilled work usually requires little or no judgment and involves simple duties that can be learnt quickly on-the-job. Some unskilled work requires strength and physical fitness. Examples of unskilled work could include road-sweeping, cleaning, labouring on a building site and packing and unpacking deliveries.

● *Operative* ●

Operative roles involve tasks that have a direct connection to the core purpose of the business. Example of operative tasks include receiving materials, processing orders, production and distribution of products and often the operation of the equipment used to manufacture them.

● *Supervisory* ●

Supervisory roles involve organising the work that needs to be done and the other members of staff who will need to do that work (i.e. the operatives).

Supervisors share many common duties, for example, they:

▢ *perform administrative tasks to ensure that staff can work efficiently*

▢ *ensure equipment and machinery used in their departments is in good working order*

▢ *help train new employees in organisational and office procedures (e.g. teach new employees how to use the telephone system and operate office equipment).*

THINK ABOUT IT

Think about all the jobs you have done. What types of job were they? What type of job do you think you could do? What type of job do you think you would like to do?

Personal qualities

While certain jobs will require specific skills, there are a number of personal qualities that most employers look for in an employee,

GLOSSARY

Skilled work is work that requires some training and/or judgement.

Unskilled work is work that involves little or no judgement and only simple tasks.

GLOSSARY

Operative tasks are involved with the core function of the business.

A **supervisor** is the person who tells you what tasks you need to do and keeps an eye on you (and other staff) to make sure there are no problems.

regardless of the level that the employee will be working at. These personal qualities include:

- *punctuality*
- *honesty*
- *personality*
- *efficiency*
- *manual skills*
- *using initiative*

- *responsibility*
- *following instructions*
- *teamwork*
- *communication skills*
- *IT skills.*

• *Punctuality* •

Good **punctuality** means turning up on time (or even a little early) at the start of the working day. It also means arriving at meetings at the right time (or, again, a little early). If you are responsible for opening a shop, it means opening the shop at the start of business hours. If you have told a customer you will telephone them between 2 pm and 3 pm, it means doing so and not calling at 3.05 pm. An employer needs to rely on you and cannot do so if you are always five minutes (or an hour!) late.

• *Honesty* •

Honesty means not telling lies. Calling in sick because you don't feel like going to work is not honest. Telling a customer that a cheque is in the post when it hasn't yet been sent out is not honest. Saying you have ten GCSEs on your CV when you only have eight is being dishonest. If you tell lies at work, you will almost always be found out. An employer needs to rely on you and will find this difficult if you are found to be dishonest.

• *Personality* •

Employers look for people with the right personality for the job. For example, in sales and customer services a polite and enthusiastic personality is important, while in administration they will look for people who are happy to get on with the job without moaning about it. Employers usually want employees who find it easy to get along with others and bring **commitment** to their job.

• *Efficiency* •

Efficiency means doing the work to as high a standard as you can and doing so in the required amount of time. It means getting all the tasks done that you need to do within the time available. Being efficient does not mean doing a job as quickly as possible and making lots of mistakes because you did not spend enough time on it. To be efficient you need to balance the time you spend against the quality of the work you do.

Manual skills

Many employers will look for employees who have some basic manual skills. Examples of useful **manual skills** could include an ability to lift and carry boxes or large packages, an ability to sweep and mop the floor and an ability to climb step ladders to reach products or files that are high up.

Using initiative

Employers want employees who are happy to get on with the job, without asking what they should be doing every five minutes. Once you have been trained in the basic procedures and tasks of a job, you should be able to undertake necessary tasks without specifically being told to do so. For example, if something has been spilt on the floor, you could use your **initiative** to go and mop it up. If you have finished typing up a letter for someone, you could spend five minutes updating the diary.

Responsibility

Employees must be willing to accept **responsibility** for their own work. Employees need to plan their work and use their time and resources efficiently. Being responsible also involves doing your work, rather than chatting to your friends on the phone; coming into work, rather than taking a 'sickie' to go to the beach; finishing tasks on time and not forgetting to do them.

Following instructions

Employers need their employees to be able to follow instructions. These instructions might be those given verbally or in writing by a supervisor, or, for example, instructions in a manual or house style guide.

Teamwork

Teamwork involves getting on well with other people, taking on and completing specific tasks as part of a team, working cooperatively and accepting constructive criticism. Some element of teamwork is necessary in most jobs.

Communication skills

Communication isn't just about the words a person uses or the tone he or she says them in. Communication is about making a connection with another human being. Communication skills include good use of language, facial expression, being able to listen and respond and directing the level of your language to the person you are communicating with. Communication skills also include a good use of spelling and grammar in written documents.

● *IT skills* ●

Many jobs these days involve some work with computers and some jobs, such as data processing, can involve spending most of your time at a computer. Employers look for employees who have at least basic IT skills, which generally include the ability to use word processing, spreadsheet and database software, email programs and the ability to browse and search for information on the Internet.

... *you had to list your personal qualities?*

1 Look back at the personal qualities described above.

2 Which of these qualities do you have?

3 Which of these qualities do you think you should work on?

4 Ask a friend to look at your list and tell you whether they agree with you.

5 Can you think of any other personal qualities you have? Would they be useful in any of the job roles you have learnt about?

▲ **Ingredients for success**

EVIDENCE ACTIVITY

Different types of jobs

1 Look in your local newspaper and/or your local job centre and find three different job advertisements within the business, retail and administration sectors.

2 For each job, look at the advertisement and note down what skills and qualities the employer is looking for.

3 Choose one of the jobs that interests you and phone or write to the organisation to ask for a job description or person specification and note down what other skills and qualities are needed for the job.

4 If possible, talk to someone who does this job or one very similar and ask them about their working day and their main responsibilities.

5 List the personal skills and qualities needed for this job that you already have and then list those that you would need to work on or gain in order to do the job.

Different types of organisation

Britain is said to have a **mixed economy** because it consists of both private enterprise (privately owned businesses) and public enterprise (businesses owned by the government).

Types of organisation

There are four main forms of business ownership in the private sector of the economy:

▭ *sole traders*

▭ *partnerships*

▭ *limited companies (private limited companies and public limited companies)*

▭ *franchises.*

● *Sole trader* ●

A **sole trader** is a single person who owns a business (known as the **proprietor**) and who is personally liable for any of the business's debts. Examples of sole traders include small shops, plumbers, electricians and cleaners.

> **GLOSSARY**
>
> A **mixed economy** is an economy that includes private and public businesses.

> **GLOSSARY**
>
> A **sole trader** is a single individual who owns and runs a business (e.g. small shops, plumbers).
>
> A **proprietor** is a sole trader (the person who runs the business).

• *Partnership* •

A **partnership** is similar to a sole trader, but there are more people to share responsibility for the business (and responsibility for the debts). Typical partnerships include accountants, solicitors, doctors and dentists. In a partnership, the partners can share their expertise and skills. They can also share the workload, organising work rotas to allow for time off and holidays. As well as sharing in the debts, the partners also share in any profits.

• *Limited companies* •

The word 'company' suggests a group of people who have come together to set up a business. A **limited company** consists of:

▱ *shareholders who provide money and invest in the business*

▱ *a board of directors who run the company*

▱ *employees who carry out the work.*

There are two types of limited company – private (Ltd) and public (Plc).

Private limited company (Ltd)
Private limited companies have 'Ltd' after their name. They are typically smaller than public companies although some, like *Portakabin* and *Penguin Books* are very large. Shares in a private company can only be bought and sold with the permission of the board of directors.

Public limited company (Plc)
Public limited companies have 'Plc' after their name. Public companies are well-known national and international companies like *Vodafone*, *Barclays* and *BT*. The shares of public companies like *Cadbury Schweppes* and *BT* are traded on the stock exchange.

• *Franchise* •

This is one of the fastest growing sectors of the economy. In a **franchise**, the franchisee pays to use the name and the products or services of the franchiser, who receives a lump sum and a share of the profits of the business. Franchising offers a 'ready-made' business opportunity for those who have the capital and are willing to work hard, but may not have a new business idea. Franchising is common in the fast-food and restaurant industry, for example *Pizza Hut* and *Burger King* are both franchises. Another well-known example of a franchise is *The Body Shop*.

• *Local authority* •

In the UK, certain services such as refuse collection and road maintenance are the responsibility of locally elected councils. Local councils receive money from the central government and from council taxes paid by local residents. Local councils often subsidise loss-making activities such as local parks or rural bus services, which provide a real benefit to the community.

• *Government agency* •

Government agencies are administrative units of government and include, for example, the *Department of Health*, the *National Health Service*, the *Department for Education and Skills* and the *Prison Service*.

• *Non-profit-making* •

Charities are one example of a non-profit-making organisation and are part of what is called the voluntary sector. They exist to promote and support a cause or activity and, as such, do not have a profit motive. That is not to say that they do not make profits. In fact, many charities have subsidiaries that sell goods or services, but they reinvest their profits in order to support the main charitable aim. Some examples of charities are *Oxfam*, the *NSPCC*, *Amnesty International* and *Cancer Research UK*.

• *E-business* •

E-business generally refers to businesses that sell products and services over the Internet. Some businesses, such as *Amazon.co.uk*, only use the Internet to sell their products, while others, such as *Dixons*, *Homebase* and *Office World*, use the Internet in addition to their shops.

> **GLOSSARY**
>
> An **e-business** is a business carried out electronically (e.g. using the Internet).

• *Size of business* •

In the UK, businesses range in size from small to medium to large. Examples of small businesses could be a plumber working as a sole trader, who does not employ any staff, or a small shop with maybe five employees. Examples of medium-sized businesses could be a gym that employs a number of fitness trainers, administrative assistants, managers, cleaners and so on, or a gardening centre that employs sales assistants, gardeners, cashiers and so on. Examples of large businesses could be a bank or an insurance company that employs thousands of employees.

• *Types of customer* •

Different businesses will have different types of customer. For example, the customers of supermarkets, restaurants and leisure centres will be members of the public. The customers of factories and office suppliers will be other businesses. The customers of banks, insurance companies and solicitors could be members of the public or other businesses.

GLOSSARY

Internal customers are colleagues and people in other departments.

Businesses will also have **internal customers** – for example, the person in the company next in line to receive the product, such as sales representatives. Some businesses might also sell to intermediate customers, for example, distributors who buy large quantities of products and sell them on to retailers or other businesses.

CASE STUDY – BRIKBY STORES

Francis is the owner of a small corner shop, *Brikby Stores*. He is a sole trader. His shop is open from 6.30 am to 8 pm and he only takes a one-hour break each day. Francis employs Sarah to help him clean the shop and serve customers, but she only works two days a week from 9 am to 4 pm. When Francis started the business, he invested £10,000 to buy goods, fittings and equipment. At the moment the business has debts of £50,000. Francis is considering asking his brother to become a partner in the business.

Questions

1 List two advantages and two disadvantages of Francis being a sole trader.

2 What would be the advantages for Francis of taking his brother on as a partner? What would be the disadvantages?

3 If you were Francis' brother, would you agree to becoming a partner?

▲ **Francis works long hours to make his business viable**

Functional areas

Even for small businesses with only one or two employees there are different kinds of task which must be carried out if the firm is to be successful. The main functional areas are:

- *human resources*
- *finance*
- *administration*
- *production/service*
- *marketing*
- *sales*
- *customer service.*

In larger businesses, each of these functional areas is likely to have its own department.

● *Human resources* ●

The **human resources** function involves ensuring that the business recruits the right people for each job. It also involves ensuring that training and development are provided to employees as necessary and keeping records of all employees, past and present.

● *Finance* ●

The **finance** function deals with all financial matters within the business. Finance or **accounting** tasks can include:

- *obtaining financial information from different departments*
- *recording financial information (commonly known as book keeping)*
- *working out payment of staff wages/salaries*
- *providing information about the amount of money (capital) needed to run the business efficiently*
- *analysing and interpreting financial information*
- *providing information about the business performance to teams and shareholders.*

● *Administration* ●

The **administration** function deals with the internal housekeeping of an organisation. The main role of the administration department is to provide centralised office services for all other departments in the business. This may include:

- *collecting and distributing mail*
- *dealing with and responding to enquiries*
- *organising meetings*
- *typing letters, memos and faxes*
- *filing and keeping records*
- *cleaning and maintaining the workplace*
- *photocopying documents*
- *dealing with emails*
- *operating the switchboard.*

● *Production/service* ●

In businesses which **manufacture** products, the **core function** is known as the production function. In businesses which provide a service, it is known as the service function. For example, in a chocolate factory, production will involve turning raw material (e.g. cocoa beans, sugar, etc.) into finished products. For an insurance company, the core function will be providing the insurance service. The tasks carried out within the production/service function will vary depending on what the business does.

▲ **Factory production lines manufacture goods for sale**

• *Marketing and sales* •

In some business the marketing and sales functions are combined, while in others they are two separate departments staffed by different people.

Marketing

The **marketing** function involves identifying and satisfying customer needs and wants by carrying out market research and promoting new products. Marketing tasks can include:

▭ *sending out questionnaires to customers*

▭ *organising direct mail campaigns*

▭ *organising advertising campaigns*

▭ *coordinating special offers.*

GLOSSARY

The **marketing** department deals with publicity and finding out about customer needs.

Sales

The **sales** function involves identifying potential customers and encouraging them to buy the product or service. The role includes direct interaction with customers and may also include providing some element of customer service. In retail outlets, the sales function is provided by sales assistants. In many other businesses, the sales function is provided by sales representatives who travel around the country visiting customers and prospective customers.

GLOSSARY

The **sales** department deals with selling products or services.

• *Customer service* •

The **customer service** function involves providing information and advice to customers, dealing with customer queries and complaints and may also include providing after-sale service in the form of technical help or organising replacement items. Large businesses may have a customer service helpline and/or website, while in smaller businesses the customer service role may be carried out by sales staff. Many supermarkets and other large retail outlets have a customer service desk.

GLOSSARY

The **customer service** department deals with customers, providing information, service and advice.

GIVE IT A GO: functional areas

1 Visit a business or organisation in your local area.
2 Find out what the different functional areas are within the organisation.
3 Find out how many people work in each of the functional areas.
4 Find out what qualifications you need to start work in each functional area.

Location

The location of a business is simply where it is. The location of a business can be very important. Different elements of location include:

- *the geographical location*
- *regional variations, for example, whether it is in the north or the south, in Scotland or in Wales, and so on*
- *whether it is European or international, or whether it is just domestic (in the UK only)*
- *how accessible it is to its customers*
- *how close it is to home (both for the employees and the customers).*

• *Geographical* •

The geographical **location** of a business means whether it is in a city, whether it is urban (in a town), rural (in a village or the countryside) or coastal (by the sea).

City

Locating in a city can be expensive, but it can also provide more access to passing customers as well as a wider base of potential employees. City locations can also bring prestige or may just be the traditional location for a particular type of business.

Urban

Like cities, **urban** locations can also be expensive, but provide a good customer and employee base. Urban locations are generally cheaper than city locations and can be more accessible for deliveries, staff and customers than rural locations.

Rural

Rural locations are usually cheaper than urban or city locations. However, they are not generally suitable for large retail businesses as there are not enough passing customers. Rural locations can be popular in certain service industries, especially for smaller businesses that do not need a wide staff base.

Coastal

A coastal location can provide good access to and from ports and so is particularly relevant to a business in the import and export sector. Coastal locations are also popular for businesses in the tourism industry, such as hotels and restaurants.

• *Regional variations* •

Regional variations can affect the cost of running the business and also the availability and variety of staff. Locating in the south of England, especially the south-east, can be very expensive, compared to locating in some of the northern towns and cities. Locating somewhere where unemployment is high can provide a wider base of staff – often at a cheaper cost than locating in a more prosperous area.

• *European* •

The European Union, the Single Market and the introduction of the Euro (European currency) have created many opportunities for businesses to operate throughout Europe. Attractions include:

- *no trading barriers*
- *free movement of workers between all countries in the European Union*
- *easier payment transactions between countries that use the Euro*
- *free movement of goods between countries in the European Union.*

• *International* •

Large **multi-national companies** operate in many different countries. These companies benefit from a very wide customer base, a large variety of staff and the opportunity to locate manufacturing plants closer to the raw materials.

• *Accessibility* •

A business needs to be accessible (easy to reach) to its employees, its suppliers and, of course, its customers. Retail outlets need to be accessible to the general public, for example, on high streets and in retail parks. Employees will find it easier to access businesses that are located near public transport or main roads.

• *Proximity to home* •

As you have seen, it is important for a business to be accessible to both its employees and its customers. Distance can also be important. Customers may be willing to travel further to buy some products but not others. For example, a customer does not want to travel far to buy a loaf of bread, but may be prepared to travel further to buy a new car.

CASE STUDY – CADBURY

Choosing the right location for Café Cadbury

◀ Location is important for *Café Cadbury*

Café Cadbury has a target market of 25–45-year-old females with high disposable incomes who are regular café users. With this knowledge, the company is able to research the right locations. The location of *Café Cadbury* must meet the following criteria:

- a prime site location in the main shopping area of a city with 100,000 people
- a double shop frontage for maximum visibility
- a high number of shoppers all year round – average weekly footfall of 50,000, peaking at 5000 per hour during the week and at 10,000 per hour on Saturdays

- a size between 2000 and 2500 square feet
- planning permission for catering and retailing.

Find out more at the *Cadbury* website – a link is available at **www.heinemann.co.uk/hotlinks** (express code 1211P).

Questions

1 How did *Cadbury* choose the location of its café?

2 How important are locational factors for *Cadbury*?

EVIDENCE ACTIVITY

Different types of organisation

1 Find three examples of each of the following, within the business, retail and administration sectors:
   • sole traders
   • partnerships
   • private limited companies
   • public limited companies
   • franchises
   • local authorities
   • government agencies
   • non-profit-making organisations
   • e-businesses

2 For each of the businesses, identify where it is located and what products it sells or services it provides.

Lifestyle

Your lifestyle will affect the job you choose and your job will also affect your lifestyle.

Lifestyle

• *Effect of lifestyle on job choice* •

In deciding the kind of job you want to do, you need to take into account the lifestyle you would prefer. For example, if you attend or play in regular sporting fixtures, **shift-work** might make this difficult. If you have a young family (or are planning to start one soon) a job with **flexible** working hours or the opportunity to work part-time might be more suitable.

Your beliefs may also play a role in your job choice – for example, if you are a vegetarian, you might find it difficult to work for a company that undertakes animal testing, or in a meat factory. Your beliefs might also lead you to work in a particular sector, such as charities or the health care sector.

• *Individual wants and needs* •

Thinking about your likes and dislikes can be a good starting point. Do you want to spend your working life indoors/at sea/working with

> **GLOSSARY**
>
> **Shift-work** means working non-normal hours (e.g. 2 pm to 10 pm, 10 pm to 6 am); it often involves working one shift for one week and then a different one the next week.
>
> Being **flexible** means being able and willing to make changes.

people? Does the idea of giving a presentation fill you with excitement or dread? Would close contact with computers fulfil or frustrate you? Once you start asking and answering such questions you begin to eliminate the poor matches and start to focus on possibilities.

● *Flexibility of location* ●

If where you live is a central factor influencing your career decisions then at least you know where to start looking! However, there may be constraints. There will possibly be fewer jobs, less choice and, for certain opportunities, more competition. What you want may not even exist in the area you intend to live in, so you may have to broaden your scope both geographically and in terms of the jobs you will consider. You will need to be flexible both in your choice of career and in the skills you have to offer.

● *Social aspirations* ●

Think about what sort of person you want to be. Do you want to just make enough money to get by or do you want to rise up the career ladder quickly? Do you want to have a big house and a flashy car? Do you want to go out for drinks or meals with your friends or have dinner parties? What sort of people do you feel comfortable with? Answering these questions can help point you in the direction of the job that will be right for you.

● *Limitations of working hours* ●

Do you have any personal commitments that might limit the hours you can work? For example, if you have a young family, you may need to be available for taking children to school and collecting them. If you have relatives to care for, you may need to be available at short notice to take them to the hospital. You might play in a sports team every weekend, which would mean that you would not be able to work at weekends.

● *Personal relationships* ●

Your personal relationships could have an effect on your choice of job as well. For example, you might choose to work close to friends. You might not get along with your family and so choose to work further away. You might have a partner and/or children to think about – will the job you choose allow you to spend quality time with them?

● *Other/social reasons for being at work* ●

There may be other lifestyle factors that affect your choice of job, for example, what you hope to get out of your working life. Do you want to work in a business where you can make lots of friends, or would you prefer to work alone?

WHAT if?

... you could have your ideal lifestyle?

1 What would your ideal lifestyle be?

2 Can you think of any jobs that would fit this lifestyle?

3 Could you do any of these jobs now, or would you need further training or experience?

Job

● *Effect of job choice on lifestyle* ●

Whatever job you choose, it will inevitably have an effect on your lifestyle. You will be committed to working certain hours. Your income must cover your cost of living. It will affect your ability to socialise and to buy necessities as well as luxuries. Your job may be very tiring and limit the activities that you can undertake outside of work.

● *Shift working* ●

Shift working will have a very strong effect on your lifestyle. It will be difficult, if not impossible, to commit to any regular activities. Your sleeping patterns may need to be adjusted on a weekly basis. You might find it difficult to fit in shopping, paying bills and so on, without very careful planning.

● *Flexitime* ●

Flexitime involves working a specific number of hours, but having the ability to choose when those hours are. For example, you could start work at 11 am and finish at 7 pm instead of working 9 am to 5 pm. Flexitime is particularly useful for employees who have children or other relatives to care for. It can also be useful for employees who commute to work because they can avoid peak charges on public transport or avoid the rush hour.

GLOSSARY

Flexitime is the ability to start and finish work at different times (as long as an agreed number of hours are worked).

● *Hours of work* ●

Your hours of work will affect your social life. For example, if you work evenings, you may find it difficult to arrange time out with friends. Your hours of work can also affect how you organise your daily life. For example, will you be able to go to the bank or shops during opening hours or will you need to find other ways to do these tasks?

● *Starting and finishing times* ●

Starting and finishing times will affect your sleep patterns. For example, if you have to start work very early in the morning, you will need to go to bed earlier than you might prefer.

● *Stress levels* ●

Some jobs will have higher stress levels than others, but most jobs can bring some element of stress. If you have deadlines to meet, you may feel stressed. If you make a mistake or have trouble getting on with a colleague these can also make you feel stressed. When you are stressed about your work, you will usually find it difficult to stop thinking about the problem, even outside work hours. Stress can affect your mental and physical health and cause you to get ill more often.

● *Personal and professional ambitions* ●

Your personal and professional ambitions may change as you progress in your job. When you start, you might only be looking to earn enough money to be able to get your own place or pay for holidays. As you become more interested in the job, you may find, for example, that you want to train further, so that you can get ahead in your career. The people you work with may affect your personal ambitions, too. For example, you might hear about the wonderful holidays they have been on, and realise that you would like the opportunity to travel.

● *Personal skills and qualities* ●

If you enjoy your job, you are more likely to develop your personal skills and qualities in doing the job. If you find your job very stressful or boring, you may start to resent it and your skills and qualities could suffer.

● *Professional qualifications* ●

Some jobs provide the opportunity to gain professional qualifications while working. These can increase your career prospects and also your earning potential.

● *Personal qualities* ●

Your job may provide the opportunity to improve some of your personal qualities. For example, a job in sales is likely to improve your ability to get on with other people and to deal with the public. A job in administration could improve your organisational and **time-management** skills.

● *Physical and other limitations* ●

Some jobs may not be suitable for people with certain physical or other limitations. For example, if you have very poor vision that is not corrected by glasses, you would not be able to do a job that involved driving. Asthmatics might not be able to do jobs where they are exposed to a lot of dust or animal hairs. Jobs that require a lot of heavy lifting and carrying need good physical strength.

GLOSSARY

Time-management means keeping on top of tasks and making sure you meet deadlines.

● *Qualification levels* ●

Some jobs require a specific level of qualifications. For example, many jobs require a C or above in GCSE English and Maths, or a key skill qualification in Communication or Application of Number. Other jobs may require NVQs or BTECs, while others may require university degrees. If the job you really want to do requires higher level qualifications than you have, then you need to think about how to gain those qualifications, or find out if there are similar jobs which you are qualified to do.

 THINK ABOUT IT

Think about the jobs or work experience you have done. How did they affect your lifestyle?

EVIDENCE ACTIVITY  **P5**

Lifestyle

1 Think of three jobs that you would like to do.

2 For each one, identify any effects the job would have on your lifestyle.

3 For each one, identify any aspects of your own lifestyle that would make the job particularly suitable for you, as well as any lifestyle factors that would make it difficult for you to do the job.

▲ **Your desired lifestyle may affect your choice of job**

END OF UNIT ASSIGNMENT

Task 1

1 Choose three job roles that interest you within the business, retail and administration sectors.

2 For each one, describe what the job role involves.

3 For each one, describe the skills and qualities needed to perform the job.

4 Choose the job role that most appeals to you and explain why it requires the specific skills and qualities that you outlined above.

Task 2

1 Choose three different organisations within the business, retail and administration sectors of different types (e.g. a sole trader, a limited company and a non-profit-making company) where you would like to work.

2 For each one, describe the type of business and the functional areas within that business (make sure you fully describe the core production/service function of the business).

Task 3

1 Choose three different job roles that interest you.

2 For each one, describe how your lifestyle would be affected by working in that job role.

3 Explain why your lifestyle would be affected by the organisation you choose to work for.

unit 2

• •

Working in business, retail and administration

In this unit you will learn about working in the business, retail and administration sectors. You will find out about different terms and conditions that may apply, including benefits. You will learn about what you might expect from the induction process when you start work and examine a number of different procedures that an employer may have in place for assessing staff development. You will also find out about disciplinary procedures and the processes and methods of ending employment.

To complete this unit you must:

⮑ consider the terms and conditions of different types of jobs
⮑ find out about the induction process of a job
⮑ examine the procedures in place for monitoring performance.

Terms and conditions

All jobs will have certain **terms and conditions**. These will include how much and how you are paid, what hours you are expected to work and any **benefits** that come with the job.

GLOSSARY

Terms and conditions are details of your rights and responsibilities within a contract.

Benefits are additional services on top of pay (employment) or money from the government for people who do not have enough money to survive (unemployment).

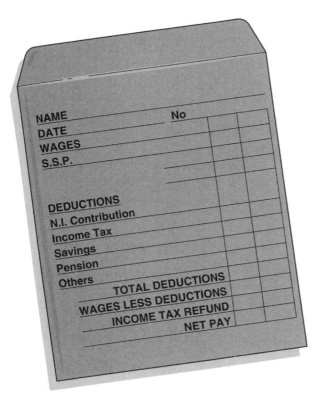

NAME _____ No _____
DATE _____
WAGES _____
S.S.P. _____

DEDUCTIONS
N.I. Contribution
Income Tax
Savings
Pension
Others
          TOTAL DEDUCTIONS
     WAGES LESS DEDUCTIONS
        INCOME TAX REFUND
                    NET PAY

▲ A payslip or wages envelope includes all elements of tax, deductions and wages or salary

Pay

Different organisations will have different methods of payment and different employees within an organisation may be paid at different intervals.

● *Hourly or salaried* ●

Some employees are paid an hourly rate. For example, someone who is paid £6 an hour and works 35 hours a week, will earn £210 a week (or around £910 a month). Other employees are paid according to an annual **salary**. For example, someone who has a salary of £15,000 a year, will earn about £250 a week (or £1250 a month).

● *Weekly or monthly* ●

Employees are usually paid either weekly or monthly. Usually salaried employees are paid on a monthly basis and employees paid an hourly rate receive their **wages** once a week.

GLOSSARY

Salary means the amount of money you are paid each year (which is usually split into 12 monthly payments).

Wages means the money you get for doing a job (usually paid weekly).

BACS is a method of paying individuals and businesses electronically.

● *Method of payment* ●

The main methods of payment are cash, cheque and bank credit transfer (BACS).

Cash

Cash payment is more common for employees who are paid by the hour and receive their wages once a week. The wages will often come in a wages envelope, on which is written the hourly rate, how many hours were worked and how much money has been deducted (e.g. for income tax and National Insurance).

Bank credit transfer (BACS)

Payment by **BACS** is very common these days, even for employees who are paid weekly. To be paid by BACS, an employee needs to have a bank account. The money will be paid into the employee's bank account on a regular basis. For salaried employees it will usually be on the same day of the month every month, for example, the 1st of every month. With employees who are paid weekly, the money will usually be paid into the bank account on the same day every week, for example, every Friday. Employees paid this way will usually receive a pay slip when their wages or salary has been paid, which will tell them how much they have earned and what has been deducted.

Cheque

Some employees may be paid by cheque (again usually either weekly or monthly). The cheque will usually be attached to a pay slip which shows how much has been earned and how much deducted. The employee will then need to take or post the cheque to his or her bank account and wait for the funds to clear (become available for use). This usually takes between three and five days, although it can sometimes be faster.

⬭ THINK ABOUT IT

Think about the jobs you have done. How were you paid? Do you think you would prefer to be paid weekly or monthly?

Work patterns

Different organisations will have different work patterns, and different departments or individual employees within an organisation may also have different work patterns. When you are offered a job you will usually be told what your expected work patterns will be, for example, what your hours of work will be, whether flexitime is available, how much annual leave you are entitled to and whether you will be expected to do overtime.

● *Hours of work* ●

The Working Time Regulations (WTR) which came into force on 1 October 1998 state that employees should not work more than 48 hours a week. Your hours at work do not include:

◻ *breaks*

◻ *time spent travelling to work*

◻ *time when you are on call, but not working*

◻ *time spent travelling to business meetings.*

Your hours of work will vary depending on the job. Some jobs will have set working hours, for example, 9 am to 5 pm Monday to Friday. Others may specify a set number of hours, but your employer or you will decide on a weekly or monthly basis when those hours are worked. You might also be expected to work a minimum number of hours and be asked to work overtime from time to time.

● *Shift systems/patterns* ●

Some jobs involve working **shifts** – for example, factory work, nursing and farming are all jobs that can involve working shifts. With most shift systems, your actual working hours may change on a weekly basis.

GLOSSARY

Shift-work means working non-normal hours (e.g. 2 pm to 10 pm, 10 pm to 6 am); it often involves working one shift for one week and then a different one the next week.

GLOSSARY

Flexitime is the ability to start and finish work at different times (as long as an agreed number of hours are worked).

For example, one week you might be working from 5 am to 1 pm and the next you might be working from 1 pm to 9 pm.

Some employers offer **flexitime**, where you must work a specific number of hours, but can choose when those hours are (as long as they are within the organisation's business hours). For example, you might get in earlier, so that you can leave in time to go to the bank or to collect children from school.

▲ Shiftworkers may change their hours often

● *Annual leave* ●

The Working Time Regulations state that all workers must be given four weeks' paid holiday per year. The year begins on 1 October for workers who started employment before 1 October 1998. For new workers, the year begins on the anniversary of the start of their employment.

Some employers may offer more than four weeks' paid holiday, or the allowance may go up the longer you work for the organisation. You will usually need to give notice of when you want to take your annual leave. How much notice you need to give will depend on the organisation. Some organisations may state specific dates when employees cannot take leave, for example, at particularly busy times of year.

• *Days off* •

Sometimes employees may need to take time off at short notice. For example, this could be because of illness, an emergency or a death in the family. There are various legal **entitlements** covering time off:

- *Maternity leave: all employees are entitled to 26 weeks paid maternity leave regardless of length of service.*

- *Paternity leave: eligible employees can take up to two weeks paid leave to care for their new baby and support the mother.*

- *Parental leave: employees – both mothers and fathers – who have completed one year's service with their employers are entitled to 13 weeks' unpaid parental leave to care for their child.*

- *Parents of disabled children are entitled to 18 weeks' parental leave up to the child's 18th birthday.*

- *Sick leave: employers must pay Statutory Sick Pay to employees for the first 28 days the employee is off sick. Employees will require a doctor's note after eight or more days of sick leave. After 28 days of sick leave the employee will need to apply for Sickness Benefit.*

- *All employees are also entitled to take a reasonable amount of unpaid time off work to deal with an emergency or unexpected situation involving a dependant.*

• *Overtime* •

Some organisations offer the opportunity for employees to work **overtime**. Overtime is when you work extra hours on top of your contracted hours of work. Employees are usually paid at a higher rate for working overtime. Your employer cannot make you work more than 48 hours a week, however you can voluntarily sign an agreement to opt out of this legal limit if you want to.

GIVE IT A GO: work patterns

1 Interview five adults (e.g. members of your family or friends of the family) to find out what their work patterns are.
2 What work patterns do you think would suit you best?
3 List **two** advantages and **two** disadvantages of working set hours.
4 List **two** advantages and **two** disadvantages of working shifts or flexitime.

Benefits

Benefits are extra perks that employers give their employees on top of their salary or wages. Benefits can include pension schemes, bonuses, discounts on products or services and free meals.

• *Bonuses* •

Some organisations pay their employees **bonuses**. This may be an annual payment which is a small share of the organisation's profits for that year. Some bonuses are linked to the employee's performance, while others may be offered to all employees. Employers may also offer bonuses for specific reasons, the early completion of a large job, for example.

• *Meals on duty* •

In some businesses employees may be offered free meals while they are on duty. This can save the employee money, because there will be one less daily meal to pay for.

• *Uniform* •

Some employees are required to wear a uniform. Usually the employer will provide the uniform, but sometimes employees have to buy it themselves. Wearing a uniform may save employees money, because they do not need to buy lots of smart clothes to wear to work.

• *Use of facilities* •

Some businesses may provide workers with free use of on-site facilities. These could include a gym, an Internet café or a car park, for example. Other businesses may provide discounted membership to gyms and other facilities.

• *Free transport* •

Some companies may provide free transport – for example, a company bus from the train station to the office, or into the nearest town at lunchtimes. In some companies, employees may be provided with a company car. The cost of any travel to and from work-related meetings outside the business will usually be **reimbursed** to employees.

• *Luncheon vouchers* •

Some companies offer employees luncheon vouchers, which can be used in a number of outlets, such as *McDonald's* and *Marks & Spencer*, to buy lunch. This can save employees money in the same way as free meals on duty can – that is, there is one less daily meal that they have to buy food for.

• *Season ticket loans* •

Commuting to work can be expensive, especially if employees need to use peak-time public transport. Some businesses offer employees interest-free or low-interest loans to buy season tickets. A season ticket can reduce the daily cost of travel considerably.

● *Special offers and discounts on products and/or services* ●

In some organisations, employees may be entitled to special offers or discounts on products. For example, many banks and building societies offer their employees discounted rates on loans or mortgages. Employees in the retail sector are often entitled to quite large discounts on the products they sell. Employees in the leisure industry may be entitled to special offers on holidays.

● *Pension* ●

Some employers pay into a **pension fund** for their employees. This will provide the employees with some income or a lump sum when they retire. Some employers also offer employees the opportunity to contribute to a pension themselves, which may be cheaper than taking out a private pension.

GLOSSARY

A **pension fund** is a type of saving that will provide you with an income or lump sum after you retire.

● *Health schemes* ●

Some employers pay for private health care or private health insurance for their employees. This can mean that employees have to wait for less time for health treatment or operations. It could also mean that they save money on dental care and eye care.

▶ **Health schemes can be valuable**

WHAT **if?**

... you could choose your own benefits?

1 Look back at the benefits described above.

2 If you could choose one, which would it be?

3 Why?

EVIDENCE ACTIVITY  P1

Terms and conditions

1 List three jobs that interest you within the business, retail and administration sectors.

2 Find out what the terms and conditions of these jobs would be (pay, work patterns and benefits).

3 From the list of terms and conditions, identify which job would be most suited to you and explain why.

Induction and training

The **induction** process is the process that introduces new employees to the organisation, to their job, to the people they will be working with and to the rules and guidelines for working within the organisation. A good induction process ensures that new starters are settled in quickly to their new job.

Starting work and training

• *Who to report to* •

The induction process should set out to whom you should report for different things. For example, your line manager may be the person to whom you report on the day-to-day tasks of your job, while you might need to report sales issues to a sales manager, finance issues to a finance manager and so on.

As part of the induction process, new employees will usually be given an organisational structure chart, which outlines the different levels of staff and who is responsible for each aspect of the organisation.

• *Expected behaviour* •

The induction process will usually include an introduction to the organisation's code of conduct and behaviour. For example, there may be guidelines on punctuality, appropriate language and how to deal respectfully with colleagues and customers.

• *Uniform in the workplace* •

For new employees who are expected to wear a uniform, the induction process may include instructions on how it should be presented, who is responsible for cleaning it, whether the employees need to buy the uniform and so on. Where there is no uniform, the induction process may include instructions about the organisation's **dress code**. For example, whether suits need to be worn, what level of jewellery is acceptable and so on.

● *Sickness procedures* ●

New employees will need to be told what the organisation's procedure is for sickness. This will vary depending on the organisation, but will usually involve calling your line manager as soon as possible to explain the situation. The induction process should also set out the organisation's requirements for doctor's notes and the rules regarding payment of Statutory Sick Pay.

● *Bereavement rules* ●

The Employment Relations Act 1999 gives employees the right to time off without pay in the event of the death of a spouse, child or parent. There is no automatic right to time off in instances of the death of another relative or a friend. Some organisations may provide time off with pay and this will be explained to new employees during their induction.

> **GLOSSARY**
>
> A **dress code** gives rules about how to dress.

> **GLOSSARY**
>
> **Bereavement** is when a family member or close friend has died.

CASE STUDY – MOBILENILE

Bereavement leave policy

Bereavement leave applies regardless of length of service. Employees may be granted up to a total of five days paid time off following the death of any of the people listed below:

- own child
- next-of-kin or nominated next-of-kin
- partners
- parents
- parents-in-law, if the employee is responsible for funeral arrangements.

Employees may be granted up to two days paid time off following the death of an immediate close relative not listed above.

Where appropriate, employees may be granted up to one day's paid leave to attend a funeral of a close friend or other relative.

Questions

1 Why does *MobileNile* grant employees time off following the death of someone close to them?

2 How far do you agree with this policy?

● *Arranging annual leave* ●

During the induction process, new employees will be introduced to the organisation's system for arranging annual leave. This may include, for example, how much notice must be given, how many days leave employees are entitled to, any time of year when employees cannot take leave and any days when leave will be compulsory, such as during a Christmas shutdown.

• *Training to help employees understand and deal with procedures* •

An important part of the induction process is training about the organisation's policies and procedures. This may include:

- 🔖 *safety and emergency procedures*
- 🔖 *smoking policy, including designated smoking areas, if relevant*
- 🔖 *security procedures*
- 🔖 *grievance procedures*
- 🔖 *disciplinary procedures*
- 🔖 *health and safety policies*
- 🔖 *emergency procedures*
- 🔖 *accident reporting*
- 🔖 *general administration procedures*
- 🔖 *restricted areas, access and passes.*

The organisation

GLOSSARY

Statutory regulations are rules and laws that have been set out by government.

Induction on the organisation may include a general introduction to the organisation, its structure, **statutory regulations**, training, company policies, equipment, documentation and computer software.

• *The organisation* •

New employees will usually be told about the organisation's missions and goals. These might include goals of profit, levels of service and how customers and employees should be treated.

• *Organisational structure* •

An induction will usually include an introduction to the structure of the organisation. In a large organisation, this may include an overall organisational chart, with a more detailed chart for the new employee's department, which would include the names and positions of everyone the employee will need to report to.

• *Statutory regulations* •

Some organisations may need to operate within statutory regulations, which are rules set out by the government for certain industries or sectors. Statutory regulations will also include those regarding health and safety, some of which will be relevant to all organisations. It is important that new employees fully understand these regulations so that they do not accidentally do something that could cause legal problems for their employer.

• *Training* •

Induction training will often also include specific training in a number of areas, depending on the job role and organisation.

Health and safety and fire regulations

All employees should receive training in the health and safety procedures of the organisation and also in the procedures to be followed in case of an emergency, such as a fire. For example, it is very important for all employees to know where the fire exits are and where the outside meeting point in the case of a fire is located.

Handling heavy equipment and use of dangerous substances

In addition new employees, where relevant, may receive training on how to lift and handle heavy equipment and the correct use of dangerous substances.

▲ It's important to know where the fire escape is

Company policies

As well as covering policies related to employee and employer responsibilities, the induction process will also cover a wide range of company procedures and policies with regard to how the business is run.

Returning/exchanging goods

It is important that new employees are aware of any policies regarding the return and/or exchange of goods. For example, a sales assistant will need to know whether they can refund a customer who does not have a sales receipt, whether they must exchange faulty goods or can provide a refund, and so on.

Range of after-sales services

It is important that *all* employees are aware of the range of after-sales services that the organisation provides – not just the employees who work in customer services. For example, they will need to know about any technical help-lines and be able to pass a caller directly to this help-line if possible, or give them the direct number, if not. They will need to know who will be able to help a customer with a complaint and ensure that the customer is given all available information, where necessary.

House styles of layout of documents

Induction training will usually include an introduction to any forms or other standard documents used within the new employee's role. They will also need to be introduced to any house style for the layout of documents, such as letters, reports and memos.

▷ *Most business letters follow a basic format. The wording of any business letter shoud be clear and precise.*

▷ *Memos are used for internal correspondence and communication and are generally less formal than business letters.*

Procedures

Induction training will also introduce new employees to the **procedures** that they need to follow in their normal working days. For example, there may be specific procedures about how to file documents, both on an organisation-wide level and within the employee's specific department. New employees will also need to be introduced to the procedures to follow in case of emergencies, such as fires, bomb alerts or chemical spills. Any responsibilities that the new employee will have in the case of an emergency must be fully explained.

Type and range of equipment

New employees who will be using equipment on a regular basis will need to receive training in how to use it safely and correctly.

Documentation in use

Induction training will usually include an introduction to the rules for the use of particular organisational documents, such as forms to complete when sick or applying for annual leave, order forms, and so on.

GLOSSARY

Procedures are steps that have been set out for specific tasks or situations (rules and guidelines).

GIVE IT A GO: training

1 Visit a local employer in the business, retail and administration sector.
2 Find out what training the employer offers its employees in:
   a general transferable skills
   b health and safety procedures and regulations
   c specific job-related skills.

GLOSSARY

Software means a program on a computer (e.g. spreadsheet program, word-processing program or web browser).

• *Computer software* •

Any employee who will be using a computer will need training in how to use relevant **software**. While the new employee may have experience in general office software, the organisation may also use custom-built software which will be new to the employee. Some organisations will also provide basic training in some of the general office software for those employees who need it.

◀ **Training on the company IT system is necessary**

Employment documents

The induction process will also include an introduction and explanation of the employment documents relevant to the new employee, for example, their employment contract and the staff handbook.

● *Contract of employment* ●

A contract is an agreement between people or organisations to deliver goods or services, or to do something on jointly agreed terms. When a new employee is taken on, he or she must be given a written contract of employment within 13 weeks of starting work.

The contract of employment must include the following:

▭ *name of employer*

▭ *date employment started and whether any previous employment is regarded as continuous with it*

▭ *rate of pay, or the method of calculating it, and how often it is paid*

▭ *hours of work*

▭ *entitlement to holidays, holiday pay, sick pay and whether or not a pension scheme exists*

▭ *the length of notice required to be given by each side*

▭ *job title*

▭ *type of employment (e.g. permanent or temporary)*

> *place or places of work*

> *disciplinary and grievance procedure.*

During the induction process, your **line manager** or a member of the human resources team will usually go through your contract with you to make sure that you fully understand it. When you are happy that you understand it and accept the terms and conditions set out within it, you will then be asked to sign it.

• *Staff handbook* •

A staff handbook explains how the company operates, its aims and objectives and, usually, general terms and conditions of employment. In fact, it will often tell you everything you want to know about the company. It may also outline procedures and guidelines in relation to house style and use of documentation. In some cases it may provide a summary of everything that was covered during the induction process, so that you can double-check anything you are not sure of.

The staff handbook usually describes:

> *the workplace*

> *the terms and conditions of employment*

> *staff facilities and benefits*

> *company policies and procedures*

> *customer service procedures*

> *equal opportunities*

> *data protection*

> *emergency procedures*

> *health and safety procedures*

> *the company administration system.*

WHAT if?

... you could write your own staff handbook?

1 Choose a job that you have done (e.g. your current job, a previous job, a work experience placement).
2 Think about what you would put in the staff handbook. Would you put everything in the list above? Do you think there would be other information that would be more useful to employees?
3 List the headings and make brief notes of what would come under them.

EVIDENCE ACTIVITY   P2   P3

Induction process

1   In your own words, describe the purpose of induction.

2   Choose a job that you have done (e.g. your current job, a previous job, a work experience placement) or a job in a local business.

3   Describe the induction process for this job, either from your own experience, or by interviewing someone who does the job now.

Procedures

Most organisations will have a number of procedures set up for tasks or circumstances that may occur frequently. These procedures help employees to know what to expect from the organisation. Some common procedures include those for staff development, appraisal, disciplinary action and ending employment.

Staff development

Different organisations will provide different kinds and levels of training. There will often be procedures set down for staff development, which can include:

- *training in the specific skills needed for the job and in more general and transferable skills*
- *development of employees' knowledge and understanding of the products and services the organisation sells or provides*
- *the provision of mentoring schemes*
- *working with others and in teams*
- *organisational and legal requirements.*

Training and development are essential not only for employees, but also for employers and the whole business.

• Skills •

Some jobs will require very specific training, for example, in custom-built software or in the use of specialised equipment. However, working in any organisation will provide the opportunity, formally or informally, to develop general and transferable skills, such as dealing with customers, using the telephone, using computers, managing your time and workload and so on. Good employers will have procedures for providing and improving these skills in their employees.

GLOSSARY

Transferable skills are skills which can be used in all or most job roles (e.g. communication skills, IT skills and punctuality).

Dealing with customers

Most organisations will have procedures or guidelines in place for dealing with customers. It is important to any organisation that its customers are treated consistently by all staff. Procedures for dealing with customers could include:

- *standard greetings – e.g. 'Good morning, you're speaking to [employee name] at [organisation name]. How can I be of assistance?' or 'Hello. Welcome to [shop name]. Is there anything I can help you with or would you prefer to browse on your own?'*

- *courtesy guidelines – e.g. always saying 'please' and 'thank you'; saying 'have a good day' to customers when they leave*

- *always giving customers an order number or a contact name*

- *informing customers of the data protection offered.*

Using the telephone

Many organisations will have specific guidelines or procedures for using the telephone. This ensures that customers will enjoy a **consistent** approach whenever they call the company. Procedures could include:

- *always answering the phone within a certain number of rings*

- *a standard greeting when answering the phone – e.g. 'Good morning, you're through to [company name]. My name is [employee name]. How can I direct your call?'*

- *transferring callers directly, rather than asking them to phone back on a different number*

- *always taking the customer's name and number at the start of the call*

- *making sure callers are not left on hold for more than a specified amount of time.*

▲ A consistent telephone manner impresses customers

● *Knowledge* ●

There are likely to be procedures in place to ensure that employees always have the most up-to-date information about the organisation and its products or services. These could include:

▭ *regular memos or emails sent to employees*

▭ *a requirement for employees to check the company Intranet on a daily basis to check for any new information*

▭ *meetings to tell employees about large changes in organisational structure or the organisation's mission*

▭ *a requirement for employees to read a trade journal on a regular basis.*

● *Understanding* ●

Procedures for ensuring employees understand the organisation and its products and services may include regular meetings with line managers and procedures and guidelines for asking for further explanation or information when necessary.

● *Mentoring* ●

Some organisations will have formal mentoring procedures in place, whereby an employee at a lower level or who is new to the organisation is provided with a **mentor** who has been doing the job for a while and therefore knows a lot about it. The mentor is someone the employee can go to for advice about the job, about the organisation and also about general working issues. A mentor is there to support the employee, to be a good role model and to listen and respond to any problems the employee raises.

Some mentoring procedures will involve job shadowing, where the employee follows the mentor around and watches everything he or she does in their working day. The employee can then learn the ropes of the job from someone who has more experience.

> **GLOSSARY**
>
> A **mentor** is someone who acts as a guide, teacher and advisor.

● *Working with others* ●

An organisation may have procedures to follow when working with others. This could include guidelines on showing respect to colleagues, listening to and responding to colleagues' requests and suggestions and being polite and helpful towards colleagues.

● *Working in teams* ●

In many organisations, **teamwork** is essential to the success of the business. In such an organisation, it is very likely that there will be procedures in place to help with efficient teamwork. This could include guidelines on agreeing a team leader, on allocating tasks within a team

> **GLOSSARY**
>
> **Teamwork** is working with other people to complete a task or project.

and on providing feedback and help to other team members. It could also include guidelines on the organisation and running of team meetings and the importance of all members of a team meeting their responsibilities, so that the team as a whole can succeed.

THINK ABOUT IT

Think about three times when you have had to work in a team or with others. You can include work in school or college. What skills did you use? How did working with others help with the task? Did it cause any problems?

● *Organisational and legal requirements* ●

There will be a number of organisational and legal requirements that play a part in the procedures of the organisation. Organisational requirements could include company-wide policies on smoking, on providing customer service and on fulfilling the organisation's mission. Legal requirements could include procedures that meet the requirements in legislation, such as:

- *the Trade Descriptions Act and Sale of Goods Act*
- *health and safety and fire safety legislation and regulations*
- *employee rights*
- *employment legislation.*

Appraisal

An **appraisal** usually takes the form of an annual meeting between an employee and his or her line manager. During the appraisal employees have the opportunity to discuss any problems they have encountered, celebrate their successes and set goals for future achievement. Line managers provide employees with feedback on their performance over the year, praise successes and give constructive criticism to help improve in areas where the employee has problems.

Organisations that undertake appraisals will usually have a procedure set out for how they work. This will usually include aims and objectives of the appraisal, the criteria which are to be looked at during the appraisal and the recording documentation that should be used for the appraisal.

● *Aims and objectives* ●

It is important that both the employee and the line manager fully understand the aims and objectives of the appraisal. For example, an employee may not be allowed to discuss pay or a line manager may not be allowed to discuss other staff's comments about the employee. The overall **aims** and **objectives** of an appraisal will usually be to look at an employee's performance over the year and work together to provide goals for both the employee and the employer.

Appraisal objectives could be to:

- *increase motivation*
- *develop relations between the employee and line manager*
- *update job descriptions*
- *enhance the quality of the service provided to customers*
- *improve staff performance and assist them in their professional development*
- *recognise the achievements of staff*
- *help staff who are having difficulty with their performance, through appropriate guidance, counselling and training*
- *inform those responsible for providing references for staff in relation to appointments.*

● *Criteria* ●

An appraisal procedure may include specific **criteria** that need to be discussed for all employees, sometimes with a score being agreed upon between employee and line manager. Examples of criteria could include:

- *punctuality*
- *quality of work*
- *meeting deadlines*
- *teamwork*
- *dealing with customers.*

● *Outcomes* ●

The appraisal procedure will set out what the expected outcomes of the appraisal may be. This will usually involve setting goals for the employee to achieve as well as commitments on behalf of the employer. For example, an employee goal might be to reduce the time it takes them to answer phone calls or to increase individual sales by five per cent. An employer commitment might be to provide training in time management or to provide the employee with an opportunity to lead a team.

> **GLOSSARY**
>
> An **aim** is a plan, goal, desire or target.
>
> **Objectives** are goals, plans, or what you want or need to happen.

> **GLOSSARY**
>
> **Criteria** are conditions, elements or characteristics of data.

● *Recording documentation* ●

As part of the appraisal procedure, there will usually be a specific document (or documents) that need to be filled in. The contents of the document are usually agreed between the line manager and the employee and they will both get a copy to keep. The document is also usually referred to in the next appraisal, in order to check whether the employee has fulfilled the goals and whether the employer has fulfilled its commitments.

WHAT **if?**

... *you had an appraisal today?*

1 Think about the job you currently do (e.g. a part-time job) or your most recent work experience (or you can use your school or college work, instead).

2 List three successes that you feel you have had.

3 List three weaknesses that you would like to improve on.

4 List three ways in which your employer (or school/college) could help you to improve.

5 Write three goals that you would like to achieve over the next year in your job (or on your course).

GLOSSARY

Disciplinary and grievance procedures are procedures for dealing with unwanted or dangerous behaviour.

Disciplinary/grievance

Disciplinary and grievance procedures provide a clear framework for dealing with unacceptable behaviour by the employee (disciplinary) as well as unfair or inappropriate treatment by the employer (grievance).

They are necessary to ensure that everybody is treated in the same way in similar circumstances; to ensure that issues are dealt with fairly; and to ensure that the procedures and outcomes are compliant with current legislation.

▶ **Disciplinary and grievance procedures can resolve problems**

• *Guidelines and codes of practice* •

When the Employment Act 2002 came into force in 2003, statutory disciplinary and grievance procedures became implied in every contract of employment. These procedures are as follows.

- *The employer must inform the employee of any allegations in writing prior to holding a disciplinary and grievance meeting.*

- *The employer must hold a meeting with the employee before any action is taken.*

- *The employer must then notify the employee of the outcome of the meeting and of his or her right to appeal.*

- *If the employee wishes to appeal, he or she must inform the employer, who must then invite the employee to a further meeting.*

- *The appeal must be conducted by a more senior manager than the person who conducted the original hearing.*

- *At the appeal meeting the employer must give the employee a proper opportunity to explain himself or herself.*

- *After the meeting, the employer must inform the employee of the final decision.*

The Advisory, Conciliation and Arbitration Service (ACAS) provides codes of practice on disciplinary and grievance procedures for employers and employees to follow. The codes of practice in themselves form guidelines for drawing up rules and procedures and for dealing with disciplinary and grievance matters.

• *Procedures* •

New employees should be informed of the employer's disciplinary and grievance procedures. These should be set out in writing and give full details of the organisation's rules of conduct, what acts could lead to disciplinary action and what employees' rights are under the procedures.

• *Industrial tribunal* •

There are a number of reasons that employers cannot use to justify getting rid of an employee. These include pregnancy, sex, race, trying to join a union and refusing to do unsafe work. If you have been fired for any of these reasons, you can claim unfair dismissal and take your employer to an employment tribunal, no matter how long you have worked there.

A **tribunal** can order an employer to give you your job back but will usually make them pay you compensation. A tribunal hearing is public.

> **GLOSSARY**
>
> A **tribunal** is a trial or hearing to find out if someone has done something wrong.

● *Sources of advice* ●

There are a number of sources of advice for the employee (and employer) in matters of disciplinary action or grievance. These include ACAS, HCIMA and CAB, but there may be other sources of advice specific to your area of work or the industry in which you are employed.

Advisory, Conciliation and Arbitration Service (ACAS)

The main aims of ACAS are to:

- *prevent and resolve employment disputes*

- *conciliate in actual or potential complaints to industrial tribunals*

- *provide information and advice*

- *promote good practice in the work place.*

ACAS can be used by employers and employees to help them work together to resolve industrial disputes.

GIVE IT A GO: ACAS

1 Visit the ACAS website – a link is available at **www.heinemann.co.uk/hotlinks** (express code 1211P).

2 Find out three facts about the service that ACAS provides.

3 List three situations that ACAS could help with.

▶ ACAS can help arbitrate disputes

Hotel and Catering International Management Association (HCIMA)

If you work in the hotel and catering sector, HCIMA can provide advice on employment disputes. There are other industry-specific organisations and trade unions that should be able to help if you work in another sector. Your colleagues should be able to tell you which organisations are relevant and there may be representatives among your colleagues from the trade unions or industry organisations.

Citizens Advice Bureau (CAB)

CAB offers free, confidential, impartial and independent advice and helps to solve nearly six million problems every year, including debt and consumer issues, and problems involving benefits, housing, legal matters, employment and immigration. CAB will be able to provide advice with an employment issue, or will be able to put you in touch with a specialist who can.

Termination

Termination of employment means ending of employment. There are number of reasons for termination:

- ▭ *redundancy*
- ▭ *dismissal*
- ▭ *job restructuring*
- ▭ *resignation.*

• *Redundancy* •

This is the situation that results when an employee's contract of employment is ended because that job no longer exists or that person is no longer needed. An employee could be made **redundant** for the following reasons:

- ▭ *the closure of the business*
- ▭ *the introduction of a modern technology to replace part of the workforce*
- ▭ *a desire to cut costs by reducing the wage bill*
- ▭ *an economic slow down – e.g. a recession.*

In some cases, employers may first offer voluntary redundancy, so that those employees who would be happy to leave can do so, and so hopefully prevent the need for forced redundancy. When employees are made redundant, they are usually given a redundancy payment, which allows them to keep paying their bills while they look for another job.

> **GLOSSARY**
>
> **Redundancy** happens when a company needs to cut down on staff (it often comes with a lump sum to make up for losing the job).

• *Dismissal* •

Over the years, the rules for dismissing employees have become more and more complicated. The heart of the matter lies in the difference between what the courts regard to be 'fair' and 'unfair' **dismissal**.

For an employer to fairly dismiss an employee they must have a valid reason for dismissing the employee and both parties must agree that the reason for dismissing the employee is sufficient.

Within the employer's guidelines on disciplinary and grievance procedures there will usually be a list of actions that are considered 'gross misconduct' and which will automatically result in dismissal. These could include:

> *theft*

> *fraud*

> *physical violence*

> *serious breaches of confidence.*

GLOSSARY

To **dismiss** means to sack someone from their job or end employment.

WHAT **if?**

... *you were the boss?*

For each of the situations below decide whether or not you would dismiss the employee. Give your reasons for your decision.

1 An employee regularly arrives at least half an hour late for work. He has already been warned twice.

2 A supervisor forgot to warn her workers about a faulty machine. As a result of this an employee was seriously injured while using the machine.

3 A sales assistant in your clothes shop has been giving 20 per cent discounts to his friends. This has happened at least three times.

4 A receptionist has twice turned up for work drunk. He has already been warned once about this.

5 An employee has been spending a lot of time chatting to her friends online.

• *Job restructuring* •

GLOSSARY

Restructuring is when the structure or organisation is changed (e.g. having fewer managers and more operatives).

Sometimes changing the structure of the organisation can lead to job losses. The **restructuring** may be necessary due to reduced funding or to mergers with other organisations. In cases of job restructuring, job losses are usually in the form of redundancies, or employees may be provided with the opportunity to take early retirement.

• *Resignation* •

If an employee wants to **resign** he or she must give the amount of notice stated in the contract (this is often four weeks, but may be more in some organisations). If there is no contract, or a notice period is not mentioned, the employee can give the minimum one week's notice. An employee is entitled to resign without giving any notice if the employer commits a serious breach of the employment contract.

• *Procedures* •

The organisation should have procedures in place for termination of employment. These procedures will set out the rights and responsibilities of both the employee and the employer. It is important for employees to read these procedures carefully and make sure they understand their rights and responsibilities.

• *Records* •

All **records** should be kept up to date and in a safe place because they will be vital should a case be pursued at an employment tribunal. Since the burden of proof is on the employer to show that the dismissal is not unfair or unreasonable, keeping records is very important. The types of record that should be kept by employers include:

- *minutes of meetings*
- *attendance records*
- *notes of telephone calls*
- *copies of correspondence.*

EVIDENCE ACTIVITY

Procedures

1 Why is it important for you to monitor your work?

2 Why it is important for your employer to monitor your performance?

3 Describe a procedure for monitoring performance that you have experienced. (If you have not experienced any yourself, then interview someone who has.)

END OF UNIT ASSIGNMENT

Task 1

1 Identify **six** jobs that interest you – three in retail and three in administration.

2 Find out what the terms and conditions are for these jobs (pay, work patterns and benefits).

3 Compare the jobs in retail and decide which one offers the best terms and conditions.

4 Compare the jobs in administration and decide which one offers the best terms and conditions.

5 Compare the best retail job with the best administration job and decide which of the two would be best for you.

Task 2

1 Describe the purpose of induction and explain why it is important to:
 a the employer
 b the employee.

2 Choose one organisation and describe the induction process there, including details of how it helps a new employee to understand the terms and conditions of their job.

Task 3 P4 P5 M3 D2

1 Explain the importance of monitoring performance in the workplace for:
 a the employer
 b the employee
 c the customer.

2 Give three examples of how work procedures are used to monitor the performance of individual employees and, for each one, describe how the procedure works.

unit 3

Introducing customer service

In this unit you will find out about the basics of customer service. You will learn that different types of customer will have different needs and expectations. You will find out how important good communication skills are and how to practise and improve these skills. You will learn how to create a good first impression and why this is important in customer services. You will find out about how to help customers and why it is important to know about the products and services you sell and offer.

▶ **Good customer service is vital to a business**

To complete this unit you must:

⇨ describe different types of customer and their needs and expectations
⇨ prepare yourself and your work area for customer service
⇨ communicate well in customer service situations
⇨ provide good care and service to your customers.

We live in an era where the customer is always right. Gone are the days when customers were thought of as an interruption or when answering customer queries was seen as doing them a favour. Whether you are involved with customers on the telephone or deal with them directly, you must make sure that you give the right impression about the business and also give your customers what they are looking for.

Different types of customers

To be successful, a business needs to know about the needs and wants of its customers and work hard to satisfy these needs and wants.

Internal customers

When we think about customer service we think of staff serving customers over a counter or over the phone. But customer service happens within the business as well.

An **internal customer** is someone in your own organisation who is next in line to receive the product. Examples might be a production line worker who receives a partly completed product from another worker or a sales representative who receives a finished product to sell on.

While most companies focus thousands of pounds on external customer service in hopes of keeping customers, less attention is paid to the effect poor internal customer service can have on customer satisfaction. For example, poor internal customer service on a production line could result in problems with the product, or late delivery.

● *Managers* ●

Managers are responsible for:

▭ *decision making*

▭ *problem solving*

▭ *planning and setting targets*

▭ *making sure targets are reached*

▭ *organising the working environment.*

In business terms, managers want the business to reach its targets (e.g. selling a certain number of products, delivering a product on time) and make a profit. In personal terms, they are also employees and so like to get pay rises, promotion and benefits (e.g. company cars, pensions, gym membership). Good managers also want their staff to be happy.

● *Colleagues* ●

Colleagues are the people you work with regularly, the other members of your team. They are usually on the same level as you. For example, if you are a clerk in a wages department your colleagues would be the other clerks. In a small shop, your colleagues might be everyone else who works in the shop, including the manager or owner.

Good internal customer service starts with good relationships among colleagues. If everyone in the team gets on with each other the team will work better. Happy employees are better team players and a company with happy employees will be more **productive**.

> **GLOSSARY**
>
> **Colleagues** are people you work with.

> **GLOSSARY**
>
> **Productive** means able to get lots of work done in the time available.

◀ **A happy team works better**

CASE STUDY – SAINSBURY'S

Valuing colleagues at Sainsbury's

At *Sainsbury's* we are committed to providing a working environment in which everyone feels valued, respected and able to contribute to the business as well as employing a workforce that recognises the diversity of our customers and values them. We reward our employees for the results they achieve.

Find out more at the *Sainsbury's* website – a link is available at **www.heinemann.co.uk/hotlinks** (express code 1211P).

Question

Why do you think it is important for *Sainsbury's* to value its employees?

A **contractor** is someone brought in to an organisation to do a specific task and who will no longer work there when the task is finished.

Permanent means there is no fixed time to end (e.g. permanent job).

The **sales** department deals with selling products or services.

The **distribution** department deals with getting products to customers.

The **production** department deals with making products.

Finance means having to do with money; the finance department deals with the organisation's spending and receipts.

The **consumer** is the person who uses a product or service (not always the person who buys it – e.g. children are consumers of toys, but their parents probably buy them).

• *Contractors* •

A **contractor** is someone who works for a company for a set period of time. Companies may take on contractors instead of permanent staff to finish a one-off project. Sometimes companies take on contractors at times when they are very busy. For example, a toy factory might take on contractors to make extra toys in time for Christmas.

Permanent employees enjoy access to company benefit schemes such as pensions, healthcare and training. A company may also provide its employees with full sick pay. Contractors do not usually get these benefits.

• *Other departments* •

To satisfy customers, a company needs good teamwork between different departments. For example, the **sales** department needs to work with the **distribution** department; the **production** department needs to work with the **finance** department. All employees need to be aware of the importance of customer service, even those who never have to speak to a customer in person.

Good internal customer service involves providing other departments with services, products and information so that they can do their jobs. It involves listening to and understanding their concerns and working together to solve problems and to help the organisation succeed.

External customers

The external customer is the **consumer** of the product or service. If external customers' needs are not met, they will not buy the product or use the service. An external customer could be:

- *an individual (e.g. buying an item in a shop, using a gym)*
- *another business (e.g. buying stationery, booking a hotel for a sales representative)*
- *a central or local government department (e.g. buying computers, paying for a report)*
- *an organisation in the voluntary sector (e.g. a charity renting shop premises, a meals-on-wheels service buying food).*

• *Businesses, private customers and groups of people* •

Businesses and groups of people can be customers, as well as individuals. Some businesses sell only to private customers, some sell only to other businesses and organisations and some sell to a mix. For example, your corner shop may sell you food, newspapers, butter, bread and other products. All these products were bought from somewhere else. Your corner shop is a seller because it sells you goods and at the same time it is a customer of other businesses.

Table 3.1 Examples of types of external customer

Customer	Examples
Business customers	• Insurance company buying stationery from an office supplies retailer • A factory paying for health and safety training for its employees
Private customers	• A couple going to watch a film at the cinema • A parent doing the weekly shop at the supermarket
Groups of people	• A football team going for a meal to celebrate winning a trophy • A youth club buying a new pool table

GIVE IT A GO: types of customer

1 For each of the businesses below, decide what types of customers it would have.
   • A mobile phone shop
   • A car dealership
   • A children's nursery
   • A five-star hotel
   • A small family dental practice
2 Pick one of the businesses above and work out what other businesses it might be a customer of.

● *Customers of different age, nationality or ability* ●

Age

Our age determines the types of products we buy. If you look around your own shopping centre you will see different age groups in different types of shops. Shops selling CDs or computer games will have more young customers, as will fashion boutiques and chain stores such as *Next*. *Marks & Spencer* will attract older customers and so will men's tailors and exclusive dress shops.

Manufacturers make different versions of the same type of product for different age groups. A good example of this is toiletry products. If you visit a store such as *Boots*, you will see different age groups buying different types of hair product, for example.

▶ **Young people have different buying patterns**

Different nationalities

It is important for a business to examine the cultural or traditional expectations of all its customers to ensure it respects them and their cultures. The products and the way they are marketed should also be considered in this light.

Millions of people from other countries visit the UK every year. Wherever you work, it is very likely that you will need to deal with customers from overseas. You will need to take into account that they may not speak English very well and that they may have different expectations to customers who live in the UK.

Overseas customers

Many businesses start selling internationally by responding to an enquiry from a foreign company. Thousands of UK firms receive such requests annually, but most firms do not then become successful exporters. To succeed in overseas sales, a business needs to:

- *properly respond to enquiries*

- *carry out research on foreign customers*

- *recognise the difference between **domestic** and **international** sales.*

Selling to overseas customers might mean that a business needs to provide different product specifications, different information and different prices.

• *Disabled customers* •

By law you must not treat a disabled customer less favourably unless you reasonably believe that either the disabled customer or someone else may come to some harm if you did not. Your reason for providing less favourable treatment in these circumstances must be genuine.

Customers who have difficulty moving around

Many different disabilities can cause problems with moving around or standing. People who use walking aids (e.g. walking sticks, crutches, etc.) may find it hard to use their hands while they are standing, for example, to count out money or fill in a form.

Ways to help:

- *Always offer a seat.*

- *Offer help with coats, bags or other belongings.*

- *Offer to open heavy doors.*

- *Offer a wheelchair or powered scooter if they are available in your premises.*

GLOSSARY

Domestic means in the UK.

International means worldwide.

Customers who use wheelchairs

Sometimes you may know in advance that a customer with a wheelchair will be visiting your premises, but most of the time you will not.

Ways to help:

▭ *Speak directly to the wheelchair user.*

▭ *Try to put yourself at the wheelchair user's eye-level to avoid stiff necks.*

▭ *Come round to their side of reception desks or high counters.*

▭ *Offer help with heavy doors.*

▭ *Don't lean on or push the wheelchair unless they ask you to.*

• *Angry or confused customers* •

Not every time you deal with customers starts as a positive experience. A customer whose complaint has not been handled well is likely to be frustrated and angry. To provide good customer service, you need to learn how to handle angry customers.

Sometimes customers get angry because their queries have not been dealt with properly, for example, they have been given the wrong information or bought faulty products. Take it seriously, but not personally. The customer is angry, but not necessarily angry at you. Sometimes customers' anger may not have anything to with you or your organisation; they could just be having a bad day, be in pain, or might just be cranky.

 THINK ABOUT IT

Have you ever been angry with a sales assistant in a shop? Why were you angry? Was the problem sorted out? How? What other reasons can you think of for customers being angry? What ways can you think of to help them?

Needs

However good your product or service is, the simple truth is that no one will buy it if they don't want it or believe they don't need it. Knowing and understanding customers' needs is at the centre of every successful business, whether it sells to individuals or to other businesses. Once you know your customers' needs, you can use that information to persuade potential and existing customers that buying from you is in their best interests.

• *Information* •

Providing the right information about a product is a major part of customer service. Customer service requires a good knowledge of the products being sold in order to provide customers with:

▷ *information about the product or the differences between products (e.g. what they are made of or how their performances compare)*

▷ *a demonstration of the product*

▷ *details of any after-sales service (e.g. maintenance and repair services)*

▷ *in the case of technical products (e.g. a DVD recorder), accurate and relevant details, explained in a way that does not confuse customers or make them feel embarrassed.*

• *Enquiry* •

Businesses have to respond promptly to customers' enquiries to be able to satisfy their needs and wants. Businesses use the information from customer enquiries to improve their service or existing products or to provide new services or products. It is important to know about the services and products that the business provides or sells, in order to respond to enquiries. If you cannot provide exactly what a customer is looking for, you may be able to suggest suitable alternatives.

• *Buying goods or services* •

Customers have needs and wants which they satisfy by buying goods and services. When we need something like food, how we actually choose to satisfy that need depends on our desire, taste, lifestyle and the amount of money we have. For example, if you are hungry you have the choice of what to eat and where to eat it. You could have a meal at home, buy a take-away or eat in an expensive restaurant. We are all different and so we all spend our money in different ways. The crisp flavour you like is not necessarily the same one that your friend or your brother or sister likes.

• *Routine and non-routine needs* •

For customers

For customers, **routine needs** are for products or services that are needed on a regular basis and do not usually require much thought. For example, buying bread and milk, renewing car insurance or television licences and going for a dental check up.

Non-routine needs are those which occur less often and tend to need a lot of thought and research. For example, buying a house, a new car or a computer, looking for a new job and finding a nursery place for a child.

GLOSSARY

Routine needs are needs that occur often, or common needs.

Non-routine needs are needs that occur less often, or unusual needs.

For people working in customer service

For people working in customer service, routine needs are those which they deal with on a regular basis. If you work on a mortgage phone line for a bank, advising customers about the bank's mortgage products would be a routine need, even though they are non-routine for the customer. Non-routine needs might be someone asking about savings or investments, or a journalist wanting details of the mortgage products for an article.

THINK ABOUT IT

Think about the job you do or have done in the past, or a work experience placement you have been on. Were you satisfying customers' routine or non-routine needs? What were the routine needs in your own job and did you ever have to deal with non-routine needs? How did you deal with them?

Expectations

Customers' expectations tend to be quite high and are always increasing. Customers expect businesses to be responsive, reassuring, polite, competent, thoughtful and reliable. If a business does not meet these expectations it could lose customers and become less competitive. Customers want:

- *to be taken seriously*
- *efficient service*
- *anticipation of their needs*
- *explanations in their terms*
- *basic politeness*
- *to be informed of the options*
- *not to be passed around*
- *to be listened to (and heard)*
- *dedicated attention*
- *knowledgeable help*
- *friendliness*
- *to be kept informed*
- *good value for money*
- *honesty*
- *feedback*
- *professional service*
- *good after-sales service*
- *respect.*

● *Good customer service and care* ●

There are many areas covered by customer service. Perhaps the most obvious one is the way the customer is treated in a shop or at the checkout.

A tired shopper who has just struggled in from a crowded and noisy street laden with bags and parcels can have their spirits lifted by a polite and well-mannered salesperson. Such first impressions can be very important. The customer may have just left another shop where he or she was less than impressed with the service. Saying 'Please' and 'Thank you' and being polite and thoughtful should become second nature. Seeing customers out of the shop and opening the door for them are all part of good manners.

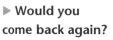

WHAT if?

... you went out for pizza with your friends?

How would you react if you ordered a vegetarian pizza and it took two hours for the pizza to be served, it was cold and dry and it had chicken on it? How would you react if you complained and the manager apologised, saying that they were very busy and the normal chef was off sick?

▶ **Would you come back again?**

GLOSSARY

Your **impression** is what you think of someone or something.

● *Giving the right impression* ●

In order to provide good customer service you need to give your customers the right **impression** about you, your business and the product or service you are selling. Try to look at yourself and your business through the customers' eyes. Are you the type of business or person they are expecting to deal with?

The impression created by all levels of staff when dealing with present and potential customers is vital to securing the future of a business. Giving the right impression involves how staff are dressed, the language staff use, the tidiness of the premises, the decoration of the premises, the background music and many other things.

• *Prompt attention* •

Customers expect businesses to respond promptly to their needs and queries. To provide good customer service, you need to reply quickly, completely and clearly. In order to keep customers, it is important to **respond** as soon as possible to any enquiries. Depending on the business, there will be different expectations for time of response. In a supermarket, you do not want to stand at the checkout for an hour, waiting to pay for your goods. When you are buying a house, however, you would expect the process to take some weeks. When phoning a customer services phone line, you expect your call to be answered within a few minutes. When you send an email for technical help, you might expect a response within 24 hours.

> **GLOSSARY**
>
> To **respond** is to answer or fulfil a request.

• *Good communications* •

Businesses need to find ways to communicate well with their internal and external customers. Businesses usually communicate with their customers in a number of different ways (for example, face to face, newsletters, letters, emails, websites, telephone, etc.). Good communications help businesses to find as much information as possible about customers' complaints, needs and wants.

CASE STUDY – TIM-TOM GO

Communication with customers

Having developed a range of new products and services, it is important that everyone within the company is familiar with these developments (internal communication) so that they can better communicate with current and potential customers (external communication). At *Tim-Tom Go* internal communications include the Intranet and a newsletter that informs employees of new and ongoing projects and important events. Notice boards are attractively set out to give clear visual messages and soon a poster campaign will begin promoting the importance of good customer service. The company also holds regional and sub-regional conferences known as 'Update Roadshows' to improve face-to-face communication. Roadshows are held in Europe for subsidiaries in France, Belgium, Germany and the Netherlands, and Italy.

The website is a very powerful, successful and cost-effective external communication tool.

Questions

1 How does *Tim-Tom Go* communicate with its internal customers?

2 How does *Tim-Tom Go* communicate with its external customers?

EVIDENCE ACTIVITY  P1

Needs and expectations

1 Choose a business that you have worked for (e.g. your current job, a previous job, a work experience placement) or visited.

2 Identify the internal customers within the organisation and what their **(a)** needs and **(b)** expectations are.

3 Identify the external customers that the organisation deals with and what their **(a)** needs and **(b)** expectations are.

Prepare yourself and your work area

In businesses where members of the public come to the premises the appearance of both staff and the premises are very important. Examples of such businesses are shops, restaurants, cinemas, leisure centres, doctors' surgeries and solicitors' offices. However, appearance is also important for businesses where the public do not often visit, such as factories, insurance offices, advertising agencies and so on. In these businesses, appearance is important both for internal customer service (if your desk is a mess and your personal hygiene is not good your colleagues may find it more difficult to work with you) and for any external customers who might visit (e.g. a representative of a large business client visiting a factory to see how it works).

> **GLOSSARY**
>
> **Appearance** means what something or someone looks like.

Prepare yourself

Preparing yourself means paying attention to your **appearance**, your attitude towards customers and towards your colleagues, the standards and guidelines within your organisation and your knowledge of the services or products that you are providing or selling.

> **GLOSSARY**
>
> **Enthusiasm** means interest, being keen or wanting to do something.

• *Positive attitude* •

You need to be enthusiastic about the products you are selling or about the service you are providing. If you do not show **enthusiasm**, why should a customer? When dealing with the public and with your colleagues you need to be polite and show an understanding of their needs. Salespeople often need to tailor their attitude and selling technique according to the customer they are serving. They need to stress the points about their product or service that will appeal to that particular customer. For example, a car salesperson might stress the safety **features** of a car to a parent with a young family, stress the comfort features to someone who will be driving for long hours and stress the MP3 player and surround-sound speakers to a younger person.

Salespeople also need to make sure they provide the right level of attention for the particular customer they are serving. For example, some customers will want to browse on their own without someone telling them all about the products; others may want to go straight to a member of staff for detailed information about the product they are there to buy. It is important not to put pressure on customers to buy something that does not suit their needs. If they end up regretting their decision to buy the goods, they might well choose not to visit that retail outlet again.

When a colleague asks you to help with a task or gives you a particular project to work on, you need to show your willingness to do the work. If you constantly grumble when asked to do things, this could make your colleagues resent you or could even result in you losing your job.

> ### GLOSSARY
>
> A **feature** is a characteristic or element (e.g. features of a mobile phone might include a camera and polyphonic ring tones).

THINK ABOUT IT

Think about the last time you made a non-routine purchase (e.g. bought a new stereo or television). How did you decide which product to buy? How did the salespeople help you make your choice?

Have you ever felt pressured into buying something that you later regretted? How did this make you feel about the salesperson who persuaded you? Did it put you off going back to the shop again?

• *Personal presentation* •

In businesses that deal face to face with the public or with business clients, it is important for staff to appear neat and clean. Where the business requires staff to wear name badges or identity cards, these should be clearly visible. Even if you do not deal with customers face to face, it is still important to be clean and tidy. The way you present yourself will affect your colleagues' impressions of you. If you take the trouble to make yourself look businesslike, they will be more likely to believe that you can act in a businesslike manner and take the trouble to do your work well.

Dress code

Different businesses will have different expectations of their staff's appearance. Some businesses (especially shops) will provide uniforms for their staff. Although you do not need to think about the clothes you wear, if you have a uniform, you still need to make sure that you are clean and presentable in other ways (e.g. your hair is clean and brushed, your teeth are clean so your breath does not smell unpleasant, your nails are clean, etc.).

▲ **It is important to look clean and smart when you are dealing with the public**

Some offices will have a **dress code** that states what staff should wear. Different businesses will have different levels of dress code. For example, a solicitor's office might expect all staff to wear smart suits, while an advertising agency might expect staff to be smart but casual. You should make sure that you follow the dress code that is expected of you. Sometimes this might include a limit on the amount of jewellery or make-up. Remember that you can always make up for these limitations outside work when you go out with your friends.

Posture

Your **posture** can affect the impression people have of you. If you slouch and look at the floor a lot, customers or colleagues may feel you look shy or scared and might be put off from talking to you. If you sit or stand straight you will look more confident. If you stand with your hands in your pockets they may think you don't care much about your work. If you stand with your arms crossed or on your hips, they may feel you look cross or bossy and might not want to come up to you. Good posture can also make you feel more confident – not just look more confident.

● *Personal space* ●

When communicating face to face with people it is important to respect their space. Try to stand at arm's length from others while talking. If you stand closer than this, it could make them feel uncomfortable. If you stand further away they may think you are scared of them, or that you do not have time to give them your attention. It is usually not appropriate to touch customers, even if you think you are doing so to show you find them important, although it may be appropriate to shake hands. Everyone has a different level of comfort when communicating with strangers and yours may be different to your customers'.

● *First impressions* ●

First impressions are very important in business. A shop might sell the very best products, but if the floor is very dirty and the staff are scruffy, the customers may not get the chance to find out about the products. They will see the dirt and the poor appearance of the staff and will expect the products to also be of poor quality.

You never get a second chance to make a first impression. The impression you give your customer in the first 60 seconds or so will last the whole time of your business relationship – and it could be a very short one.

● *Knowledge of products or services* ●

Giving information about a product or service is a very important part of customer service. You should memorise as much of the basic information as possible, for example, the price, the location of a product, the delivery time for a large item or the call-out time for a service.

What you cannot memorise, you should keep close to hand. For example, for more technical details of a product, there might be a specification sheet; for details of special discounts or special services, there might be a list in a ringbinder or on the computer.

The more knowledgeable about the products or services you are, the quicker you will be able to respond to customers' queries. For anything you cannot answer yourself, you should know which of your colleagues or managers will have the information so that you can still answer the query quickly, without leaving a customer waiting in the store or on the phone.

• *Organisation's guidelines and standards required for customer service* •

Every business should have a customer service **policy** that states the required standard for customer service. This will ensure that employees know what to do when they are dealing with customers and will help them to provide a high standard of customer care.

CASE STUDY – MOBILENILE

Our customer service standard

We are constantly seeking to improve the way we work and the quality of service we offer. Our salespeople set themselves very high standards to serve customers and to answer their queries promptly.

Standard 1: We will answer your letters clearly and within four working days of receipt.

Standard 2: We will see you within five minutes of any pre-arranged appointment at our offices.

Standard 3: We will provide you with information about our services or put you in touch with someone who can.

Standard 4: We will consult customers regularly about services and report on findings.

Standard 5: We will respond to complaints and send you information about our complaints policy on request.

Standard 6: We will take all reasonable steps to make services accessible to everyone, including people with special needs.

Question

Why is it important for *MobileNile* to have the above customer service standards and guidelines?

• *Teamwork* •

When you work as part of a team it is important to treat your colleagues as you would your customers. You can use customer service skills (attitude, active listening, **assertiveness**, **negotiation**, creative thinking, questioning, etc.) to manage your relationships within the team. When working in a team your own failures or poor behaviour will affect everyone else on the team.

Teamwork involves sharing ideas and working together. For example, in an *Argos* store an essential ingredient of processing customer orders is the customer service staff working with each other and with the staff behind the scenes. At the Inland Revenue, a major aspect of working together is being 'approachable and understanding at all times' when dealing with colleagues.

Prepare your work area

Any place of business needs to be safe, both for the employees and for members of the public or business clients who visit the premises. Equipment must be easily accessible to those who need to use it and the working space should be set out to provide a pleasant and efficient environment. Tidiness is also important, both in retail outlets and offices.

● *Appropriate equipment* ●

In retail outlets equipment needs to be made ready before the store is opened. Equipment could include tills, computers, pens and paper, lighting and also any equipment that is being sold and may need to be demonstrated. For example, tills may need to be turned on and filled with cash, computers may need to be turned on, as may lights, and equipment to be demonstrated may need to be turned on and prepared for demonstration (e.g. televisions tuned to a certain channel, computers loaded with a particular piece of software or game).

In offices, equipment needs to be readily available to employees. This could include computers, telephones and headsets, photocopiers, fax machines, franking machines and pens and paper. For example, computers need to be turned on, photocopiers need to be turned on and may need the paper trays filling, fax machines may need to have paper trays filled or toner changed.

GIVE IT A GO: preparing equipment for work

1 Visit a retailer in your local area.
2 Look at the sales area and write a list of the equipment you think needs to be prepared before the store is opened.
3 If possible, ask one of the sales staff how they prepare their work area and write down the steps they follow.

● *Safe and tidy work area* ●

It is essential, in all areas of business, for work areas to be safe and tidy. Untidiness can cause **hazards** such as obstacles that people could trip over, electrical dangers and health hazards through lack of hygiene. Untidiness can also make it difficult for employees to do their jobs properly – for example, because important documents cannot be found or because there is not enough space to work in.

> **GLOSSARY**
>
> A **hazard** is something that could cause harm.

● *Efficient use of space* ●

In retail outlets there needs to be enough space for customers to walk about with their trolleys or baskets. It is also important for the space to be used efficiently for displaying the goods on sale and making it easy for customers to pick up items. High shelves can make it difficult for shorter people to reach the products and narrow aisles can make it difficult for wheelchair users, parents with pushchairs or more than one customer to browse comfortably.

In offices there needs to be enough space for employees and visiting clients to walk from desk to desk or office to office. Employees' work areas need to be arranged so that they can do their jobs. For example, most employees will need space for paperwork as well as a computer and the computer station needs to be set up so that the employee can sit comfortably and see the screen easily.

• *Health and safety* •

All employers are required by law to make sure that the workplace is safe and healthy. In large businesses there will usually be a health and safety

representative who will provide information about health and safety within the business and who employees can talk to if they are worried about any health and safety problems.

▲ **Places of work must be safe for the people who use them**

Employees are required by law to take reasonable care for their own health and safety and that of others (this includes any visiting customers, as well as colleagues). They are also required to use all work items correctly. Whenever you use a piece of equipment you need to be careful to do so safely. When you move something, you need to think carefully about whether it could cause a hazard (for example, a box in the middle of an aisle in a supermarket could cause a customer to trip and hurt themselves).

It is not only when you work in premises open to the public (e.g. shops) that you need to be careful and assess risks. This is also important in offices and any other workplace.

• *Fire safety* •

Employers must make sure that safe working practices are set and followed with regard to fire safety. This could include properly marked fire exits, emergency evacuation procedures, safe storage of flammable material and providing necessary fire extinguishers. As an employee it is important to ensure that you know where the nearest fire exit is and what you have to do in the case of an emergency. It may be part of your job to make sure that any visiting customers are made safe. It is also a good idea to make sure that you know how to use the fire extinguishers.

● *Accidents* ●

It is important to know the procedures to follow in case of accidents to yourself, your colleagues or your customers. You should know which of your colleagues have first aid qualifications and where the nearest first aid box is. In cases of severe accidents, you will need to call 999 and ask for an ambulance.

EVIDENCE ACTIVITY

Prepare yourself and your work area for customer service

1 Choose a business that you have worked for (e.g. your current job, a previous job, a work experience placement) or visited.

2 Describe how customer service staff need to present themselves in this business (include details about dress code, attitude, personal presentation, etc.).

3 Describe what knowledge customer service staff need to have about the products or services in order to deal efficiently with customers.

4 Summarise the customer service guidelines or standards and how staff follow these.

5 Describe how teamwork within the business helps to improve customer service.

6 Describe how the customer service area is prepared for business.

7 Describe the responsibilities of the employer in terms of health and safety, fire safety and accidents.

8 Describe the responsibilities of the staff in terms of health and safety, fire safety and accidents.

Communication skills

Customer service is a two-way street. As well as talking to your customers you need to listen to them and encourage them to tell you what they want and need. You need to learn about the different types of communication, such as **face to face**, letter, telephone, email and Internet. You need to take on board all customer comments, whether they are good or bad. You must respond to comments and queries where you can, while passing on the information to others in your organisation who are more able to act on it.

> ### GLOSSARY
>
> **Face-to-face communication** means talking to someone in person.

Communications

Communication is essentially the interaction between people that focuses on the transfer of information. Some methods of passing on information involve writing it down. Other methods use the spoken word (sometimes known as oral methods).

• *Verbal communication* •

Verbal communication is any communication that uses language. It can include **oral communication**, such as speaking to another person over the telephone, face-to-face discussions, interviews, debates, presentations and so on. It can also include **written communication**, such as letters and emails.

Good verbal skills are important to help you communicate with customers and colleagues. Good communication can lead to more sales and to increased customer satisfaction. Failure to transmit clear messages can lead to errors and customer dissatisfaction.

• *Non-verbal communication* •

Non-verbal communication includes body language, eye contact, facial expression, posture, gestures and tone of voice. Non-verbal communication is very important in customer service, in terms of what your non-verbal communication puts across to your customers and how you understand your customers' non-verbal communication. When dealing with international customers and customers from cultures other than your own, it is important to consider carefully your own non-verbal communication. Certain gestures can have different meanings for different people and some people will be more tolerant of physical contact than others. For example, in the UK, it is common to shake hands at the end of a deal, but in other countries and cultures this physical contact may be unwelcome, while in others more physical contact might be common, such as cheek kissing or hugging.

• *Body language* •

Body language is a type of non-verbal communication. Your body language can affect both your own state of mind and the impression you give to others. Slumped shoulders, a frowning face, bowed head and lack of eye contact can make you feel quite low and can give the impression that you are not interested in your customers, that you are afraid of them or that you lack confidence. Smiling, standing straight with shoulders back and making eye contact with your customers can make you feel and look confident. Your customers will be more likely to believe you know what you are talking about and will feel happier to take advice from you.

Other elements of body language include:

- *fiddling (can make you seem nervous)*
- *crossing your arms (can make you seem impatient or bored)*
- *putting your hands on your hips (can make you seem cross)*
- *leaning forward (can make you seem interested)*
- *nodding or shaking your head (can show you agree with or understand a customer without interrupting them).*

● *Types of communication* ●

Face-to-face communication

Face-to-face communication is when you are talking to someone in person. It usually refers to a one-on-one meeting, but can also include, for example, talking to a couple, a family or a group of friends who are coming to buy a product or service. Face-to-face communication also includes elements of non-verbal communication such as eye contact, body language and tone of voice.

Letters

Business letters are:

- *the most frequently used form of external communication between one business and another*
- *a written record that can be used to send almost any type of information*
- *usually on headed paper*
- *usually set out in fully blocked style*
- *written in a more formal language than personal letters.*

Email

Email has become the primary means for delivering short written messages within organisations that are networked. As email between organisations becomes more common, it is increasingly taking the place of faxes, particularly as whole documents can be sent as email attachments. Email provides many cost advantages when compared with the use of paper or telephone. It also allows for fast communication between outlets and offices in different countries – where telephone communication may be difficult to arrange due to differing time zones.

Telephone

Telephone communication is a type of verbal communication. It also includes elements of non-verbal communication, such as tone of voice, though not as many as face-to-face communication. More and more companies are increasing their use of the telephone in communicating with customers. Call centres and mail order are the fastest growing operational departments for UK organisations. In telephone communication, it is essential for all employees to represent their organisation in a professional and friendly way.

Internet and Intranet

The Internet provides businesses with the ability to make information widely available. A number of businesses also use the Internet to sell products or services. For internal communication, companies will often use an Intranet. This works in the same way as a website on the Internet, but is limited to internal use only. Putting information such as phone directories, product information, health and safety procedures, etc. on the Intranet can be much less expensive than using printed documents. It also makes the information easier to keep up-to-date, as changes can be made at the touch of a button and will be immediately visible to everyone.

CASE STUDY – CADBURY

Communication in Cadbury customer service department

The customer service function at *Cadbury* involves dealing with customers on a daily basis. The customer care unit does not only deal with complaints from customers, it also deals with questions, queries and feedback. The most common method of communicating with the public at *Cadbury* is by telephone. However, they also receive complaints and feedback by fax, email and letter and usually reply using the same method. When communicating internally, telephone, fax, email and the intranet are all used in sending information between departments.

Find out more at the *Cadbury* website – a link is available at **www.heinemann.co.uk/hotlinks** (express code 1211P).

Questions

1 What methods of communication are used at *Cadbury*?

2 What are the advantages and disadvantages of these methods?

● *Confidential information* ●

When working in customer service, it is essential to know what information is confidential. There will be certain information about a business that must not be passed on to anyone outside the company. Any information that, if disclosed, could damage the business's reputation or service or affect its competitive advantage would be sensitive.

⟲ THINK ABOUT IT

Think about what damage could be caused by confidential business information being stolen by or disclosed to a competitor.

▲ **Disclosing confidential information can harm a business**

In addition to confidential business information, customer service employees may also be told confidential personal information by customers. The Data Protection Act 1998 restricts and sets down rules for the processing of sensitive information. The following are examples of sensitive personal information:

- *political opinions*
- *religious or other beliefs*
- *trade union membership*
- *physical or mental health*
- *criminal proceedings and convictions.*

Businesses that have to collect any personal information about their customers (including, for example, names, addresses and income) will have a privacy policy that sets out for customers what information will be kept and what, if any, will be passed on to outside organisations.

Skills

Anyone providing customer service – whether it is internal or external – needs to have excellent communication skills. They need to know how to use appropriate language, both written and spoken. They need to pay attention to the level and tone of their voice, to make good use of body language, as well as understanding other people's body language. They also need to develop skills in recording and relaying of messages.

● *Appropriate language* ●

Working in customer service it is important to use language that is **appropriate** to your audience (i.e. your customers). Your audience will depend on the area in which you work. For example, when dealing with business clients, it may be appropriate to use more technical language, if they are familiar with it. However, when dealing with the general public, the language needs to be clear and straightforward. When working with the general public it may be necessary to tailor the language you use to the individual customer. For example, certain slang terms might be appropriate to use with a younger customer, but not with an older customer.

Spoken language

Spoken language can be less formal than written language, but slang should generally be avoided, unless it is appropriate. For example, slang or technical language might be appropriate if working in a shop selling computer games, but you should also be aware that your customers may not always be the people who will be using the product. You need to take into account the educational level, age and social background of your customers. For example, the language used in an up-market clothes shop may well differ from that used in a budget clothes shop.

It may be necessary to deal with international customers or domestic customers whose first language is not English. If someone tells you they do not understand what you have said, it is important to try to rephrase it in a clearer way – do not just repeat what you said, or say the same thing but with a louder voice. You also need to take into account other potential communication problems such as hearing impairments. For example, if your customer is deaf or very hard of hearing, you should make sure that you face them directly while talking, so that they are able to lip read.

Written language

Written language is generally more formal than spoken language. It is important to use correct spelling and grammar. Bad spelling and grammar can cause misunderstanding. It can also cause annoyance to customers and will make your organisation look unprofessional.

GLOSSARY

Appropriate means fit for the purpose or situation.

In written language slang should be avoided even more so than in spoken language.

In some cases, when dealing with international customers, it may be necessary to get written material translated before sending it out. If the customer is happy to receive communication in English, then it is important to ensure that the English is very clear and understandable. For example, any idioms (e.g. 'It's been raining cats and dogs here' or 'I've been working like a dog') are likely to be misunderstood.

● *Tone and level of voice* ●

When speaking to customers it is important to pay close attention to your tone and level of voice. Your tone of voice can indicate your emotions – for example, tone of voice can be sarcastic, patronising, frustrated, angry and so on. The level of voice should be carefully balanced. If it is too quiet the customer may not be able to hear everything you say, or may feel you are nervous or lacking in confidence. If it is too loud you may come across as angry or frustrated with the customer.

● *Welcoming* ●

In customer services it is important to be welcoming and friendly. In a reception area, it is important to greet customers as soon as possible and to find out what they want. In certain shops it may be appropriate to welcome customers as they come in and ask if they need any help.

Speak clearly and smile as you speak. Take care with your tone of voice and make sure it is welcoming and that you do not sound bored or frustrated.

Facial expression, smiling and eye contact

Make sure your facial expression is welcoming. Smile, but do not grin as this could make you seem sarcastic. Think of yourself as calm and confident and this will show in your facial expression. Do not frown or raise your eyebrows. Make sure you keep eye contact with the customer. If you look away or look at your feet you can appear nervous or bored. Keeping eye contact will ensure customers feel they have your full attention.

Gestures

Make sure your own **gestures** (e.g. nodding to show you agree with the customer, leaning forward to show interest) let customers know they have your full attention. Watch customers' own gestures to try to understand their mood. Customers who are leaning forward are likely to be interested and enthusiastic about what you are saying. Customers who are fiddling or looking away are probably losing interest. Customers who are talking with many hand movements could be very

> **GLOSSARY**
>
> **Gestures** are hand and body movements that have meaning (e.g. nodding your head or waving).

enthusiastic about something or, equally, could be very angry about something.

• *Assisting* •

It is important to offer and give help to customers. Opening doors for customers with lots of bags, will make them feel good – and make them more likely to come back. Packing customers' shopping and offering to carry it to their cars can often be much appreciated. Offering to get something from a high shelf is also good customer service. If your business does not have the product or service the customer is looking for, as well as suggesting alternatives that your business does have, you can suggest other local businesses that might be able to help. Although you will be sending them elsewhere, the attention and thoughtfulness will be remembered and they will be more likely to come back to your business when they want something you do sell.

• *Questioning* •

Questioning is very important in customer services. Your first contact with a customer should usually be in the form of a question. For example, 'How can I help, Sir?', 'What are you looking for?'. Questioning will help you find out about the needs of your customers. It is important to listen to the answer. From the answers a customer gives, you can provide targeted help or you can follow up with more detailed questions, such as 'What is your budget for this item?', 'How soon do you need the job done?', which can further your knowledge of the customer's needs.

• *Listening* •

Improving your listening skills can make a huge difference to your success in communicating with customers. Customers need to know that you fully understand them and their needs. Here are some listening tips that will help you:

- *don't interrupt unnecessarily*
- *don't switch off half way through*
- *don't hurry people*
- *try to put yourself in the customer's place.*

Listen to what the customer has to say. The more you learn about your customers the more likely you are to sell to them. The more interested you are the more interesting you will appear to them.

• *Telephone skills* •

On the telephone we are limited to using only 30% of our available communication skills, which means we must work even harder than in face-to-face communications.

When answering the telephone you need to beware of ruining a professional image with comments that could give the wrong impression, such as:

⊃ *'He's still at lunch.' (= he's taking a long break)*

⊃ *'She's not in yet.' (= she's late)*

⊃ *'He's left already.' (= he's slipped off early)*

⊃ *'She's at the dentist.' (this information is too personal)*

⊃ *'He's just popped out.' (= and does so all the time)*

⊃ *'I don't know where he is.' (= internal communication is bad)*

⊃ *'He's tied up.' (= he's too busy to talk to you)*

◯ THINK ABOUT IT

Think about times when you felt frustrated over the phone when talking to a salesperson or customer service representative. What made you frustrated? What could the employee have done to make your experence more pleasant?

▼ **Make sure you record all relevant information when taking messages**

• *Recording and relaying messages* •

When taking messages for other people, it is vital to collect and write down all the relevant information. The following checklist will help you to make sure you haven't forgotten anything:

⊃ *who the call is for*

⊃ *the date and time of the call*

⊃ *the name of caller (and the company, if relevant)*

⊃ *the caller's telephone (and/or fax) number*

⊃ *the reason for the call*

⊃ *whether the call is urgent*

⊃ *a convenient time to return the call*

⊃ *your name*

⊃ *details of anything you have agreed with the caller.*

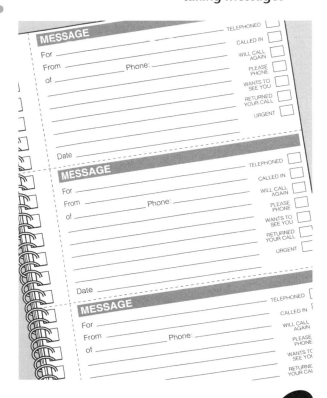

EVIDENCE ACTIVITY   P4

Communication skills

1 Choose a business that you have worked for (e.g. your current job, a previous job, a work experience placement) or visited.

2 Describe how customer service staff use non-verbal skills to improve their communication with customers.

3 Describe how customer service staff use verbal skills to improve their communication with customers.

4 Describe the different methods of communication that are used within the organisation.

5 Describe the personal communication skills that are necessary in a customer service employee in the organisation.

6 Describe the procedure for recording and relaying messages.

Care and service

Customer service does not end with the selling of the product or completion of the service provided. It is extended after the sale to provide the best possible service for the customer. Customers may be tempted to buy products, particularly expensive ones, and then regret their purchase afterwards. Businesses usually have a refund and exchange policy. Others may offer a guarantee on products, especially the expensive ones. Examples of after-sales services include dealing with complaints about faulty items, extending guarantees and providing maintenance through warranties on products.

Care

Good customer care will satisfy customers, give you a sense of achievement and provide you with the chance of further promoting your business. Good customer care means a happy customer and bad customer service means an unhappy customer. Improving customer care is one of the ways businesses can attract more customers and compete with other businesses.

• *Attentiveness and attitude* •

Attentiveness
Showing attentiveness involves listening carefully to your customers, questioning them to gain a better understanding of their needs and showing that you have understood these needs by recommending the

right product or service. While persuading a customer to buy the most expensive item may seem like a good money-making strategy for your business, if customers regret their decisions they are unlikely to return to your business at a later date. If you show that you understand their needs, including the **budget** they have available, they are more likely to come back later and therefore make your business more money in the long-term.

Attitude

Make sure you maintain a positive attitude. Provide positive solutions for customers, not negative ones. For example, suggest alternatives rather than just saying, 'We don't have that' or 'We don't do that.' Be enthusiastic about your products or services, letting customers know why they are better than those of your competitors. Take into account the customers' needs and wants. Make customers feel at ease and show that you are interested in them.

> ### GLOSSARY
>
> A **budget** is the amount of money available for a task or project (business); to budget is to look at how much money you have coming in and decide what you can afford to pay for different things (personal).

◯ THINK ABOUT IT

Think about a time when you have been served by a good salesperson. What was the salesperson's attitude? Why do you feel he or she was a good salesperson?

• *Selecting and providing accurate and appropriate information* •

The information that you provide to customers must always be accurate. It should also be appropriate to the individual customer. For example, if a customer asks for the price of a computer and whether they will be able to get Internet access with it, you should not instead give them a long explanation about how much RAM it has and the state-of-the-art sound and video cards.

When giving information make sure to:

- *be clear and accurate*
- *give correct information*
- *avoid jargon*
- *talk with confidence*
- *get the facts and record the information*
- *confirm your customer understands the information you have supplied*
- *answer questions if you can or offer to find out the information if you cannot.*

• *Exceeding customer expectations* •

Give customers more than they expect. Whether it's spending a few extra (non-billable) minutes helping one client solve a problem, taking others to breakfast a few times a year, or becoming the expert they can call for solid research, give your customers more than they pay for.

CASE STUDY – NICETIME

Exceeding customer expectations

Nicetime wanted to deliver extended services and improved public access at the same time as introducing a more flexible working week. *Nicetime* opened one of the customer enquiry centres in Sussex every Thursday evening and Saturday morning. This was achieved using volunteers among the staff. The extended service helped 543 customers. This represented 3.1% of the callers between December 2001 and July 2002.

Questions

1 What are the advantages for *Nicetime* of providing access to customer enquiry centres Thursday evenings and Saturday mornings?

2 Find three businesses that provide customer services that exceed your expectations.

3 Describe these services.

◀ *Nicetime* **have improved their customer services**

• *Under-promise and over-deliver* •

If you intend to make promises, you must be prepared to keep them, no matter what the cost. The easiest way to lose the respect of customers is by guaranteeing things that you are either unable or unwilling to deliver. When you tell someone that you intend to do something, it is your responsibility to see to it that you follow through.

You must know what you can and cannot commit to. Never lie, never cheat and never ever over-commit. For example, if you think you can probably deliver a product the next day, promise to deliver it by the day after. If you think the service will probably cost £500, promise to provide it below £700. If you are then able to deliver the next day or do the work for £500, the customer will be pleased because you have exceeded his or her expectations.

Service

Research shows that businesses spend six times as much on recruiting a new customer than they do on keeping an existing one. Every business – no matter how small – should have a strategy for dealing with customers. Listening to customers can help in all areas of your business, from developing new products to finding out more about your competitors.

● *Assisting and offering help* ●

Customers should be assisted before the sale and also after the sale is completed. A salesperson should offer assistance before sales in terms of providing knowledge and information about the product features, price and delivery. However, assistance does not end with the selling of the product. Extended after-sale assistance provides the best possible service for the customer.

Assisting customers should also start from the top. Richard Branson has been known to phone customers to discuss their problems with a product or service.

GIVE IT A GO: help and assistance

1 Visit a local supermarket.
2 Find out what extra services are offered to help and assist customers.

● *Communicating* ●

Communicating with your customers is an essential part of customer service. This can involve letting them know what services are available, providing after-sales advice and maintenance and making sure they are happy with the product you have sold them or the advice you have provided.

● *Availability of products and services and delivery time* ●

Customers buy goods or services to satisfy their immediate needs and wants. Customers therefore expect to find or receive a product when they want it. For example, if you need a computer to do your coursework, there is no point in buying one that will not be available for six months. Businesses expect to receive stock or raw materials that they order on time. Delays can lead to losses.

● *Delivery time and date* ●

All warehouses and the stockrooms attached to shops and businesses need an efficient and accurate stock control system that allows additions and withdrawals from stock to be immediately and accurately recorded. Good sales practice involves speedy delivery of goods and services. Having paid for a product, customers like to receive it straight away. Sometimes though, especially with bulky items, it is difficult to find enough space in the shop to store them. Orders have to be made to the warehouse or the stockroom. Some businesses offer free delivery for customers who live in the local area as part of the service. It is important to make sure that goods are delivered at a time convenient to the customer and that the goods turn up when you have said they will.

● *Responding to changes in customer needs* ●

Businesses succeed by responding to changes in customer needs. For example, supermarkets used to provide for fairly basic food needs, whereas these days they provide for people with varying budgets, they provide more exotic foods and they provide food for vegetarians and people with food allergies. They also provide non-food products, such as crockery, books, magazines, medicines and so on.

In order to respond to changes in customer needs, businesses need to know what these new needs are. An important part of customer service is talking to and questioning customers in order to understand their current needs and predict their future needs.

CASE STUDY – SAINSBURY'S

Sainsbury's responds to growing interest in travel and style

Due to the growing interest in travel and style, *Sainsbury's* source from around the world new and different food and drink products and ideas. Responding to the increasing interest in homestyle, we launched a stylish range of homewares in September 2003.

Find out more at the *Sainsbury's* website – a link is available at **www.heinemann.co.uk/hotlinks** (express code 1211P).

Question

Give four benefits for *Sainsbury's* of responding to customers' growing interest in travel and style.

● *Seeking assistance* ●

In some circumstances you might find it difficult to handle customers, for example, if they are rude or angry. In such circumstances it is a good idea to seek help from your supervisor or manager who may be better able to deal with such situations. If a customer needs information about a product that you do not know yourself, you will need to get help from a colleague, supervisor or manager who does. It is important to know who to go to for help in each situation. For example, one colleague may specialise in a certain product range, your supervisor may have more knowledge about special discounts available and your manager may be more suited to deal with large and unusual orders. Make sure you seek **assistance** quickly, as soon as you know that the customer has a need that you cannot personally fulfil. Do not try and 'wing it' as it will be obvious to the customer that you are doing so.

> **GLOSSARY**
>
> **Assistance** means help.

● *Organisational limitations and guidelines* ●

Organisational limitations

Providing good customer service is sometimes easier said than done. The standards and expectations of customer services depends on many organisational factors such as business strategy, culture, mission statements and management style, support and attitude. These factors might help or hinder customer service performance.

Organisational factors that can help customer service performance include:

- *management with vision, energy, dynamism and a positive outlook*
- *putting customer needs and wants at the very centre of the business*
- *the ability to change, improve and adopt new ideas*
- *staff commitment, motivation, ability, training and development*
- *lack of bureaucracy*
- *a flexible system that can respond to changes in the market.*

Organisational guidelines

Most businesses have a customer service policy or guidelines for staff who deal with customer service. They do not just make it up as they go along. The policy is a guarantee to the customers that the business is dedicated to achieving customer satisfaction. Guidelines could, for example, state that you aim to achieve 100% order accuracy, 30-day money back guarantee, speedy service, fast corrective action on customer issues, promise of low prices, free delivery and so on. Each statement in the policy or guidelines may have a few sentences in small print to explain in more detail the terms, conditions and process. Make sure that you fully understand the customer service policy or guidelines and that you fulfil any promises made within it/them when dealing with customers.

● *Keeping records and information* ●

Businesses need to find out who their customers are and what their customers' needs and wants are. It is therefore important to keep accurate records and information about customers' profiles. Businesses will keep details about customer habits and preferences. They will also keep information about customers' personal details, such as names, addresses and telephone numbers, so that they contact them in the future either to sell other products or services or to ensure that the customer has received satisfactory service.

Details of customer feedback and complaints need to be kept in order to improve products and to improve future service. New strategies or guidelines for service may be developed on the basis of analysing feedback and complaints.

EVIDENCE ACTIVITY  P5

Providing good care and service

1 Choose a business that you have worked for (e.g. your current job, a previous job, a work experience placement) or visited.

2 Describe how customer service staff select and provide accurate and appropriate information.

3 Describe any methods the organisation uses to exceed customer expectations.

4 Describe what services the organisation offers to assist and help customers.

5 Identify which members of staff would be able to provide customer service staff with further information or help when needed.

6 Summarise the organisation's guidelines for delivery and providing customer service, including any after-sales services on offer.

7 Describe the procedures for keeping records of customer feedback and complaints.

END OF UNIT ASSIGNMENT

Elegant Steps is a small designer shop in Brentwood in Essex. The shop sells quality designer shoes for men, women and children. One day a middle-class woman walks into the shop to buy a designer pair of shoes for a wedding party. This woman is very demanding and spends over an hour asking questions and trying on many different shoes in the shop. Eventually the woman decides to buy a dark blue pair of shoes for £250. Two weeks later the woman comes back to the shop angry and complaining that the new pair of shoes hurt her feet. She demands a refund although the shoes have already been worn. The shop policy states that neither refund nor part-exchange is acceptable without a receipt and if the shoes have been worn.

▲ **Customers' complaints may be unreasonable**

Task 1 P1 D1

1 Identify the needs and expectations of the customer.

2 Describe whether her needs are routine or non-routine from her point of view and from your point of view (as the salesperson).

3 Describe how you would respond to all of the customer's needs.

Task 2

1 Describe how you would need to present yourself as a salesperson working at *Elegant Steps*.

2 Describe how the shop would need to be prepared for customer service, including health and safety aspects.

Task 3

1 Describe the communication skills you would need to work at *Elegant Steps*.

2 Describe the communication skills and strategies that you would need to use with this customer.

3 Think of and describe a solution to the customer's problem and how you would effectively communicate the solution to her.

4 List the questions that you would ask the customer **(a)** when she first comes in to buy the shoes and **(b)** when she comes back to complain.

5 Describe how you will show the customer that you have listened to her and that you understand her needs.

Task 4

1 Describe the skills and strategies that could be used at *Elegant Steps* to provide good service.

2 Describe how you can provide consistent customer care to this customer.

3 Describe how you can provide consistent customer care in general at *Elegant Steps*.

4 Explain why it is important to provide good customer service to this customer.

5 Explain why it is important to provide good customer service to everyone, when working at *Elegant Steps*.

unit 4

Personal effectiveness

This unit will help you look at your own skills and potential in relation to working in the business, retail and administration sectors. You will learn how to assess your skills, behaviour and interests and use this assessment to create a personal audit. You will learn how to identify your strengths and your weaknesses, how to match your strengths to specific job roles and how to set goals and targets for improving your skills. In addition, you will find out how to create a personal statement and a portfolio that displays evidence of your job-related skills.

◀ **How well do you know yourself?**

To complete this unit you must:

▭ carry out a personal audit of your skills, behaviour and interests, to help find suitable jobs

▭ explore, assess and improve your strengths and weaknesses in relation to suitable jobs

▭ prepare a personal statement and portfolio to prepare for employment.

Personal audit

A **personal audit** involves looking at yourself and your experience to assess what skills you have. The skills you look at include **vocational**, personal and **inter-personal skills**. You also look at your own behaviour and how to change it where necessary and your interests, which could provide useful skills for the workplace.

Vocational skills

Your vocational skills come from any work-related experiences and any practical qualifications you have gained. These are very important to employers, as they show that you are able to handle basic work-related tasks and take responsibility for your own work.

● *Work-related experience* ●

Work-related experience comes from paid work you have done, such as part-time or temporary jobs, but also from any work-experience placements you have been on and any **voluntary** work you have done.

Part-time jobs

Many students do part-time or holiday work. As well as earning you extra money, a well-chosen job can provide excellent work experience. It can give you a taste of different working environments and provide a competitive edge for when you enter the workplace full-time.

You should keep a record of any part-time or temporary work that you do – even if it's just for a few days. Note down the organisation you worked for, how long you worked there, what your main duties were and who you had to report to. It is also useful to keep notes of any problems you had in the job and how you solved them.

If you have not done any part-time or **temporary work**, you might want to explore the possibilities in your area for doing so.

Work experience

Most schools and colleges require students to do some work experience. This may involve working in a placement for a period of two weeks, or perhaps one afternoon or day a week over a longer period. Some students also arrange work experience themselves, for example, during holidays from school or college.

Work experience can be very useful to find out about working practice in your chosen area, build useful contacts, show **motivation** to possible employers and gain more skills.

Keep a note of any work-experience placements you have been on. Record the place and length of the placement, what your main tasks were, who you had to report to and what skills and experience you gained while there.

If you have not already done so, think about arranging a placement yourself (e.g. during the holidays). Employers will be very impressed with someone who has organised their own work experience, because it shows motivation and enthusiasm for the business.

Voluntary work

There are many opportunities to do voluntary work. It can involve working in a charity shop, helping deliver meals on wheels, spending time visiting sick children in hospital or older people who are unable to get out and about, and many other things.

Doing voluntary work can provide lots of work-related experience as well as opportunities to improve **transferable skills**, such as working with others, communication skills, organisational skills and so on.

If you would like to try some volunteering, you can find opportunities in your local area at the *do-it!* website – a link is available at **www.heinemann.co.uk/hotlinks** (express code 1211P).

• *Practical qualifications* •

Practical qualifications show your motivation and enthusiasm to employers. Some might also be of particular use for specific jobs. Examples of practical qualifications include first aid and swimming certificates and the Duke of Edinburgh's Award, but you may well have or be working toward other practical qualifications.

Keep a note of any practical qualifications you gain and keep any certificates you were given on completion of the qualifications.

First aid

In many organisations, employers are required to have trained first-aiders available, so having a first aid qualification can be very useful. Some schools and colleges provide first aid courses for students and staff. St. John Ambulance also provides first aid courses.

> **GLOSSARY**
>
> **Motivation** means wanting to do the job well and enjoying it.

> **GLOSSARY**
>
> **Transferable skills** are skills which can be used in all or most job roles (e.g. communication skills, IT skills and punctuality).

Swimming certificates

Most primary and secondary schools provide swimming lessons for pupils and students. Sometimes these will lead to swimming certificates and sometimes people attend swimming classes at their local leisure centre and gain swimming certificates there.

The Duke of Edinburgh's Award

The Duke of Edinburgh's Award is a programme of activities for young people. It is widely recognised by employers and educators. Benefits of undertaking The Duke of Edinburgh's Award include:

- *developing self-confidence and self-reliance*
- *gaining a sense of achievement and responsibility*
- *discovering new skills, interests and talents*
- *developing leadership skills and abilities*
- *discovering new opportunities*
- *making friends*
- *experiencing teamwork*
- *improving problem-solving and decision-making skills*
- *increasing motivation*
- *enhancing self-esteem*
- *developing communication skills.*

▶ The Duke of Edinburgh's Award develops young people's skills

You can find out more about The Duke of Edinburgh's Award at the organisation's website – a link is available at **www.heinemann.co.uk/hotlinks** (express code 1211P).

GIVE IT A GO: practical qualifications

1 Find out more about a practical qualification you would like to gain (e.g. The Duke of Edinburgh's Award, first aid certificate).

2 Find out what you would need to do to get this qualification (e.g. do a short course, a long course, etc.).

3 If you can, book yourself on the course and gain the qualification.

Personal skills

Examples of personal skills include appearance, dress, posture and body language. You may be able to think of others.

● *Appearance* ●

Being skilled in personal appearance does not just mean knowing how to look professional, or indeed what the latest fashions are. It involves changing your appearance to suit the situation. For example, a receptionist in a solicitor's office will need to look smart and professional, whereas a sales assistant in a youthful clothes shop or record store may need to concentrate more on fashion, while also looking smart.

All situations need you to pay attention to personal hygiene, so keep yourself, your hair, your nails, your teeth and so on, clean.

● *Dress* ●

Your ability to dress to suit the occasion – or the workplace – is very important to employers. While some organisations may have uniforms or specific dress codes, others will just have unwritten **expectations** of employees. Make a note of your experiences of dressing formally, in uniform, smartly, casually and scruffily – and link these experiences with the situations, to show you know how to dress **appropriately**.

Formal

Formal dress includes black-tie, dinner dress, and other kinds of dress. Formal dress may be required at special occasions, such as weddings and award ceremonies. Some jobs may require you to wear formal dress on a regular basis (for example, in some catering jobs), while others may require you to wear formal dress on occasion.

GLOSSARY

An **expectation** is what is expected (e.g. your employer will expect you to come to work on time).

Appropriate means fit for the purpose or situation.

Uniform

You will probably already have experience of wearing a uniform, as most schools in the UK require their students to wear one. There are also many jobs that require employees to wear uniforms. While you may have been someone who pushed the limits of the school uniform rules, in a work environment it is important to follow uniform guidelines very strictly. If you are required to wear a uniform in your job, you have less to worry about at the start of the working day!

Smart

The definition of 'smart dress' will vary from organisation to organisation. For example, it could mean you need to wear a suit to work or it might mean you need to wear a shirt and tie (or skirt and blouse). If you are required to dress smartly at work, look at how the other staff dress. Try to dress as smartly as, or even a little bit more smartly than, everyone else.

A few general rules for being smart include:

- *don't wear jeans or T-shirts*
- *wear shirts or blouses*
- *don't wear skirts above the knee*
- *don't wear shorts*
- *don't show any midriff*
- *don't wear more than one pair of earrings*
- *don't show any other visible piercings (e.g. take out nose rings and eyebrow rings, etc.).*

Some organisations still require women to wear skirts or dresses, but this is becoming much rarer these days and smart trousers will usually be just as acceptable.

Casual

As with smart dress, the definition will vary from organisation to organisation. Look at what others are wearing and take your cue from them. Sometimes casual dress includes jeans (but not with rips or other effects), while sometimes it does not. If in doubt, don't wear them.

Scruffy

While scruffy dress may need to be kept for your free time, there are some situations where you are required to dress scruffily (or at least in clothes that can be dirtied or damaged). Examples could include working in a dirty environment, such as a building site, farm or factory. You also might be expected to dress scruffily for certain out-of-hours activities, such as going on a cross-country walk for charity.

⬭ THINK ABOUT IT

Think about the way you dress. Do you always wear the same kind of clothes or do you wear different clothes for different situations? Have you ever been to a wedding? If so, what did you wear? If you have a part-time job, what do you wear for it? What do your colleagues wear? Do you think you are dressing appropriately?

• *Posture* •

Your **posture** can affect the impression people have of you. If you slouch and look at the floor a lot, people will see you as shy or scared. If you sit or stand straight you will look and feel more confident. If you stand with your hands in your pockets you will look as though you do not care. If you stand with your arms crossed or on your hips, you may look cross or bossy. Good posture makes you feel more confident – not just look more confident. It is also good for your future health.

• *Body language* •

It is important both to understand and to use body language. Slumped shoulders, a frowning face, bowed head and lack of eye contact can make you feel low and show lack of interest, fear or lack of confidence. Smiling, standing straight with shoulders back and making eye contact can make you feel and look confident.

Fiddling indicates nervousness, crossed arms indicate impatience or boredom, leaning forward indicates interest and enthusiasm and nodding or shaking of the head (at the right moment, of course) will show agreement or understanding.

Inter-personal skills

Inter-personal skills are all about relating to other people. They are very important in any kind of work.

• *Getting on with people* •

Getting on with people can be a very tough challenge. Unfortunately, getting on with people does not just mean being able to talk to and have fun with your friends. In life, but especially at work, it is necessary to get on with people who you do not like or who are very different from you. While some people find it very easy to get on with anyone, most people find it more difficult.

Some tips to help you get on with people include:

▭ *be friendly to all people*

▭ *try your best and then move on*

> **GLOSSARY**
>
> **Posture** means how you sit, stand or hold yourself.

⟁ *communicate assertively (but not aggressively) with other people*

⟁ *be easy going with other people*

⟁ *be polite*

⟁ *aim to please others*

⟁ *be a good listener*

⟁ *respect others (and show this respect).*

If you can develop your ability to get on with other people, this will be very useful in your working life and will be noticed by employers.

● *How you would relate to others in a work situation* ●

Empathy is a very useful skill to have and to develop. Empathy involves seeing a situation from other people's point of view: understanding what they want and why they want it.

It is too easy to forget that your colleagues are human too. They have their own weaknesses, habits and needs and sometimes these get pushed aside in the daily rush of work.

Listening and **observing** will help you build your empathy skills and so improve your ability to relate to others in a work situation. It is also important not to jump to **conclusions** or make early **judgements**. Remember that the other person may just be having a bad day.

> ### GLOSSARY
>
> To **observe** means to watch something or someone.
>
> A **conclusion** is what you decide about something.
>
> A **judgement** is what you think of something or someone.

WHAT **if?**

... *you had to work in a team?*

1 What skills would you need to work in a team?

2 Do you have these skills, or do you need to work on them?

3 What could you do to practise these skills?

Behaviour

The way you behave affects the people around you. It also affects the way these people see you.

● *Expected behaviour* ●

Being able to behave as is expected of you is an important skill in life as well as in the workplace. Sometimes it will be obvious what behaviour is expected of you, for example, doing your job to the best of your abilities, dealing politely and helpfully with customers and so on.

However, sometimes you may need to work this out yourself. It is useful to get into the habit of observing those around you closely. In the workplace, look to see how the successful employees behave and use them as your role models. Likewise, look to see how the less successful employees behave and try to avoid this behaviour yourself.

• *Acceptable behaviour* •

Essentially, acceptable behaviour is the same as expected behaviour. Tips for behaving acceptably include:

- *respect other people*
- *understand other people's point of view*
- *do not jump to conclusions*
- *behave toward others as you would like them to behave toward you*
- *respect confidentiality (of personal information and organisational information)*
- *respect others' property (do not steal or knowingly cause damage to others' property)*
- *respect the beliefs of others.*

• *Unacceptable behaviour* •

Examples of unacceptable behaviour include:

- *harassment*
- *bullying*
- *discrimination*
- *making demeaning or offensive comments or gestures*
- *taunting people*
- *ignoring or isolating a person or group*
- *spreading malicious rumours or insulting people*
- *showing confidential information to people who do not have the right or permission to see it*
- *treating anyone unfairly*
- *misusing power or position*
- *making unwelcome sexual advances (e.g. touching, standing too close, showing offensive materials)*
- *making threats or comments about job security without foundation*
- *deliberately undermining someone with constant criticism.*

● *Modifying behaviour* ●

Learning how to change your behaviour where necessary is an important skill. Sometimes you may be unaware that your behaviour is unacceptable until you are either told by someone or realise it through others' actions. If you do discover that an element of your behaviour is causing problems, you should do your utmost to change it.

This can sometimes be quite difficult, so you could try practising with changing small things, then the big things will be easier to change when necessary. For example, you could try making sure you always wear a bicycle helmet when cycling, or try to always say 'please' and 'thank you' to bus drivers, sales assistants and your family.

GIVE IT A GO: modifying behaviour

1 Choose a behaviour that you want to work on. Try to choose something quite small or simple, such as cutting down on your swearing, finishing homework early or washing cups and plates up as soon as you have finished with them.

2 Identify the strategies you will use to modify the behaviour. For example, for swearing you could have a swear box, where you put 10p into it every time you swear on your own and 20p every time you swear in front of someone else.

3 Use these strategies to modify your chosen behaviour.

▶ **Helping others is appreciated**

Interests

We all have some interests in life. For example, some people are interested in music, while others are interested in animals, drawing, travelling or talking to new people. Our interests can sometimes help us guide our career choice and build skills for work.

For employers, interests or hobbies can indicate an employee's ability to relax and switch off at the end of the working day. Having interests outside of work helps reduce stress levels. Interests can also provide an employer with insights into their employees' or potential employees' personalities. For example, social interests can indicate a caring and outgoing nature; an interest in writing or drama can indicate good communication skills; an interest in computing or engineering can indicate practicality; an interest in art can indicate creativity.

The table below shows some examples of interests, but it is quite likely that you will have others.

Table 4.1 Examples of interests and what they might demonstrate

Interest	Commentary
Animals	An interest in animals can indicate a caring nature and responsible attitude. To care for an animal you need to find out how to do so and commit time and effort to that animal, so it also demonstrates research skills, the ability to learn new things, time management skills and the ability to see a task through. Campaigning for animal rights, or raising money for animal charities shows commitment to your beliefs.
People	An interest in people (e.g. socialising with friends, helping people less fortunate, etc.) can show a caring nature, an outgoing personality, an ability to get on with others, as well as good communication skills.
Plants	An interest in plants (e.g. cultivating a garden or a vegetable plot) can show commitment, time management skills and an ability to see a task through. It can also show an ability to research and to learn new things, because in order to care for plants, you need to know how to do so.
Drawing	An interest in drawing demonstrates a creative personality and attention to detail.
Talking	An interest in talking can indicate good communication skills and a willingness to improve them. It can also demonstrate an ability to get on with others.
Music	An interest in music can show creativity. If the interest extends to playing music (e.g. in a band or orchestra) then it also shows commitment, responsibility and time management. It can also show the ability to learn new things and to improve oneself.
Film	An interest in film can show creativity and an ability to see others' points of view. It may also increase communication skills. If it extends, for example, to writing film reviews for a school paper, it would also show commitment, research abilities and writing skills.
Theatre	An interest in theatre shows creativity. If it extends to participating (e.g. acting or helping out backstage) it can also show commitment, teamwork, time management and organisational skills.
Travel	An interest in travel can show an openness to new ideas, an ability to research and a willingness to learn new things. If it extends to saving money for travelling and actually going on trips, it can show financial management skills as well as organisational skills.
Hobbies	A hobby is generally something you do outside of your workplace or school/college and only for your own pleasure. There are many hobbies, some of which fall into the other interests listed above. Having a hobby to which you commit time and effort can show commitment, time management skills, organisational skills, financial management skills and many other skills and abilities, depending on the actual hobby.

◯ THINK ABOUT IT

Think about your interests. Do any of them help improve your personal or interpersonal skills? Could any of your interests lead you to a job? What kind of job? Can you extend any of your interests to gain other skills (e.g. starting or joining a club)?

EVIDENCE ACTIVITY  P1

Different types of jobs

1 Write a list of all your work-related experience (e.g. part-time or temporary jobs, work-experience placements, voluntary work) stating:
   a when and for how long you worked there
   b what your main tasks were
   c who your line manager or supervisor was
   d why you left (if you did).

2 Write a list of your personal skills (e.g. appearance, dress, positive body language).

3 Write a list of your inter-personal skills (e.g. getting on with others, how you relate to others in a work situation).

4 Describe your attitude to behaviour. Are you able to behave as expected in a work situation? Have you had any problems due to unacceptable behaviour? How have you had to (or would you) modify your behaviour to suit a particular work situation?

5 Write a list of your interests (e.g. animals, people, plants, drawing, music, film, theatre, travel, other hobbies, etc.).

GLOSSARY

Your **potential** is how far you could go in your career, or what you could achieve.

Potential

Understanding and improving your **potential** as an employee involves assessing your own strengths and weaknesses, setting goals and targets to improve these and identifying job roles and careers that match your own abilities and strengths.

Assessment

GLOSSARY

To **empower** is to give power to.

The best place to start a job search or develop an education plan is with a study of you. Taking time to discover or confirm your strengths will **empower** you to make key decisions about your career and help you focus on rewarding opportunities.

• *Identify strengths and weaknesses* •

Self-assessment

Self-assessment is an important skill in life, as well as in work. You need to be able to identify your achievements and strengths and build on them, but you also need to be able to see your own weaknesses and work on improving yourself in those areas.

Examples of questions you can ask yourself include:

- *Do I always get my assignments in on time?*

- *Do I do the work to gain a pass or do I always aim for a distinction?*

- *Am I able to explain my views to my friends?*

- *Do I think about others before myself?*

- *Do I spend my money as soon as I have it or do I save up for special purchases?*

- *Am I able to follow rules or do I always push the limits?*

These are just examples. There are many questions you will need to ask yourself in order to identify your strengths and weaknesses. Some people find it easier to identify their weaknesses than their strengths, while others find it difficult to admit to weaknesses.

Assessment by others

Other people's assessment of you can provide a very useful insight into your own strengths and weaknesses. There are many sources for this assessment, for example:

- *friends*

- *relatives*

- *colleagues*

- *teachers*

- *employers*

- *acquaintances (e.g. people on the same sports team, in the same orchestra, in the same club as you, etc.).*

You will probably have some formal assessments available, such as school or college reports, references from work-experience or jobs, letters of recommendation or personal statements from **acquaintances** and so on. These documents are a very useful resource for identifying your strengths and weaknesses. Read them with an open mind and take on board any criticisms they contain, as well as any praise and recognition of achievements.

GLOSSARY

Acquaintances are people you know and who know you.

WHAT if?

... you looked back at all your old school reports?

1 Think about the kinds of reports you get (or used to get) at school.

2 How do they make you feel (e.g. proud, happy, depressed, angry)?

3 How do you think your reports progressed throughout your time at school? Did they always say the same things? Did they get better as you got older?

4 Can you remember anything that always seemed to appear on every school report (e.g. 'Needs to talk more in class', 'Needs to work on punctuality'.)? If so, this is probably a problem area for you and you need to work on it.

5 If you (or your family) have kept your reports, have a look at them to see if you remembered right. Maybe they were better than you remembered?

Strengths

In assessing your potential for employment, you need to look closely at your strengths in areas relevant to work. Some of these are described below, but there may be others that are relevant to specific job roles.

● *Ability to listen and ask appropriate questions* ●

We often take listening for granted, not realising that it is a skill that can be learnt. The ability to listen can be improved with use and will help in all your relationships: at work, at home and with friends.

Listening does not just mean standing or sitting still while someone talks. It means taking in what the other person is saying and responding to the speaker appropriately. It includes asking questions to clarify what you do not understand or to prompt the speaker to provide more information. It also involves paying attention to your own body language to show your interest, enthusiasm and understanding.

▲ **Listening and understanding other people is a skill**

● *Confidence levels* ●

Your confidence levels include your overall self-confidence as well as your confidence in a specific task or subject. Overall self-confidence is something that can be built over time. **Acknowledging** your own achievements and praising or rewarding yourself for them will help with this, as will identifying weaknesses and working to improve them. Confidence levels in a specific task or subject can be increased by building your knowledge about it. For example, if you lack confidence in selling a product, it will help to find out more about that product and learn its benefits and selling points. If you lack confidence in a specific task, asking for guidance as well as doing your own research (e.g. reading user manuals) will build your confidence.

● *Ability to follow instructions* ●

Following instructions involves carefully listening to or reading the instructions and ensuring you understand them. If you do not understand the instructions you will not be able to follow them, so you should always ask or look for more **clarification** where necessary. Once you understand the instructions, you then need to go through the necessary steps to complete the task.

You should have plenty of experience in following instructions from doing assignments at school and college. You may also have experience from work placements or part-time jobs, or from learning the steps to go through in a particular hobby or interest.

● *Good timekeeping* ●

Good timekeeping includes turning up on time for classes and for work. It also involves managing your own workload to ensure that all deadlines are met. Good timekeeping is an essential skill in any job.

● *Administrative abilities* ●

Administrative abilities can include:

- *organising your workload*
- *organising files*
- *using general office software (e.g. word-processing, spreadsheets)*
- *using office machinery (e.g. photocopiers, fax machines)*
- *organising a diary of appointments.*

Many administrative abilities can be learnt and extended from managing your school or college work. For example, organising your notes and textbooks, so that you know where to find information when you need it; creating a study timetable; typing up and presenting assignments using a word-processing program.

● *Customer focus* ●

Customer focus involves putting the customer's needs first. While it is of particular relevance to retail work, it is something that needs to be kept in mind in all jobs. Overall, it is the customers who pay your wages or salary. If you do not meet their needs and expectations of good customer service they will not use the organisation.

Some skills and abilities that you will have gained in school or college work will help with customer focus. For example, the ability to tailor an assignment to what is asked for can be extended into the ability to tailor your work to what the customer asks for.

● *Getting on with other people* ●

Getting on with other people is an important skill. In the workplace, as well as in life, you will need to spend time with people who you do not like or do not share any interests, views or values with. It helps to look beyond the surface and try to understand some of their motivations and desires. Any dislike you feel needs to be pushed to the background, otherwise it will come across in your dealings with them. You will probably have experience of working with other people from school or college and from outside activities, so you will probably have a good idea of whether you are strong in this skill or not. (Look back at pages 95–96 for some tips on getting on with other people.)

● *Using initiative* ●

GLOSSARY

Using **initiative** means working on your own (e.g. to solve problems and decide what work needs doing).

Using **initiative** involves thinking for yourself, rather than always asking what to do or how to do it. An example at home would be changing a light bulb rather than waiting for a parent or partner to do it. An example at school or college would be going to the library or using the Internet to find further information on a subject rather than relying on your textbook or the factsheets your teacher gives you. An example in the workplace would be offering a customer a seat if they look very tired or filling the paper tray in the photocopier before being asked to do so.

● *Learning new skills* ●

Learning new skills does not just involve what you learn at school or college. For example, it can include learning a new recipe so you can cook dinner for your friends or using the Internet or library to learn some phrases in another language to prepare for a holiday.

You should be constantly on the lookout for opportunities to learn new skills – both for improving your career and for your own personal benefit and sense of achievement. The ability and willingness to learn new skills is very important in the workplace and will greatly improve your chances of moving on in your chosen career.

THINK ABOUT IT

Think about how you learn new skills. Do you learn by doing (e.g. practise a task a number of times and then you can do it)? Do you need to make notes of the steps and knowledge needed? Do you prefer to draw pictures and diagrams? Do you like to read a book to learn something or do you prefer to listen to someone explain it to you, or perhaps you find it best to watch someone doing the task?

These questions will help you identify the learning methods that are best for you (everyone is different, so you need to find your own way). Knowing how you learn best will help you improve your learning skills and will help you to enjoy learning new skills, rather than seeing it as a chore.

Weaknesses

Your weaknesses will include any of the skills described above where you need to improve. Identifying your own weaknesses and planning how to improve them is a skill in itself. Make use of your own assessment of yourself and the assessments of others to identify the areas where you need to improve.

Looking at and improving your weaknesses should be an ongoing task – not something you do in preparation for employment and then never think of again. To do this you need to be self-aware and constantly question whether you can improve yourself and your working practices. It helps to look at yourself from someone else's point of view. For example, imagine you are your boss or line manager and ask yourself whether you are doing everything they would want you to.

GIVE IT A GO: strengths and weaknesses

1 Get a piece of A4 paper and draw a line down the middle.
2 On the left, list all the strengths, talents and positive qualities that you have.
3 On the right side, list all the weaknesses you can think of.
   If your left-hand column is much longer than your right, you may want to focus more on the areas where you could use improvement. If your right-hand list is longer than the one on the left, then you may be too self-critical and not recognising or finding your personal strengths.
4 Look at your list of weaknesses and pick one to concentrate on improving over the next week.

Matching strengths to job roles

Having a thorough understanding of your own strengths, qualities and skills will help you to decide on a job role that is most suitable for you. Even if you manage to get through the application and interview process, if you end up working in a job that does not match your strengths, you will probably find it difficult to keep that job.

● *Personal strengths matched to different jobs* ●

By matching your personal strengths to different jobs, you should be able to find a career that will interest and enthuse you – one that will make you want to get up in the mornings!

Some of your personal strengths may be relevant to all or many jobs, but your overall **analysis** of yourself should show that you will be more suited to some jobs than others. For example, if you are very strong in getting on with others, then a job in retail might be more suitable. If you have excellent organisational abilities then a job in administration might be more suitable. Your interests can help you further narrow the field. (Though make sure you don't narrow it too far, or there might not be any jobs available!) For example, if you have a strong interest in animals and very good organisational skills, then you could consider a receptionist job in a veterinary clinic. If you have a strong interest in music and get on well with others, then you could consider working for a music retailer.

Looking at the job descriptions and personal specifications for jobs that interest you will also help to match skills and strengths to jobs.

Job descriptions

A **job description** will set out the daily tasks that the successful applicant needs to do in the job. It may also include more general tasks or responsibilities. Below are some examples of tasks and responsibilities that might appear in a job description:

- *greet clients and see that they are met by the relevant member of staff*
- *use the switchboard to answer calls and direct them to the correct member of staff*
- *photocopy documents*
- *sort and distribute mail within the department*
- *overall responsibility for updating the staff holiday rota*
- *organise travel arrangements for two managers.*

Personal specifications

Personal specifications set out the type of person that is required, rather than the specific skills or tasks involved. This could include:

- *good sense of humour*
- *outgoing personality*
- *professional attitude*

GLOSSARY

Analysis is looking at or studying something.

GLOSSARY

A **job description** gives details of the tasks and responsibilities involved in a job role.

GLOSSARY

Personal specifications give a description of characteristics, personality and skills needed for a job role.

● *thoughtfulness and respect for others*

● *enthusiasm*

● *professional and smart appearance*

● *ability to use initiative.*

Skills and qualifications

If specific skills or qualifications are required for a job role, this will usually be indicated in the advertisement or job description. If a job advertisement asks for people who have a childcare qualification, for example, and you do not have one then you would be unlikely to get the job at this time. If a job requires a full driving licence and you have not yet passed your test, you would not be in a position to apply for it.

It is important to read all the information carefully, so you do not waste your own time or the employer's time by applying for a job you would not be able to do. You may discover that the job roles you are particularly interested in require qualifications or skills that you do not have at the moment. If so you should think seriously about working to gain these skills and qualifications. However, it is also worth looking into other job roles in the same area, as there could be potential to gain the relevant skills or qualifications while doing that job, then moving on in a year or two to the one you really want.

▲ **Qualifications can help you get the job you want**

WHAT **if?**

... *you were a data processor?*

1 What vocational skills would you need?
2 What personal skills would you need?
3 What inter-personal skills would you need?
4 Which work skills would you need to be strong in?
5 Do you have all these skills? Could you be a data processor?

Action plan

Once you have identified your skills, interests, strengths and weaknesses and have found some job roles that interest you and match well with your strengths, you need to create an action plan.

An action plan involves setting goals and targets and a timescale in which you plan to achieve those goals and targets. While at the moment your action plan might be geared towards getting a specific job, as time goes by you will need to develop new action plans to help you progress on your long-term career path.

• *Goals* •

Goals are generally long-term (rather than immediate) things that you want to achieve. It is likely that you will have a number of goals. Examples of goals could include:

- *getting a specific job*
- *gaining a specific qualification*
- *getting a pay rise or promotion*
- *learning how to use a particular piece of software*
- *passing your driving test.*

• *Targets* •

In order to achieve your goals, you need to break them down into smaller, short-term targets. For example, targets for getting a specific job could include:

- *improve your communication skills*
- *find out more about the job role*
- *ask for an application form*
- *write a CV*
- *write a letter of application*
- *practise your interview techniques.*

Breaking down your targets into **manageable** tasks is also important. If you set targets that are too general or too difficult, then you may fail in your goal. For example, in the list above, improving your communication skills could be split down into:

- *explain a product to a friend and find out how much they understand*
- *describe your day to a friend. Then ask them for feedback on your communication skills*
- *learn how to spell four new words every day.*

• *Timescale* •

Your action plan needs to be time specific. You need to identify when you want to achieve your goals (e.g. in two months, by the end of the year, etc.) and you then need to set out deadlines for targets and tasks (e.g. get more information about the job by Tuesday, write the CV by next Monday). Try to make sure you are realistic in setting the deadlines and take into account other commitments you have – for example, if you have a number of assignments to do for college one week you may have less time available than in a normal week.

• *Content* •

The content of your action plan should include:

- *personal development*

- *work-based development*

- *how you will evaluate, monitor and review your progress.*

• *Personal and work-based development* •

Personal development is development you do in your own time, for example, practising body language in front of the mirror, learning how to drive, doing research into a specific industry, etc. It also includes any studying you do on your own or on a school or college course.

Work-based development is development that you do at work. This can include specific structured training that your employer provides. It can also include observing your colleagues and asking your line manager for tips and advice. It also includes doing your job, in the process of which your skills will improve.

• *Evaluation, monitoring and review* •

You need to build into your plan opportunities to evaluate, monitor and review your own progress. For some targets or goals, this could involve testing yourself or asking a friend to help test you (e.g. testing your spelling, testing your knowledge of driving theory, testing how much you can remember about a specific product). For other targets you need to be self-aware in order to assess how you have progressed.

You should review your action plan frequently, adding new goals or targets or rewriting the tasks as necessary. Remember that failing to achieve a goal or target is in itself a useful learning experience. Use any feedback you get as well as your own self-analysis to identify why you failed. This will help you improve and achieve the same goal or similar ones at a later date.

THINK ABOUT IT

Think about how you would monitor your action plan. How would you analyse whether you are progressing with your goals? How often would you need to evaluate your progress? Do you have any skills that will help you review your plan?

EVIDENCE ACTIVITY **P2** **P3** **P4**

Potential

1 Identify whether you are strong or weak in each of the following skills:

a listening   **f** administrative skills

b questioning   **g** customer service skills

c confidence   **h** getting on with others

d following instructions   **i** using initiative

e time keeping   **j** learning new skills.

2 Use the list of strengths you identified in **(1)** above to match your strengths to three different job roles within the business, retail and administration sectors.

3 Use the list of weaknesses from **(1)** above to set two goals for improvement – include the individual targets you will need to achieve to fulfil each goal.

Personal statement and portfolio

You can use all the information that you have gathered about yourself (in your personal audit and in assessing your potential) to create a personal statement suitable for sending to prospective employers and a portfolio of evidence of specific skills.

Personal statement

A personal statement will most commonly take the form of a curriculum vitae (CV), but may also be used in filling out application forms, writing letters of application and phoning to enquire about jobs.

● *Curriculum vitae (CV)* ●

A CV is a summary of your skills and experience relevant to the job for which you are applying. You will need to adapt your CV each time you apply for a job in order to emphasise the skills and experience of most use in the particular role.

Your CV needs to look professional: it should be presented neatly and clearly, not have spelling or grammar mistakes and follow a recognised format. Your CV should be word-processed and printed on good quality paper – white or cream paper, *not* pink or blue.

Contents of CV

A CV should usually contain the following information:

▲ **You need a well-presented CV**

- ▭ Personal details: *name, address, telephone number, email address, date of birth, nationality.*

- ▭ Education: *in reverse order, with most recent education first – to include where you studied (name of school/college), when (academic year/s) and what grades you achieved. You could also include a separate heading* Other qualifications *where you list things like first aid certificates, swimming certificates, The Duke of Edinburgh's Award, etc.*

- ▭ Work experience: *in reverse order, with most recent experience first – to include where you worked (name of employer), when (date you started and date you left) and brief details of your main tasks and responsibilities. Where work experience is of particular relevance to the job you are applying for, you can go into more detail about the tasks and responsibilities. If you have a lot of experience, you can split it into separate headings (e.g. paid employment, voluntary work, work-experience placements; or you could split it into retail experience, administrative experience, customer service experience, according to the requirements of the job).*

- ▭ Skills: *This section should emphasise those skills which are useful or necessary for the job you are applying for. Examples of skills to include here are technical and IT skills, skills in foreign languages, ability to drive and any skills that are specific to the job (e.g. experience with photocopiers, cash registers, etc.).*

- ▭ Interests and activities: *Include any hobbies or leisure activities (e.g. sports, music, drama, membership of clubs and societies, etc.). Try not to just write a list of your interests, but show how these interests are relevant to the employer (e.g. positions of responsibility in clubs, time* **commitment** *to sporting or musical activities, specific achievements within the interest, etc.).*

- ▭ Referees: *You should include the names and contact details of two people who have agreed to provide references. These people should be as relevant*

GLOSSARY

A **commitment** is a promise, duty or obligation.

as possible to the job you are applying for (e.g. if you are applying for a job in retail, the supervisor of your part-time shop job would be relevant; if the job requires specific qualification, then your course tutor might be relevant). Never include details of referees without their permission.

▷ *Some CVs also include a brief personal statement, which allows you to put across elements of your personality that are relevant to the job. For example, 'I am an outgoing person who gets on well with people. I am enthusiastic and willing and able to learn new skills.'*

Check and proofread

Check your CV against the job description and/or personal specification to ensure that you have provided evidence of all the skills and qualifications needed.

Read your CV over a number of times to check for spelling mistakes (look up any words you are unsure of in a dictionary) and to ensure that it looks tidy and professional. Ask a friend, colleague, course tutor or careers advisor to look over your CV and suggest improvements.

GIVE IT A GO: curriculum vitae

1 Look at the list of sections (pages 111–112) that are usually on a CV.
2 Pick one of the sections and try to write down everything you *could* include in that section.
3 Now choose a job you would like to do. From your list in **(2)** pick the items that are most relevant to this job.

Portfolio for employment

It is very useful to build up a portfolio for employment. This will help you whenever you need to apply for jobs or make decisions about how to progress in your career. Each time you are unsuccessful in a job application you will be able to look back at the documents and notes in your portfolio and identify the areas on which you need to work. Likewise, when you are successful, you can look in your portfolio and identify the reasons for that success – skills and experience which will prove valuable when you next need to apply for a job.

Table 4.2 on page 113 outlines what your portfolio for employment should contain.

WHAT **if?**

... you had to show an employer your portfolio now?

How much evidence do you already have? Would it be enough to show that you would be a good employee? What other evidence do you need to gather or work on?

Table 4.2 What your portfolio for employment should contain

Content	Commentary
Preparation and practice of telephone skills	This can include notes that you make to prepare for a telephone call and notes you make after the call, in which you assess how well you did.
Completed application forms	Always take a photocopy of a completed application before you send it out. If you are offered an interview, you will then be able to look back to check what you said on the form. It will also help you identify any areas you need to improve on in future and can also make the task of completing future application forms quicker, as some of the information will be the same.
Word-processed and handwritten letters of application	Always take a photocopy of handwritten letters of application and print out an extra copy of word-processed ones. You will be able to check what you said if you are offered an interview and you will be able to use it for improving future letters of application.
Letters of acceptance	You need to keep these safe so that you know when the job starts, when the deadline is for accepting it and so on. It is also a useful boost for your ego!
Letters of refusal	While these may be depressing, they can provide you with valuable information for future job applications. Some letters of refusal may explain why you were not offered the job and this can prove useful in deciding what skills you need to improve on.
Preparation for interviews	You should make notes of all interviews you prepare for and how you do so. This includes deciding what clothes to wear, how you plan to behave in the interview, organising how to ensure you get to the interview in plenty of time, lists of questions you would like to ask the interviewers and lists of skills and experience that you want to emphasise in the interview. These notes will prove valuable to you in identifying why you failed (shows you what skills you need to work on) and also why you succeeded (shows you what strategies work well). You will then be able to look back at your notes when preparing for future interviews.
Evidence of interviews (or practice interviews)	You may be given feedback after an interview which you can use to improve your interview techniques. If you undertake practice interviews, the interviewer will tell you what you did well and what you need to work on. You should also undertake self-analysis of all interviews (practice ones or real ones) after they are finished.
CVs used for specific job applications	You should keep a copy of all the CVs you send out (which should all be different as you will be tailoring them to specific jobs). It is useful to make a note on the CV stating what the job was and when you applied for it and stating whether or not you were successful. This will help you produce better CVs in the future.
Your personal audit, list of strengths and weaknesses and your action plan	It is useful to keep these in your portfolio for employment as you will need to refer to them when applying for jobs.

EVIDENCE ACTIVITY

1 Use all the information you have gathered in this unit to draw up a rough hand-written curriculum vitae aimed at jobs in the sector that most interests you.

END OF UNIT ASSIGNMENT

Task 1 P1

1 Using the list of skills you wrote earlier (see page 100), draw up a detailed personal audit of your:
- vocational skills
- personal skills
- inter-personal skills
- behaviour
- interests.

2 Word-process your audit and put a printout in your portfolio.

Task 2 P3

Using your audit and the lists of strengths and weaknesses you wrote earlier (see page 110), describe your strengths and weaknesses, and give examples of where you have demonstrated them.

Task 3 P2

Using your personal audit and analysis of your strengths and weaknesses, identify five job roles within the business, retail and administration sectors that would suit you.

Task 4 P4

Draw up a detailed action plan for turning your weaknesses into strengths and improving your strengths. Pay close attention to the skills you need to improve for the job roles identified in Task 3.

Task 5 P5

Use a word-processing program to create a professional looking curriculum vitae based on the handwritten one you created for the Evidence Activity at the top of this page. Make sure you update it with any new information from tasks 1–4.

unit 5

●●●●●●●●●●●●●●●●●●●●●●●●●●●●●●●

Social responsibility at work

This unit will help you to recognise the contribution which you can make to your working environment. It looks at your social responsibilities in terms of the environment and the legal requirements and explores your potential influence on society and the environment through your work.

To complete this unit you must:

▭ understand the environmental issues relevant to your work
▭ explore how the law affects you and other people in the workplace.

Environimental issues in work

The environment is the world in which we live and work and everything around us. Your actions in the workplace will have an effect on the environment and the environment will also affect the way in which you work.

Environmental issues which are relevant to work include:

▭ *energy conservation and recycling*
▭ *cleaner environment*
▭ *health and hygiene*
▭ *methods of transport.*

Energy conservation and recycling

Energy includes the energy used to light and heat our homes and offices, the energy used to travel around (e.g. petrol), the energy used to run our computers and other machines and the energy used in harvesting raw materials and in manufacturing products. Most of this energy comes from non-renewable sources (sources that will not always be there). For example, there is not an **inexhaustible** amount of coal on the earth, nor is there an inexhaustible amount of oil. These resources will run out one day.

It is therefore important for the environment to conserve energy and to use **alternative** sources of energy where possible (e.g. solar power, wind power, water power, etc.). Conserving energy is also important for businesses as it saves on costs – and therefore increases profits.

In addition to energy, other resources are limited and will not be available forever. For example, there is a limited amount of metal available on the earth and the number of trees in the world has reduced considerably in recent years. Materials made out of plastic use oil, which is a resource that will one day run out.

Because of these limitations in the availability of resources (e.g. oil, wood, coal, etc.), it is important to act responsibly to ensure that they last as long as possible.

GLOSSARY

Inexhaustible means without limit, endless.

Alternative means different.

▶ **Alternative energy sources are vital for the future**

Strategies for conserving energy and recycling include:

- *minimising use of materials*
- *using **biodegradable** materials*
- *reusing materials*
- *recovering materials*
- *disposing of materials correctly.*

● *Tips for saving energy* ●

- *Turn the lights off before you leave a room (as long as no-one else is in there).*
- *Switch off electric appliances when they are not being used.*
- *When making a hot drink, only boil the amount of water you need.*
- *Use desk lights instead of over-head lights in open-plan offices where desks are not always occupied.*
- *Switch lights off when there is enough natural light coming into the room.*

● *Tips for minimising use of materials* ●

- *Proofread documents thoroughly on-screen before printing them out.*
- *Use email rather than printed memos.*
- *Use email rather than faxes.*
- *Store files electronically, rather than on paper, where possible.*
- *Keep staff handbooks and phone directories on the organisation's Intranet, rather than one paper copy on every employee's desk.*

● *Use of biodegradable materials* ●

Technological advances mean that many plastic products are now available in a biodegradable version. These include food containers, carrier bags, cutlery and pet toys (though there are many more). Ensuring that you always use a biodegradable alternative where it is available will help the environment.

● *Reusing materials* ●

Many items used in shops and offices can be reused. For example, printer and fax cartridges can be refilled rather than thrown away. Out-of-date computer equipment can be sent to charities that provide computers to developing countries or poor families. Office furniture can be given away to charities or sold when the office is being redecorated, rather than being thrown away or burnt. Sometimes furniture and equipment can even be dismantled and used to make new furniture and equipment.

• *Recovering materials* •

Much of the waste created in the manufacturing of products, or in the running of an office or shop, can be put to use elsewhere. For example, sawdust can be used to make MDF, left-over glass or metal can be melted down to use in other products, the clippings from hole punches can be put in the recycling bin, rather than just thrown out.

• *Recycling* •

Many materials that are often thrown out can be recycled instead. Examples of materials that can be recycled include:

- *paper*
- *glass*
- *most metals*
- *many types of plastic*
- *batteries*
- *computers*
- *cars*
- *organic material (e.g. fruit and vegetable peel, egg shells, garden waste, etc.)*
- *furniture.*

▲ **Most towns have recycling sites**

● *Disposing of materials* ●

Always think before you throw something in the bin. Can it be recycled? Can it be reused? Can someone else make use of it? If your organisation does not have separate bins for different kinds of material to recycle or reuse, take these materials to a recycling centre yourself. If the organisation itself is not prepared or able to provide these facilities then organise a rota among your colleagues for collecting waste material and disposing of it responsibly.

● *Costs and savings* ●

Although it may cost an organisation initially to set up recycling facilities and other environmental **strategies**, in the long run it will usually save money and may even provide extra income.

Conserving energy will save an organisation money – and therefore increase its profits. Some recycling plants offer payment for materials such as glass, plastic or metal. Other organisations may pay for material that you might think of as waste – e.g. shredded paper, compost, used printer cartridges, old computers.

GLOSSARY

A **strategy** is a plan, technique, method or way of doing something.

Conserving means saving.

CASE STUDY – THE CO-OPERATIVE GROUP

Recycling at the Co-op

The *Co-op* is in favour of recycling provided that it saves resources, prevents pollution and is economic.

The *Co-op* has the largest network of consumer recycling facilities in the UK. The *Co-operative Group* has committed itself to provide facilities for paper, cans, glass and plastic at all stores over 15,000 sq. ft where the *Co-operative Group* control the car park and disposal facilities are available.

Co-op Brand specifications take into account the need to avoid excessive packaging and to avoid the use of different materials, which would hamper recycling.

The *Co-operative Group* implements recycling policies in its offices and warehouses.

Find out more at the *Co-operative Group* website – a link is available at **www.heinemann.co.uk/hotlinks** (express code 1211P).

Questions

1 What strategies does the *Co-op* use for recycling?

2 Use the Internet to search for other businesses that support the environment.

Cleaner environment

Creating a cleaner environment involves paying attention to air quality, pollution levels, litter and waste disposal. Within the immediate working environment it also includes paying attention to anti-smoking and anti-alcohol policies, lighting and radiation.

● *Air quality* ●

Air quality is affected by exhaust fumes from cars, emissions from power plants and manufacturing plants and gases and toxins put out by certain chemicals.

Strategies for improving air quality include:

▷ *finding alternative methods of transport (see pages 124–127)*

▷ *reducing use of electricity and other energy (see page 117)*

▷ *reducing use of chemicals in cleaning processes*

▷ *reducing personal use of chemical sprays (e.g. hair sprays, deodorant and antiperspirant sprays, etc.)*

▷ *choosing organic food where possible.*

● *Pollution levels* ●

Pollution levels are causing holes to appear in the ozone layer of the earth's atmosphere, which protects us from dangerous rays from the sun. Pollution levels also cause illnesses and diseases (e.g. it is thought that the increase in asthma could be caused by pollution) and damages the environment (e.g. killing plants and animals).

One of the worst offenders in terms of pollution is the car. Reducing the use of cars and the number of cars on the road is a very important element in protecting the environment.

In addition, many manufacturing processes can cause chemical pollution (to water as well as air). It is important for businesses to be responsible in the way that they dispose of chemical waste, as well as creating strategies to reduce the chemical waste they do produce.

● *Litter* ●

You should never throw litter on the ground or anywhere other than in a proper bin. As stated above, think before you throw anything away and recycle or reuse it wherever possible. If there is no bin nearby, then keep the rubbish until you do find a bin. Keep a carrier bag or two on you, so that you can carry rubbish around without damaging your belongings until you can throw it away. If you see a piece of litter in the street, why not pick it up and **dispose of** it yourself? The more people who do this, the less litter there would be.

GLOSSARY

To **dispose of** means to throw away (or put in the recycling bin, etc.).

● *Waste disposal* ●

Disposing of waste correctly is very important, both for the environment and for hygiene and health reasons. If you work in a business that produces potentially dangerous waste (e.g. syringes, bodily fluids, dangerous chemicals, etc.) you need to ensure that you dispose of this waste in the correct bins. You should have been provided with training in this during your induction but, if you are unsure, ask your line manager.

Remember – think before you throw anything away!

● *Public health policies in the workplace* ●

Anti-smoking regulations

The vast majority of workplaces these days have a non-smoking policy. Some employers provide a smoking room or smoking area and others require employees to go outside to smoke and may provide ashtrays outside the building. Other employers may require their employees to not smoke at all on the premises – including outside.

Smoking is now banned in many public places (e.g. on trains and buses, in shopping centres, etc.) in order to protect the health of the employees who work there.

◀ Smoking is banned in many places

If you are smoker, it is essential that you respect these rules and regulations and only smoke where you are allowed to do so. Your smoke can cause discomfort to non-smokers and regular exposure to smoke (passive-smoking) can cause serious and even fatal illnesses.

Even if there are no rules in your workplace that ban smoking, you should be respectful toward non-smokers and avoid smoking in their presence. You might also like to take the opportunity to think about your own health – if it can cause these problems to non-smokers, what is it doing to you? Your doctor will be able to give you advice on how to give up smoking if you are ready to do so.

 THINK ABOUT IT

What do you think of smoking? Do you smoke? Do your friends smoke? Why do you think it is important for smokers to think about others when they are smoking?

Anti-alcohol regulations

Many organisations will have specific rules on the use of alcohol and there are also legal regulations that need to be followed. You should never drink and drive, for example, so if you drive regularly as part of your job, do not have a glass of wine or pint of beer with your lunch. Although you are allowed a small amount of alcohol when driving, the safest thing is not to drink at all if you are driving.

Alcohol reduces your reaction time, so if you work with any kind of machinery, you should avoid alcohol during working hours. If you do not, you could be responsible for causing serious or fatal injury to a colleague, yourself or a customer.

The more alcohol you drink at a given time, the longer it will take to leave your system. This means that if you have a heavy drinking session one night, you may well still have alcohol in your system the next day. It is a good idea, therefore, to drink only small amounts.

The recommended weekly limit for men is 21 units and for women 14 units. A unit is equivalent to a small glass of wine, half a pint of beer or a small measure of spirits. It is also advisable not to drink more than three units in any 'session'. If you drink more than these amounts, you could be causing your body considerable damage and could develop dangerous diseases such as cirrhosis of the liver.

If you feel you may have a drinking problem, there is help and counselling available to you. For example, you can ask your doctor or find the number of a local alcoholics anonymous branch in the phone book and give them a call.

• *Lighting* •

Legal requirements on lighting are contained within the Workplace (Health, Safety and Welfare) Regulations 1992, which state, 'Every workplace shall have suitable and sufficient lighting'. Regulations for those working with computers are contained within the Health and Safety (Display Screen Equipment) Regulations 1992.

Radiation

Exposure to radiation can come, for example, from working within the nuclear industry, medical and dental practices, some manufacturing, construction and engineering industries, schools and colleges.

If you work somewhere where you could be exposed to radiation, your **induction** will provide instructions and guidelines for reducing the risk to your health. It is very important to follow these guidelines. You should be told the names of those employees who are responsible for maintaining safety in regard to radiation. If you are not, then make sure you ask.

Health and hygiene relating to work

Health and hygiene issues relating to work include:

- ▭ *personal cleanliness*
- ▭ *health care policies for employees*
- ▭ *private health insurance.*

Paying attention to health and hygiene is an important aspect of providing a pleasant environment to work.

• *Personal cleanliness* •

Personal hygiene is important in any workplace. Your hygiene affects others around you and poor hygiene can spread germs and illnesses, as well as making your colleagues and customers uncomfortable.

One element of personal hygiene includes washing your hands:

- ▭ *when you get up in the morning*
- ▭ *when you start work*
- ▭ *after using the toilet*
- ▭ *between handling raw and cooked foods*
- ▭ *after breaks for eating, drinking or smoking*
- ▭ *after coughing, sneezing or blowing your nose*
- ▭ *after touching your hair*

GLOSSARY

Exposure means being close to something (e.g. exposure to some chemicals can cause illness or death).

Induction is training given to new employees when they start work in an organisation.

> *after handling refuse or waste materials*

> *after handling cleaning chemicals*

> *at regular intervals at other times.*

You also need to keep yourself and your clothes clean. Brush your teeth, wash your hair and brush your hair regularly. Have a shower or bath regularly and use anti-perspirant and/or deodorant to reduce body odours. If you are ill with something contagious (catching) you should not come into work as you will spread the illness to your colleagues and customers. Cover your mouth when you cough, use paper or cloth handkerchiefs to blow your nose and dispose of them safely or clean them regularly.

... you worked in a restaurant?

1 Why would personal hygiene be of particular importance?

2 What could be the effects of employees not being hygienic?

3 What strategies would you need to use to stay hygienic?

• *General health care policies for employees* •

Some organisations provide their employees with health care policies. This may include providing regular health check-ups, health advice and free or reduced-cost treatment.

• *Private health insurance* •

Some employers pay for private health insurance for their employees. This may provide employees with an income if they are ill for a considerable amount of time, it could provide refunds of money paid for dental or optical care and sometimes it will also cover the cost of private medical or surgical treatment, where the NHS waiting list is very long.

Alternative methods of transport

Using alternative methods of transport is a very important strategy in the reduction of energy use and pollution levels. Strategies that employers can use to help include:

> *encouraging car-sharing schemes*

> *providing bike racks and shower facilities*

> *promoting the use of public transport*

> *paying mileage for employees who use cycles on business errands*

> *avoiding unnecessary travel (e.g. using IT systems such as videoconferencing and email instead of travelling to meetings)*

> *looking at alternative methods of distribution (e.g. rail shipping).*

• *Walking* •

Looking for jobs that are close to your home, or considering moving home if you get a job quite far away, could enable you to walk to work. A half-hour walk to and from work will keep you fit and help the environment as well. Walking to work can also help you wake up in the mornings, while walking home gives you time to wind down after a stressful day.

• *Cycling* •

There are more and more cycle routes being created in cities now, as well as cycle routes that run alongside large roads between towns and cities. If there is a safe cycle route that you could use, consider cycling to work. Cycling produces no pollution and it is also very good exercise. If you do cycle, make sure you stay safe by wearing a helmet and reflective clothing, so that cars can easily see you. If you have to cycle on the road you will need to learn about road safety and will need to pay close attention to the traffic around you.

• *Motor vehicle* •

While cars are very convenient and allow people to get from place to place very quickly, they are very heavy polluters. If you have to drive to work, you should try to find colleagues who want to car share. This involves taking it in turns to drive to work and filling up the car, so that it is taking more people. If you find four other people to car share with, you will producing four times less pollution than if you each drove to work on your own. Consider using park and ride schemes, so that you do not contribute to congestion in towns and cities.

Before you get in your car, think about whether it is necessary to drive. If you do not have much shopping to do, walk to the shops instead. If you're going to visit friends, consider taking the bus instead. If you're going to the gym, why not walk or cycle – you'll get even more exercise and the benefit of some fresh air, as well. Consider sharing shopping trips with friends or relatives, or doing your supermarket shop less often.

• *Using public transport* •

Using public transport (where it is available) to get to and from work can be **beneficial** to you as well as the environment. You can use the time to read a book, plan your working day, talk to friends or even do some work. If you are driving, you have to concentrate, so the time spent travelling becomes wasted time.

Trains

Most large towns and cities have at least one train station. Using trains to travel to and from work helps reduce pollution. Using trains for

> **GLOSSARY**
>
> **Beneficial** means helpful or of use.

business travel means employees can work while travelling and therefore waste less of their working day. Some companies provide employees with season ticket loans for train travel to and from work. This can reduce travelling costs considerably.

Trams

A number of cities are introducing trams or light railway systems. Trams use smaller vehicles and narrower rail tracks than conventional trains, which means they can be **constructed** within existing built-up areas. They also run at a lower cost than trains and can easily be expanded during busy periods. Trams also contribute less pollution than buses.

Underground

Some large cities such as London and Glasgow have an underground train system. Travel on the underground is often reasonably cheap and can provide a much more **convenient** method of travelling than the car in cities where congestion is very high and parking expensive and difficult to find.

Bus

A bus can usually carry between 20 and 70 passengers, depending on its size. It is therefore much more efficient than a car, which generally only carries five passengers. Most buses use diesel fuel, which is less polluting and more efficient than ordinary petrol. In addition there are a number of bus companies within the country that have introduced alternative

> **GLOSSARY**
>
> **Constructed** means built.

> **GLOSSARY**
>
> **Convenient** means fitting, suitable.

▲ Rural bus services are improving

fuels (see below). In small towns and **rural** areas buses are likely to be the most widely available form of public transport. While there are still rural areas that have no or very few bus services, this is improving and many local councils now subsidise bus routes (pay extra money to keep the services available).

If you have a bus service available that will get you to work, you should make use of it, rather than driving. You may need to make a few changes to your **schedule**, such as getting up a little earlier, but in the long-term it will benefit you as well as the environment.

> **GLOSSARY**
>
> **Rural** means set in the countryside or in a small village.

> **GLOSSARY**
>
> **Schedule** means timetable.

GIVE IT A GO: buses

1 Find a job advertised in the local paper or job centre that interests you.
2 Find out if there are buses that could get you there on time.
3 Find out how much it will cost each day.
4 Find out if there are any special weekly or monthly bus passes you could buy to make the cost cheaper.

● *New developments in transport* ●

There is much new development in transport which is aimed at reducing pollution levels and cutting down on the use of non-renewable sources of fuel. Two examples include congestion charging and alternative fuels for public transport.

Congestion charging

Traffic congestion occurs at busy times of the day, such as in the morning or late afternoon when people have to travel to and from school and work. Cities, such as London, which suffer from very bad congestion problems, have started introducing congestion charges. This requires drivers to pay a charge if they drive in certain areas during certain times of the day. The aim of these charges is to persuade people to find alternative ways to travel, such as using public transport, walking or cycling.

Alternative fuels on public transport

Examples of alternative fuels include:

- *Liquid Petroleum Gas (LPG) – this is cheaper, cleaner and less polluting than normal petrol*

- *rechargeable electric cars and buses – these are quieter and less polluting than those using normal fuel*

- *biodiesel – this is fuel made from replaceable plant oils or used cooking oils and it is cleaner and less polluting than normal fuel.*

EVIDENCE ACTIVITY 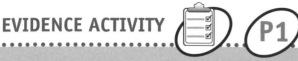 P1

Environmental issues in work

1 Choose a job role in the business, retail or administration sector that interests you.

2 List the environmental factors that are relevant to this job.

The law

There are many laws that are relevant to work. These include laws to help you at work, laws to protect your health and safety and laws that may affect you at work.

How the law helps you at work

• *Why laws exist* •

Laws are there to help you, to protect your health and well-being and to protect the health and well-being of other people and the environment. Laws help ensure that employers act fairly and responsibly to all their employees and to their customers.

• *What they are* •

Some laws that may directly affect you at work include:

- ⬭ Employment Rights Act 1996: *includes issues such as itemised pay statements, Sunday working rates, maternity and paternity leave and termination of employment rights*

- ⬭ Trade Union and Labour Relations (Consolidation) Act 1992: *deals with the rights and responsibilities of trade unions and their members*

- ⬭ Equal Pay Act 1970: *makes it unlawful to offer different pay and conditions where women and men are doing the same or similar work*

- ⬭ Sex Discrimination Act 1975 & 1986: *prevents discrimination in the workplace on the grounds of sex*

- ⬭ Race Relations Act 1976: *prevents discrimination in the workplace on the grounds of race*

- ⬭ Disability Discrimination Act 1995: *prevents discrimination in the workplace on the grounds of disability*

- ⬭ Health and Safety at Work Act 1974: *makes employers responsible for the health, safety and welfare of their employees.*

GIVE IT A GO: laws

1 Choose one of the above acts and find out more information about it.

2 Describe how your chosen act protects employees in the workplace.

● *Their purpose* ●

The purpose of many of the above laws is to reduce or cut out any form of discrimination in the workplace. This includes discrimination in hiring people and in providing all employees with equal rights. The laws also aim to protect your health and safety.

Health and Safety at Work Act

Some of the issues that the Health and Safety at Work Act covers include working hours, breaks, minimum temperatures and lighting. However, there are many other areas covered by the act.

● *Working hours* ●

Some of the rights covered include:

▭ *no more than a 48-hour working week*

▭ *for night workers, no more than 8 hours work in a 24-hour period*

▭ *a minimum of 4 weeks' paid annual leave*

▭ *uninterrupted weekly rest break of at least a full 24-hours in each 7-day period.*

● *Breaks* ●

Employees are entitled to a break of 20 minutes when they work for longer than 6 hours a day. This break should be uninterrupted and should not be taken at the start or end of the day. Employees are also entitled to a rest of at least 11 hours for every 24 hours they work (although there are some special exceptions).

● *Minimum temperatures* ●

The temperature in most workplaces should be at least 16 °C, though it should be lower where work requires considerable exertion (no lower than 13 °C). When temperatures are very high, for example during hot weather, measures such as electric fans should be provided to keep employees cool.

● *Lighting* ●

Workplaces need to be suitably and sufficiently lit. Where screens are used, the lighting needs to provide a good contrast between the screen and the background environment. Natural light should be provided wherever possible and appropriate.

Other laws affecting you at work

Employment law exists to protect both parties. Every employment contract, verbal or written, must state the terms of employment to the employee.

● *Equal opportunities* ●

Gender

People in employment should not be discriminated against because of their gender (sex). Women and men should be treated equally and given the same opportunities to learn and be promoted.

Race

Everyone has the right not to be discriminated against on racial grounds. The Race Relations Act 1976 makes it unlawful to treat a person less favourably than others on racial grounds. These cover grounds of race, colour, nationality (including citizenship) and national or ethnic origin. The Race Relations (Amendment) Act 2000, places a duty on public sector employers to promote racial equality.

▶ Discrimination on racial grounds is unlawful

Religious faith

The Race Relations Act does not cover issues of religious faith as religion is often separate to race. However, the Human Rights Act 1988 gives everyone the right to freedom of thought, conscience and religion. Employers should therefore ensure they respect their employees' religions – for example, by allowing people to opt out of working on their Sabbath day and providing employees with space and time for prayer.

Disability

The Disability Discrimination Act 1995 introduced new laws and measures aimed at ending the discrimination that many disabled people have previously faced. The Act gives disabled people new rights in the areas of:

- *employment*
- *access to goods, facilities, services and premises*
- *management, buying or renting of property.*

◯ THINK ABOUT IT

Why do you think it is important for people to have equal opportunities at work? What would be the **consequences** if there were no equal opportunities laws?

• *Equal pay* •

The Equal Pay Act 1970, as amended by the Equal Pay (Amendment) Regulations 1983 and the Sex Discrimination Acts 1975 and 1986, rules that women should be treated equally to men (and vice versa) in a similar job, or in a different job which is awarded an equal value.

• *Data protection* •

The 1998 Data Protection Act came into force early in 1999 and covers how information about living persons is used. The act includes requirements that:

- *personal data must be processed fairly and lawfully*
- *personal data that is kept should be adequate, relevant and not excessive in relation to its purposes*
- *personal data must not be kept for longer than is necessary*
- *permission must be given to keep any sensitive data (e.g. political opinions, religious beliefs, trade union membership, health and sexual life).*

• *Minimum pay* •

At the time of writing the national minimum wage is £4.85 an hour for workers aged 22 years or over, £4.10 an hour for workers aged 18–21 and £3 an hour for workers aged 16–17 (though apprentices are exempt).

• *Dangerous substances* •

The Control of Substances Hazardous to Health (COSHH) 1999 requires employers to assess likely health risks. The regulations cover:

- *substances labelled as 'very toxic', 'toxic', 'harmful', 'corrosive', or 'irritant'*
- *substances with maximum exposure limits or occupational exposure standards*
- *substantial quantities of dust*
- *any other substance that creates a comparable health hazard.*

• *Clean air* •

The Clean Air Act 1993 regulates a number of issues including:

- *smoke emissions*
- *height of chimneys*
- *content and make-up of motor fuels.*

• *Transport* •

The Road Traffic Act 1988 and the Transport and Works Act 1992 prohibit driving, attempting to drive or being in charge of a vehicle while under the influence of drugs or alcohol (beyond a certain limit). In addition, certain rail, tram and other guided transport system workers must not be unfit through drugs while working on the system. In these cases drugs will include legal drugs (e.g. sleeping tablets, some antibiotics, some allergy pills) as well as illegal ones (e.g. cannabis, cocaine, ecstasy).

EVIDENCE ACTIVITY

The law

1 Choose a job role in the business, retail and administration sectors that interests you.
2 List the laws that are most important to this job.

END OF UNIT ASSIGNMENT

Task 1 (P1)

1 Look back at the list of environmental factors that you wrote down earlier (see p.128).

2 For each environmental factor describe:
   a why it is important for your chosen job role
   b why it is important for the environment
   c the possible effects of not considering this environmental factor in your chosen job role:
      i)   on you
      ii) on the organisation
      iii) on the environment.

Task 2 (P2)

1 Look back at the list of laws that you wrote down earlier (see p.132).

2 For each law:
   a describe how it affects the employees
   b describe how it affects the organisation
   c explain why it is important to your chosen job role.

Task 3 (P3)

Explain why you think some work-related laws might be more important than others. Give examples and reasons for your answer.

unit 6

· ·

Financial management

This unit will help you learn how to manage your money. You will find out about different sources of income, including earnings from employment and income from state benefits. You will also find out about the different deductions that may be made from your pay. You will learn how to manage your personal finances, including information on attitudes toward money and how to run a current account. You will also learn how to create a personal budget.

To complete this unit you must:

- ▭ learn about different sources of income
- ▭ learn how to manage your personal finances
- ▭ understand the importance of keeping a personal budget.

Sources of income

Unfortunately money does not grow on trees. People receive money in different ways and for different reasons, including:

- ▭ *earnings from a job*
- ▭ *benefit payments*
- ▭ *income from savings*
- ▭ *income from pensions*
- ▭ *allowance paid by family, gifts*
- ▭ *borrowed money, such as loans and credit to buy goods.*

At work

Once you have a full-time job this will probably be your main source of income. Even if you are still at school or college, you may well have a part-time job or do temporary work during the holidays. In which case, this may also be your main source of income.

● *Types of employment* ●

Whether you are self-employed, a freelancer or an employee will affect the way you earn your money and also what deductions are made from it and how these are made.

Self-employed

Some people choose not to work for someone else but to start their own business. These people are **self-employed** (i.e. they employ themselves).

The income from self-employment will depend on the type of business. For example, the income of someone who owns and runs a shop will come from customers who come in and purchase goods. The income of someone who makes and sells greetings cards would come from the sales they make (e.g. to shops or to other businesses).

Self-employed people pay tax on any **profits** they make. They also pay National Insurance contributions. They may also pay into a private pension fund, but this will be up to them.

Freelance

Freelancers are self-employed. Rather than making or selling products, they sell their services to individuals or businesses. Most freelancers do work for a number of different individuals or businesses. Examples of freelancers include illustrators, web designers and editors.

As freelancers are self-employed, they are taxed in the same way as described above.

Employee

Employees work for a single employer, who controls what work is done as well as when and where it is done. The employer is responsible for deducting income and National Insurance from the employee's wages or salary. Some people have more than one part-time job, but they are still employees and not freelancers if the employer has the control and responsibilities described above.

GLOSSARY

A **self-employed** person is someone who works for themselves, either running their own businesses or taking on a number of different jobs for different clients.

Profits are money that is left over after a business has paid for materials, expenses, overheads and so on (i.e. money left over after everything has been paid for).

A **freelance** worker is a self-employed person who does jobs for a number of different individuals or organisations (e.g. photographers, illustrators or web designers).

◯ THINK ABOUT IT

What do you think the advantages are of the different types of employment? Which ones do you think would be better for your finances? Why?

• *Gross and net income* •

Your **gross income** is the amount of money you earn before any deductions (e.g. tax, National Insurance) have been made. Your **net income** is the amount of money you actually take home (or that goes into your bank account). This is true for employees and also for the self-employed. However, self-employed people have to pay income tax and National Insurance contributions after they have received money – so they have to be careful not to spend that money!

If a job advertises an annual salary of £12,000, this does not mean that the successful applicant will actually get £1000 paid to them every month. The employer will need to make deductions from this, so the employee might only end up receiving £750 every month.

• *Basic pay* •

Basic pay is the money you earn (gross income) before any additions are made. Examples of additions include overtime and bonuses (see below).

• *Payments added* •

Overtime

Some employers offer the opportunity for employees to work **overtime** – this is working extra hours on top of the time you are contracted to work. Overtime may be offered at busy times, for example, when a business has a number of large orders to send out.

Overtime is usually paid at a higher rate than normal contracted hours, although this is not always the case. However, payment for overtime is always an addition to your basic pay.

Bonuses

Some organisations will pay their employees **bonuses**. Sometimes these are offered for getting a big job finished on time or early, while some organisations pay an annual bonus to all employees based on the amount of profit that has been made that year. Bonuses are an addition to your basic pay.

Deductions

Deductions are money taken from your gross pay before you get it (though self-employed people get the money first and then have to pay these deductions out of the money they receive). Deductions include income tax and National Insurance. They may also include pensions or superannuation, union subscriptions and charitable donations.

GLOSSARY

Gross income is the money you earn before deductions (e.g. tax, National Insurance or pension).

Net income is the money that you actually get after deductions (e.g. tax, National Insurance or pension).

Basic pay is pay before overtime or bonuses.

GLOSSARY

Overtime means working extra hours on top of normal contracted hours.

GLOSSARY

Bonuses are extra money received on top of pay.

GLOSSARY

Deductions are money taken off pay (e.g. tax, National Insurance or pension).

• *Income tax* •

Everyone is allowed to earn a certain amount of money before they have to pay income tax. This amount is called a personal tax allowance. At the time of writing, the personal allowance for a person under 65 is £4895 a year. The allowances change every year and are announced in the budget.

The amount of income tax you pay will depend on how much you earn. The more money you earn, the higher the percentage will be, of your earnings, that is deducted.

• *National Insurance contributions* •

Employees and the self-employed have to pay National Insurance contributions. If you are an employee your employer will deduct the contributions from your wages or salary and will also make a contribution themselves. If you are self-employed, you will pay small monthly or quarterly contributions and then may also need to pay a lump sum every year if your profits are over a certain amount (which changes every year).

As with income tax, the more money you earn the more money you will need to pay in income tax and if you have low earnings (or profits if self-employed) then you may not have to pay any National Insurance.

• *Pensions/superannuation* •

Superannuation is another word for pension. Pensions are long-term investments that are designed to provide you with an income when you retire (stop working after a certain age). As with any form of saving, the earlier you start the more you will receive at the end. Pensions are paid to us when we get older or when we are unable to work through ill health.

If you are an employee, your organisation is likely to have a pension scheme (which may be **compulsory**). The employer will usually pay a contribution into your pension fund, but you will also pay money into it yourself and this will be deducted from your wages or salary before you receive it.

Self-employed people can set up private pension funds themselves, but they do not have to. Employees can also set up an extra private pension fund separate to their work-based fund.

• *Union subscriptions* •

Many areas of work have unions that you can join. A union is a large group of workers in a particular industry or profession. Unions can provide benefits such as legal advice and can also provide support in cases of unfair treatment or **dismissal**. If you are a member of a union, you will need to pay fees, which help run the union and provide

> **GLOSSARY**
> **Superannuation** means pension.

> **GLOSSARY**
> **Compulsory** means necessary, must be done.

> **GLOSSARY**
> To **dismiss** someone is to sack them from their job or end their employment.

members with an income if they go on strike. Sometimes union fees are deducted from your wages or salary before you receive it, or you may pay this yourself afterwards. You cannot be forced to join a union and can always opt out.

● *Charitable donations* ●

Many organisations provide the ability to **donate** to charity through 'payroll giving'. If you choose to do this, the donation will be deducted from your wages or salary before you receive it. The employer will often make a contribution as well. You do not have to pay income tax on any earnings that you donate to charity. However, you can choose to pay the income tax and the government will give it to the charity (so the charity gets a further contribution from the government).

Other

Other sources of income can include allowances from family, state benefits, interest from savings, inherited money and borrowed money.

● *Allowances from family* ●

If you are at school or college, you may get an allowance (or pocket money) from your parents or other family members.

● *State benefits and allowances* ●

If you are unable to work, able to work but looking for work or have a very low income from your work, you will probably be entitled to **benefits**, allowances or tax credits from the government.

There are many different benefits, credits and allowances available. If you are entitled to a benefit you should make sure that you get it. Your local Citizens Advice Bureau will be able to tell you what you are entitled to. Some benefits include housing and council tax benefits, which help you pay your rent as well as any council tax you are liable to pay, if you are on a low income.

If you are between 16 and 18 years old, in full time education and your family has a household income lower than £30,000 you may be entitled to an Education Maintenance Allowance (EMA) of between £10 and £30 a week. You should be able to find out more at your school or college.

● *Interest from savings* ●

If you save your money in your cupboard or piggy bank at home it will not grow. If you save it in a bank or other financial institution you will earn extra money, which is called interest. There are many different types of savings schemes and accounts available, some of which are described on page 145. If you earn interest on your savings, you will have to pay income tax on that interest. Your bank will usually deduct the tax before paying you the interest. If you have an income lower than the personal allowance (see page 137), then you will be able to claim this tax back. You can also ask the bank to stop deducting it, if you can show that your earnings are below the personal allowance.

● *Inherited money* ●

Sometimes people leave money to their relatives or friends when they die. This is known as an **inheritance**. If the inheritance is very large it may be necessary to pay inheritance tax on it. Inherited money often comes as a surprise and is accompanied by the sadness of losing a relative or friend. What you do with your inheritance (after paying any tax) will usually be up to you. While you could blow it all on a flashy car or a big holiday, it is a good idea to consider saving some of it or investing it. Another option would be to pay off your mortgage or a part of your mortgage, which could reduce your monthly outgoings. (see page 140 for a case study on inherited money.)

> **GLOSSARY**
>
> An **inheritance** is money or items left to you when someone dies.

● *Borrowed money* ●

Borrowed money includes:

- *overdrafts*
- *loans*
- *hire purchase (e.g. buying goods from catalogues, paying for large items like cars and computers over a few years)*
- *credit card balances*
- *mortgages*
- *money borrowed from friends or relatives.*

While borrowing increases your available funds in the short-term, it can prove very expensive in the long-term. The money is not a gift, so you have to pay it back. This will usually involve making regular monthly payments and almost all borrowing requires you to pay interest. While borrowing money may mean you can take the holiday you want or buy a new iPod, it will also mean that your monthly outgoings in the future will be higher. Wherever possible, it is much wiser to save up for holidays and other luxuries, because while you are saving you *earn* interest instead of *paying* it.

Out of work

If you are out of work or have a very low income, you may be entitled to certain benefits, allowances and credits. Some of these include Jobseekers' Allowance, Income Support, Child Benefit, Housing Benefit and Working Families' Tax Credit. There are many others available too, and your local Citizens Advice Bureau should be able to tell you which ones you are entitled to.

CASE STUDY – PAM HUGHES

What to do with the inheritance

Pam Hughes is 54 years old. Her grandmother died recently and left her £75,000, which she will receive next month. She plans to spend £5000 on a new kitchen, but does not know what to do with the rest of it.

Pam works as a personal assistant and earns £26,000 a year. She contributes to a final-salary pension scheme but has only been a member for ten years. She is divorced but has a partner with whom she has lived for seven years. She has two children who live with her, a 20-year-old daughter and 16-year-old son.

She owns a house in London, which has been valued at £420,000. She has £62,000 left to pay on the mortgage and will have paid it off in 12 years.

She is thinking about:

- paying off some of the mortgage
- buying a buy-to-let property
- putting the money into safe investments
- using some money to convert the loft and provide extra space for her children.

Questions

1 What are the advantages and disadvantages of Pam's ideas?

2 What do you think she should do?

3 What would you do if you inherited £75,000 tomorrow?

▼ **What should Pam do?**

• *Benefits available* •

Jobseekers' Allowance

Jobseekers' Allowance is available to unemployed people who are able to work and who are actively seeking work. It is usually only available to people between the ages of 18 and 65 (for men) or 60 (for women), although there are some exceptions.

Income Support

If you have a low income, but are unable to work (e.g. you are a single parent looking after a young child, caring for a disabled relative or too ill to work), you may be entitled to Income Support. You will usually need to be between the ages of 18 and 60, although there are some exceptions. If you have savings above a certain amount you will not be able to claim income support.

Child Benefit

Everyone who is responsible for a child under 16 is entitled to receive Child Benefit (only one person can claim it for each child). The benefit for the eldest child is slightly higher than that for the other children. The benefit is not affected by your income and it is tax-free. Child Benefit can be extended until a child is 19, if they are in full-time education (up to A level or equivalent).

Housing Benefit

Housing Benefit is available to people on low incomes to help them pay rent. It is not available for mortgage payments, although in some cases there may be other benefits available to help with these. You will not be able to claim Housing Benefit if your savings are above a certain amount.

Working Families' Tax Credit

Working Families' Tax Credit is available to people with at least one child under 16 (or 19 and in full-time education up to A level or equivalent) and whose household income is below a certain level. You and your partner must be working at least 16 hours a week and your savings must be below £8000. This is a tax credit and is managed by the Inland Revenue.

GIVE IT A GO: benefits

1 Go to your local benefits agency or Citizens Advice Bureau and find out whether you are entitled to any benefits.
2 Find out if you are entitled to an EMA.

EVIDENCE ACTIVITY P1

Sources of income

1 List all your sources of income from work.

2 List all your other sources of income.

3 Identify any other income to which you are entitled.

Managing personal finance

Managing personal finances is an important skill for everyone to learn. It is important to be able to set money aside for regular bills, such as rent, electricity, telephone and gas, as well as for unexpected expenses, such as car repairs or damage to your property. If you want to be able to pay for luxuries, such as holidays and nights out, you will need to learn how to **budget**. If you do not budget you may quickly find yourself in debt and unable to pay your bills.

Attitudes to work and money

Different people have different attitudes toward money and your attitude toward money will affect the way you manage your finances.

• Spend or save •

Some people spend any extra money as soon as they have it. Some people spend money before they have it by borrowing money. Other people save any extra money they have and wait until they have a large lump sum available before buying luxuries.

While saving money is the most sensible attitude, if you are able to manage your finances carefully there may be situations when borrowing money would be sensible. Examples of borrowings that can be worthwhile are:

▷ *a mortgage to buy a house (this is an investment in your future and can sometimes prove cheaper, on a monthly basis, than paying rent)*

▷ *loans to fund study at university (this is also an investment in your future – having a degree will increase your earning potential and you usually don't have to start paying the money back until you earn above a certain income)*

▷ *loans to start a business (this is also an investment in your future, although it can also be very risky).*

> **GLOSSARY**
>
> A **budget** is the amount of money available for a task or project (business); to budget is to look at how much money you have coming in and decide what you can afford to pay for different things (personal).

• *Gambling* •

Gambling is when you pay money for the chance of winning more money. In gambling it is never guaranteed that you will win and the chances will often be very low. Examples of gambling include playing Lotto, buying scratch-cards, betting on the horses, playing the football pools and playing on a fruit machine.

While for many people gambling is a form of entertainment and does not cost them too much money, some people can become addicted to gambling and lose large amounts of money. Gambling is a problem if you spend more money than you have available for entertainment purposes. For example, if you spend your rent money on a bet on the horses instead of paying your landlord, you have a gambling problem. Your doctor may be able to help by referring you to a counsellor or you can find the local branch of Gamblers Anonymous, who will be able to support you in dealing with the problem.

◀ **Gambling can be addictive**

• *Expectations* •

People's **expectations** of money vary. Some people want only enough money to provide for their needs (e.g. shelter, warmth and food) and a few small luxuries, while others expect to be able to go on lots of holidays, have all the newest gadgets and go out for dinner or drinks every night. It is important to manage finances carefully in order to meet your expectations. This should include budgeting for all your needs and luxuries and may involve saving up for a while before you can have the luxuries.

GLOSSARY

An **expectation** is what is expected (e.g. your employer will expect you to come to work on time).

• *Spending habits* •

Your spending habits will affect the money you have available. If you spend every spare penny you have (or more), it is very likely that you will run into problems in the future. If you suddenly lose your job or get very ill, your income will go down considerably and you will no longer be able keep up with your spending habits. Developing sensible spending and saving habits is a good way to avoid future problems.

• *Money and lifestyles* •

The lifestyle you have will be affected by the amount of money you have available. You need more money to maintain a luxurious lifestyle than a basic one. If you want a luxurious lifestyle, or even just a comfortable one with a few **material pleasures**, then you will need to work hard to achieve it. You will need to work to improve and further your career. It is not enough to sit around dreaming about winning the lottery or receiving a large inheritance from a long-lost relative. You need to make it happen by achieving your career goals.

> **GLOSSARY**
>
> **Material pleasures** are items that you buy and that keep you happy (they will be different for everyone, but could include televisions and stereos).

THINK ABOUT IT

Think about your own attitude to money. Are you a saver or spender? Do you ever gamble? What do you expect your earnings to do for you? Do you want just the basic needs or do you want a big house in the country and a private jet?

Using banks, building societies, post offices

An important part of managing your finances is learning how to use your bank account (or building society or post office account). It is almost impossible these days to survive without a bank account. Most people's wages or salary is paid into their bank accounts, as are benefits, allowances and tax credits. In addition to this, most service providers (e.g. gas companies, telephone companies, etc.) prefer to be paid by direct debit from your bank account – and many provide considerable discounts to persuade people to do so.

• *Help provided* •

Most banks (and building societies and post offices) will provide you with help and advice with using your account. They want your custom and so provide this help and advice as a form of customer service. You may also be able to get help from friends and relatives.

• *Accounts* •

There are many different types of account available, but the most important one will usually be the current account. This is the account into which your income will be paid and out of which your bills and other payments will come. Many current account holders are entitled to a cheque book, a cheque guarantee card and sometimes a debit card, as well.

Other accounts include savings accounts and loan accounts and many variations of these.

• *Short- and long-term savings* •

Savings accounts will pay you some interest on your savings. Usually they will pay a higher rate of interest if they are long-term accounts where you have to give notice (e.g. 90 days) of when you want to **withdraw** money. These can be useful for saving up for big expenses, such as a wedding, a new car or a holiday (i.e. situations where you know when you will need the money). Short-term savings accounts pay lower rates of interest but allow you to access the money quickly. These are useful for setting aside money for emergencies and unexpected **expenses**, such as paying for dental treatment or a veterinary bill.

• *Saving schemes* •

As well as ordinary savings accounts there are also a number of special savings schemes available, most of which pay higher interest rates than ordinary accounts. Examples of savings schemes include ISAs and Internet and telephone accounts.

ISAs

ISA stands for 'Individual Savings Account'. An ISA allows you to save a certain amount of money per year, without paying tax on the interest you earn. There are a number of different kinds of ISA and your bank or building society will be able to give you information on the ISAs that they offer.

Internet and telephone accounts

There are now a number of banks that do not have high-street branches. They provide all their services through the post, telephone and/or the Internet. Because they save money by not having high-street branches, they usually pay higher rates of interest on savings and sometimes also on any money in your current account.

Most high-street banks and building societies also offer you the opportunity to do most of your account management using the telephone or the Internet. This can save you a lot of time and is very useful for people who find it difficult to get to the bank during working hours.

• *Loans* •

Loans are lump sums of money that someone lends to you. Loans can come from banks or building societies, from family or friends or from loan sharks.

> **GLOSSARY**
>
> To **withdraw** means take out (e.g. money from a bank account).
>
> **Expenses** are outgoings and spending.

Loans from banks or building societies (and other reputable financial institutions) will cost you money in the form of interest. When you borrow from reputable financial institutions you have some protection by the law.

Family members or friends may be prepared to lend you money without charging you interest. This is the cheapest type of loan, but can cause problems in your relationships and friendships if you do not pay the money back when you say you will.

Loansharks are usually individuals or small groups of people who lend money and charge very high interest rates – so much interest that people often spend the rest of the lives paying the interest and never get rid of the loan. Some loansharks use violence to collect their money. You should never be tempted to borrow money from a loanshark.

▶ **Don't borrow from loansharks**

GIVE IT A GO: banks, building societies and post office accounts

1 Visit a local bank, building society or post office.
2 Find out what different types of accounts are available.
3 Find out what help is provided.
4 Find out what kind of loans are on offer.
5 Find out if they offer any incentives to new customers (e.g. gifts, money, extra services).

Running a bank or building society account

Running a bank or building society account successfully may involve using a chequebook, using credit and debit cards, paying bills and staying in credit.

● *Using a chequebook* ●

A cheque is a promise to pay and is used in place of cash. When you write a cheque out to a person or a business, they then take it to their bank who contacts your bank. Your bank gives their bank the money and puts it into their bank account. When someone pays a cheque into their bank, it usually takes between three and five days until the cheque clears (the money leaves your account and appears in theirs). You should always assume that this money has already left your account, even though your balance will not show this, otherwise you might spend the money before the cheque clears.

You should only write a cheque out if you have enough money in your account (or an agreed overdraft limit) to cover the amount of the cheque. Do not be tempted to write a cheque out a day or two before payday, when you have run out of money. Some cheques clear immediately (for example, if you are paying someone who uses the same bank as you) and there might be a problem with your wages or salary payment.

It is very important to always keep a record of any cheques you write out. Chequebooks come with 'stubs' which are left in the chequebook after you tear out the cheque. These stubs are there for you to note down the details of the cheque and will help you keep track of your money and also sort out any mistakes that may be made.

● *Credit cards* ●

A credit card is a plastic card that you can use to pay for goods or services (where the facilities are available) instead of using cash. When you pay for something with a credit card, you can avoid paying interest as long as you pay off the full balance by a certain time (usually at the end of the month or the end of the next month). If you do not pay off the full balance, you will usually be charged interest. Credit cards can be useful, providing you manage them carefully (see below for more details).

WHAT **if?**

... you had a credit card with a £10,000 credit limit?

1 What would you use the credit card for?
2 How would you use it (e.g. would you pay off the balance at the end of every month)?
3 How would you make sure that you could always make the payments?

● *Debit cards* ●

Debit cards are similar to credit cards, except the money is taken out of your account immediately or very soon after the payment. A debit card also allows you to take cash out of ATMs (automated teller machines) if you have enough funds in your account. You will be given a pin number for your debit card and you should memorise it and then destroy the paper it came on. The pin number allows you to get cash out and is also often needed for making purchases in shops.

● *Cash cards* ●

Cash cards are similar to debit and credit cards, but they only allow you to get cash out of ATMs. They cannot be used to pay for goods or services. You will usually be given a cash card if you are not able to get a debit card (e.g. your income is too small, or you are a new customer to the bank).

● *Paying bills* ●

Many bills can be paid by direct debit or standing order. This means that the money is taken from your account and paid to the business on a regular basis (usually the same day every month). This can help with budgeting, as you will always know how much money is going out. It can also help if you are not very good at remembering when payments are due. In addition, many businesses offer a discount if you pay by direct debit, as it helps them to manage their finances too.

▶ **Paying your bills on time makes sense**

• *Remaining in credit* •

It is important to manage your account carefully to ensure you stay in credit. If you write cheques out or make debit card payments that take your account into debit (i.e. spend more money than you have in the account) you will be charged fines and may also build a bad credit rating, which will make it difficult to get a mortgage or a credit card in the future.

Personal finance records

Part of good financial management is checking and keeping all your personal finance records. These include bank statements, credit and debit card statements and statements for any store cards. It also involves keeping track of home shopping and Internet accounts.

• *Checking up-to-date bank statements* •

You will receive a monthly statement for your current account. This statement will show the starting balance, the details of each payment into and payment out of your account, including payments made using a debit card, and the end balance. Some statements may also provide a total of your incoming payments and your outgoing payments, as well as any details of interest you have earned or paid.

It is important to check these statements carefully, to make sure there are no mistakes. For example, check that the amount of any cheque matches the amount you wrote on the cheque stub and check that all the standing orders and direct debits went out correctly. Check there are no payments out of your account that you are unaware of and query these immediately, in case someone is stealing money from you.

• *Credit and debit card statements* •

If you have a credit card or a store card, you will receive a monthly statement. This statement will detail all the purchases and payments you made in the period the statement covers. It will also detail any interest you have been charged, as well as any other fees, such as fees for late payment. It will tell you the total money you owe, what the minimum payment is that you will need to make and when the company must receive the money by. Many statements give an estimate of the interest you will be charged next month, although this does not take into account any new payments you might make.

Paying off the full balance before you are charged interest is the most sensible way to use credit cards. If you are unable to do this, make sure that you make at least the minimum payment by the due date (which will be shown on your monthly statement). However, it is better to pay more than the minimum amount – as much as you can – because the minimum usually only covers a little bit more than the interest. If you only pay the minimum amount it can take you years to pay off the balance and you will end up spending a fortune in interest charges.

• *Home shopping* •

There are a number of different types of home shopping, including catalogues, TV shopping and Internet shopping.

Catalogues

Many catalogues offer you credit, so that you can buy an item and then pay for it over a number of weeks. Some catalogues offer interest-free credit, provided you make the minimum payment every month and pay off the balance on time. Catalogues will send you a monthly statement detailing any purchases you have made, what your outstanding balance is (how much money you owe them), what the minimum payment is and when you need to pay it by.

TV and Internet shopping

There are many companies that offer the opportunity to buy goods through your TV (especially on shopping channels if you have a satellite or cable TV subscription) or via the Internet. In most cases, you buy the goods immediately, using a credit or debit card – although some companies will accept payment by cheque. Once your payment has cleared (which will take longer if you pay by cheque), the company will send the goods out to you. Many companies offer next-day delivery, while some will only guarantee that you will receive the goods within a certain time (e.g. 28 days).

In terms of your money, TV and Internet shopping is like going to a retail outlet, as the money will come straight out of your account, or be charged immediately to your credit card. Some credit card companies and banks offer protection for Internet purchases, so that if you never receive the goods you will get your money back.

▲ **You can buy many goods over the Internet**

• *Internet banking* •

If you have an Internet bank account, or your bank offers Internet banking, you can keep track of your account online. You can check your balance regularly, and look at your statements on a weekly or even daily basis, so that you will know much more quickly if there are any problems or there have been any mistakes. You will also be able to pay bills and set up standing orders. You can also make transfers between your different accounts, with the same bank. For example, if you have some extra money, you could transfer it to your savings account.

GIVE IT A GO: statements

1 Get a statement (e.g. for a bank account, credit card, catalogue or store card).
2 Look at the statement and identify all the information that is provided.
3 Identify how you would check that the information is correct.
4 Identify what you would do if there were any mistakes.

EVIDENCE ACTIVITY

Managing personal finance

1 Identify your spending and saving habits.

2 List any bank, building society or post office accounts that you have.

3 List any credit cards you have.

Produce a personal budget

A personal budget is a very useful tool for managing your finances. It helps you stay on top of your finances and stop problems before they start.

Personal budgeting

Personal budgeting involves finding out all the money that comes to you and that you have to pay out on a regular basis and then setting aside specific amounts of what is left over to use on your goals.

⬭ THINK ABOUT IT

What reasons can you think of to budget? Do you budget? What do you think you might find out if you produced a personal budget?

• *Planning income and expenditure to meet identified goals* •

Income and expenditure

Your personal budget will help you to plan your **income** (money that comes to you) and **expenditure** (money you have to pay out) over time to meet your goals.

GIVE IT A GO: working out your income and expenditure

1 Work out how much money you have coming in each month. (Remember! It is better to underestimate the amounts coming in.)

2 Work out how much money you spend each month. (Remember! It is better to overestimate the amounts going out.)

3 List any other sources of income, which might increase your personal finance.

4 Now work out how much money you can save each month.

Identifying goals

You will need to identify your goals. Examples of goals could be to make sure you pay all your bills and can eat well, to buy a new car in two years' time or to save up for a wedding.

You may have several goals, some small, some large, and you will need to:

▭ *decide which goals will take priority*

▭ *ensure that your goals are realistic*

▭ *work toward the lesser goals only after the really important ones have been met.*

GIVE IT A GO: identifying your goals

1 Identify ten different goals to which you or your family aspire. They could be short-term goals, such as 'Having a great holiday this summer', or long-term goals such as 'Securing a comfortable retirement'.

2 Decide whether your goals are realistic (use your notes about your income and expenditure to help you). Cross off any goals which are not realistic.

3 Put the goals that are left in order of priority.

Planning to meet your goals

Once you have identified your goals, you will need to plan how to budget for them. Banks and building societies can help with this.

GIVE IT A GO: filling in forms

1 Look in your local Yellow Pages for the telephone number and the address of one of the banks or building societies in your area.

2 Visit the bank and ask one of the personal bankers for a blank form for a personal budget.

3 List the sort of information that is needed to fill in this form.

Budgeting is important – if you don't budget you are likely to get into debt or need to borrow money. Debt is a fact of life for many people these days, and one of the most common forms of debt is caused by overspending on credit cards. If you can't trust yourself with credit cards, avoid them. If you feel that you can manage a credit card, you should subscribe to one with a low interest rate.

GIVE IT A GO: borrowing money

Think about each of the following situations. Is there a need for you to borrow money? Justify your answer.

1 You are offered a place in a college that is far from where you live. You want to buy a car to save your time and bus fare. The car costs £1500 and you don't have the money.

2 You decide to go to university to do business studies. The university fees are £1000 and you don't have the money.

3 You are appointed as a sales representative in a big car company. Your manager asks you to smarten yourself up before starting your job. The clothes you want to buy cost £750 and you don't have the money.

Income

The first thing you need to do when creating a personal budget is find out what money you receive on a regular basis. This will be your sources of income (see pages 134–135) and may come from salary or wages, savings or tips, as well as other sources of income, such as benefits and allowances.

If you receive weekly wages, it is a good idea to work out a weekly budget. If you receive benefits, you might be better off setting up a fortnightly budget, as most benefits are paid every two weeks. If you receive a monthly salary, you might prefer to create a monthly budget, although you might still find it useful to break this down into a weekly budget for your outgoings (see page 154).

A useful way to look at your income is to write it in a table, such as the one here:

Table 6.1 Sample income

Income	Weekly
Wages	£150.00
Benefits	£20.00
Savings	£0.00
Allowance	£20.00
Tips	£10.00
Other	£5.00
Total	£205.00

WHAT **if?**

... *you were self-employed?*

1 How could you work out your monthly income?

2 What would be the dangers of expecting a specific income every month?

3 What strategies could you put in place to make sure you avoided problems?

Expenditure

After you have worked out your total income, you then need to work out your total outgoings. Your outgoings will be made up of regular payments (e.g. rent, council tax, electricity, mobile phone contract, payment into savings or private pension) and irregular outgoings (e.g. holidays, leisure, unexpected bills).

As with your income, it is useful to write your regular outgoings in a table, such as this one (right):

Notice that this budget also includes an amount of long-term

Table 6.2 Sample expenditure

Expenditure	Weekly
Rent	£55.00
Council tax	£25.00
Electricity	£5.00
Gas	£5.00
Mobile phone	£8.00
Home phone	£5.00
Water rates	£2.00
TV & satellite	£13.00
Food	£20.00
Travel	£15.00
Long-term savings	£5.00
Emergency fund	£20.00
Total	£178.00

savings as well as an emergency fund. The emergency fund is something you build up to cover the irregular expenses (unexpected bills, clothes, etc.).

The money left over when you take your outgoings away from your income (in the examples above £205 – £178 = £27) is the money left over for luxuries. This could include, for example, going out with your friends or buying items such as CDs, computer games or magazines.

GIVE IT A GO: spending

1 Spend a week writing down *everything* you spend money on.

2 What do your findings tell you about your spending habits? Are they worse than you thought or better? Did writing things down make you stop and think before buying something?

3 If you needed to reduce your spending, what could you cut out? (Examples might include taking a packed lunch, instead of buying sandwiches, walking to work instead of getting the bus, buying fewer magazines, etc.)

EVIDENCE ACTIVITY   (P4)

Personal budget

Identify the tasks you will need to carry out in order to manage your finances. Identify how often you will need to do these tasks to keep on top of your finances.

END OF UNIT ASSIGNMENT

Task 1 (P1) (P2)

1 Investigate sources of income.

2 If you have a part-time job, look at one of your payslips (or wage slips). Identify the different amounts that are mentioned on the slip (e.g. basic pay, overtime, deductions for tax and NI).

Task 2 (P5) (P3) (P4)

1 Why is it important to manage your personal finances? What could happen if you do not do this? List **three** benefits of managing your personal finances.

2 A friend has approached you asking for help managing his or her income. Provide some information which would help.

3 Plan how you would manage your personal finances.

Task 3 (P6)

1 Use the information you have collected about your income and outgoings to create your own personal budget.

2 If you have money left over after taking your expenses away from your income, decide what you will do with this money (e.g. save it all, save some of it and use the rest for socialising).

3 If you find that your expenses are more than your income, decide what to do to solve this problem (e.g. reduce your expenses, get a part-time job so you have more income, find out if you are entitled to any benefits).

unit 7

Ensuring personal health and safety at work

In this unit you will learn about health and safety. You will find out about workplace policies, including what employees' and employers' responsibilities are, and about different kinds of health and safety policies. You will also find out about different kinds of hazard and risk, as well as methods for reducing such risks.

To complete this unit you must:

▻ look at workplace policies that support health and safety
▻ learn how to spot possible hazards and risks and work out their severity
▻ find ways to reduce risks to health and safety in the workplace.

Workplace policies

Responsibility for health and safety

Everybody at work has a part to play in ensuring that work is done in a healthy and safe way. While employers have duties to ensure a safe working environment for employees, employees also have a role in ensuring their own health and safety and that of the people around them, including other staff, customers, visitors and contractors.

The Health and Safety at Work Act 1974 provides the basis of health and safety law. It places general duties on all people at work, including employers, employees, the self-employed and people in control of premises.

● *The employee's responsibility* ●

Employees are required by law to take reasonable care for their own health and safety and that of others (this includes visitors and customers, as well as colleagues and contractors). They are also required to use all work items correctly. Whenever you use a piece of equipment you need to be careful to do so safely. When you move something, you need to think carefully about whether it could cause a **hazard** (for example, a box in the middle of an aisle in a supermarket could cause a customer to trip and hurt themselves).

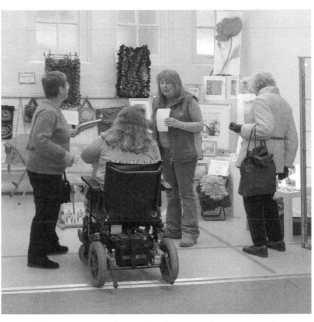

▲ **Businesses must be safe for employees and customers**

● *Supervisor* ●

Supervisors must supervise their staff's work activities to ensure that these activities do not cause **risks** to the health and safety of people in the workplace. This does not necessarily mean that supervisors need to constantly watch every member of their staff. However, they should be readily available in case of any problem and should also regularly monitor work activities to identify any possible risks.

● *Line manager* ●

Your line manager is the first person you should go to with any health and safety problems (as well as other work problems). Line managers have a responsibility to check on a regular basis that their staff are performing their duties safely and healthily. Your line manager may ask you questions as well as observe you from time to time, to ensure this is the case.

● *Health and safety representatives* ●

In large businesses there will be a member of staff who is the health and safety representative (in some organisations there will be more than one). These are the people to go to with any specific queries about health and safety. They will have received special training in health and safety and will therefore be more informed than supervisors or line

GLOSSARY

To **minimise** is to reduce or lessen.

managers. They will be able to provide you with advice on how to operate safely and healthily. They will also be able to help with **minimising** hazards and risks.

GIVE IT A GO: responsibility for health and safety

1 Visit a business in your local area.
2 Find out if the business has a health and safety representative and, if possible, interview him or her.
3 Find out about the employees' responsibilities for health and safety in the business.
4 Find out about the employer's and managers' responsibilities for health and safety.

Policies

GLOSSARY

Documentation means pieces of paper (e.g. with guidelines or procedures on).

All organisations will have some form of health and safety policy, or policies. These could include the way they implement the Health and Safety at Work Act, policies for safety, for protecting yourself and others and for personal presentation. They may also include smoking policies, eating and drinking policies, drugs and alcohol policies and emergency policies. All these policies will usually have **documentation** which sets out the main points of the policy and the written procedures that need to be followed to comply with them.

● *Health and Safety at Work Act 1974* ●

The Health and Safety at Work Act 1974 requires all employers to 'provide and maintain a safe working environment which is, so far as is reasonably practicable, safe, without risks to health and adequate as regards facilities and arrangements for their welfare at work'.

Under this Act every organisation (including the self-employed who work from home) must pay close attention to health and safety and follow the necessary procedures, according to the industry that they work in.

● *Safety in the workplace* ●

A safety policy will deal with a number of issues including:

▷ *working methods – e.g. safe lifting of heavy items, enough breaks and rest, etc.*

▷ *equipment – e.g. safe use of computers, of heavy machinery, etc.*

▷ *using hazardous substances – e.g. safe use and/or disposal of toner, correcting fluid, chemicals and bodily fluids.*

● *Protecting yourself and others* ●

Policies for protecting yourself and others will set out the responsibilities of employees and may include:

▭ *keeping your work area tidy*

▭ *following manufacturers' guidelines in using equipment*

▭ *following safety guidelines when using dangerous materials*

▭ *keeping roads, gangways and other routes free from obstructions (whether the item that is in the way is yours or not)*

▭ *safe storage of all work materials and tools when not in use.*

● *Personal presentation* ●

Policies on personal presentation may include personal hygiene requirements, dress codes, rules about the wearing of jewellery and rules for wearing protective clothing or equipment. If your job requires you to wear **protective clothing** or equipment your employer must provide this for you. If you are self-employed you must buy or hire it yourself.

GLOSSARY

Protective clothing is clothing that protects against damage, harm or injury (e.g. gloves, safety glasses and hard hats).

CASE STUDY – LAZY DAISY RESTAURANT

Personal hygiene policy

Some germs can stay alive on our hands for up to three hours and in that time they can be spread to all the things we touch – including food and other people. So wash your hands regularly throughout the day and especially at these times:

- *before* preparing food
- *between* handling raw foods (meat, fish, poultry and eggs) and touching any other food or kitchen utensils
- *after* handling raw foods, particularly meat, fish and poultry; going to the toilet; touching rubbish/waste bins; coughing or sneezing, especially if you are sick.

Questions

1 How important is staff personal hygiene at Lazy Daisy Restaurant?

2 List **three** job roles where personal hygiene is particularly important. Give reasons for your answers.

4 List **three** reasons why personal hygiene is important in **all** job roles. Give reasons for your answers.

• *Smoking* •

A smoking policy will include details on where, if anywhere, employees are allowed to smoke. It may also include a limit on the number of cigarette breaks employees are allowed to take. Some organisations may not allow smoking anywhere on the premises, including outside.

• *Eating and drinking* •

An eating and drinking policy may include where you are allowed to eat or drink (e.g. it will probably not be allowed to eat or drink near to certain machinery or hazardous materials), where on the premises you can get food and drink (if relevant) and also where you can get fresh drinking water (e.g. water coolers, water fountains or taps). The policy may also include details of when employees are allowed to take food and drink breaks.

• *Drugs and alcohol* •

A drugs and alcohol policy will set out any rules regarding the use of drugs or alcohol. Drug use will usually include the use of certain prescription or over-the-counter drugs as well as illegal drugs. It will also set out any disciplinary measures that will be taken against employees who do not follow the rules (e.g. dismissal, warning, suspension, etc.). Employees who have to drive or operate heavy machinery may have to follow much stricter guidelines on alcohol and drug use.

• *Emergencies* •

Policies for emergencies will include details of fire exits, locations of fire extinguishers, emergency evacuation procedures and employees' responsibilities in cases of emergency (e.g. ensuring customers and visitors get out of the building, checking a register of employees to ensure no-one is left inside, etc.).

▶ **Signs indicating emergency exits are important**

• *Associated documentation* •

Safety documentation should be kept separately and filed or displayed as appropriate. While many items in the staff handbook can be put on the organisation's **Intranet**, instead of on paper, safety information should be available separately as well – in case an emergency causes electrical failure, for example.

Safety documentation that an organisation may need to make available includes:

- *safety policy*
- *information for employees' poster or leaflet about 'Health and Safety Law'*
- *identification of risk assessment and control measures*
- *certificate of Employer's Liability Insurance*
- *letters and reports from local council or HSE inspections*
- *organisation inspection reports*
- *staff health and safety training records*
- *an accident book*
- *accident reporting forms*
- *a fire certificate*
- *a COSHH assessment*
- *electrical test certificate and records*
- *inspection and test certificates for lifting and other equipment*
- *noise assessment*
- *manual handling assessment.*

Health and safety policy statements

Under the Health and Safety at Work Act 1974 employers must have a written policy on health and safety at work, which must be provided to all employees. Failure to provide such written information is an offence and carries a maximum fine of £20,000.

As a minimum, policies should include the following:

- *a brief statement of the organisation's commitment to health and safety*
- *details of the organisation for safety including people and their responsibilities and any committees or working groups*
- *details of the main hazards in the workplace and **precautions** to be taken to control the risk of injury (e.g. safety rules and procedures such as accident reporting, fire and first aid).*

> **GLOSSARY**
>
> An **Intranet** is a collection of web pages that are only accessible from within an organisation.

> **GLOSSARY**
>
> **Precautions** are strategies to guard against danger, risk and error.

EVIDENCE ACTIVITY  P1

Workplace policies

1 Choose a job role that you do, have done or would like to do.

2 Describe each of the health and safety responsibilities that you would have if working in this role.

3 Describe how the employer's own health and safety responsibilities would affect you.

Hazards and risks

Definitions

In health and safety terms, a hazard is the potential to cause harm, whereas a risk is the likelihood of a hazard causing harm. For example, the presence of a poisonous substance would be a hazard, but it would only become a risk if it was stored or used unsafely or spilt.

THINK ABOUT IT

What possible hazards can you think of in a retail outlet? What possible hazards can you think of in an office environment? Can you think of how these hazards might become risks?

Hazards and risks

The most common potential hazards and risks (though there may be many others, depending on the workplace) come from the following:

- *machinery and equipment*
- *materials and substances*
- *unsafe working practices*
- *unsafe behaviour*
- *accidental breakages or spillages.*

• *Machinery and equipment* •

Employers must maintain machinery and equipment (e.g. keep parts clean and replace them on a regular basis, *before* they break), so that it is safe to use. An employee must use machinery or equipment in a safe and healthy manner as set out in the manufacturer's manuals or in the employer's safety guidelines.

Some common mistakes employees and employers make in using machinery and equipment are:

- 📎 *ignoring or not following a manufacturer's instruction before operating an electric item or machine*

- 📎 *not checking for trailing leads, broken sockets and frayed wires*

- 📎 *allowing rings and other jewellery to interfere with operating equipment*

- 📎 *poor ventilation where dangerous fumes or substances are present (e.g. where drills and photocopiers are used)*

- 📎 *leaving drawers and filing cabinets open.*

▲ **Operating instructions must be followed**

Power sources

Power sources (e.g. electrical sockets, electrical wires, electrical plugs) can cause electric shocks and other damage to people if they are not positioned and used safely. Power sources that are in bad repair or used incorrectly can also cause fires.

• *Materials and substances* •

Hazardous substances can be found in all sorts of work environments, not just in chemical factories.

Flammable material includes paint thinners, petrol, welding gases, heating fuels, metal fumes, exhaust fumes, packaging materials, sawdust, flour, sugar, toner and glue.

Some substances can cause severe problems when breathed in, when touched by bare skin, when splashed in the eyes or when swallowed. Effects of such substances can be short- or long-term and include illnesses such as asthma, dermatitis or cancer.

All hazardous substances must be stored safely according to the guidelines provided by the employer or the manufacturer. When using hazardous substances, it will often be necessary to wear protective clothing or equipment.

Any accidents with hazardous materials (e.g. spillages) must be reported immediately and the procedure followed for dealing with them. This could include simply cleaning up the spill and disposing of it correctly, or it could be as severe as **evacuating** the building, or even other buildings in the area, until it has been safely disposed of.

GLOSSARY

Evacuating means emptying a building (or area).

• *Unsafe working practices* •

Unsafe working practices include working for too long on a computer, driving for too long or operating heavy machinery when very tired or under the influence of alcohol or drugs.

• *Unsafe behaviour* •

Unsafe behaviour can cover a lot of things, including lifting objects incorrectly, smoking near flammable materials, bad posture when sitting at a desk or not keeping your work area tidy. As an employee you need to behave safely at work. As well as following safety policies and procedures, this also involves using your common sense, for example, disposing of waste properly, rather than leaving it on your desk or the floor, getting enough sleep, eating properly and keeping clean.

• *Accidental breakages or spillages* •

Accidental breakages or spillages can cause risks to yourself and other people. It is essential to clear away any breakages or spillages safely and securely. Broken glass needs to be thoroughly wrapped before it is disposed of and care needs to be taken when picking it up. If a spillage involves hazardous materials, special procedures may need to be followed in cleaning it up. Spillages of non-hazardous materials such as water or milk still need to be cleaned up, as they could cause someone to slip over and hurt themselves.

• *Environmental factors* •

Environmental factors can include ensuring that hazardous substances are correctly and safely disposed of, ensuring that fumes are kept to a minimum, that good ventilation is provided and that lighting is sufficient for employees to do their work comfortably, safely and without causing health problems.

WHAT if?

... *you worked in a dark and stuffy atmosphere?*

1 How do you think this would affect your health?

2 How do you think this would affect your ability to work?

3 What do you think could be done to improve the situation?

• *Level of risk* •

Levels of risk can be high or low (or somewhere in between). It is important to assess risks carefully so that they can be minimised.

High risks are those which could cause long-term illness or disability or could prove fatal (i.e. someone could die). High risks could include electric shock, damage to hearing, poisoning and loss of **limbs**.

GLOSSARY

Limbs are arms and legs.

EVIDENCE ACTIVITY

Hazards and risks

1   In your own words, explain what the differences are between a hazard and a risk. Give examples of each.

2   List **five** potential hazards in a retail outlet

3   List **five** potential hazards in an office workplace.

4   For each of the hazards you listed in **(3)** and **(4)** describe how these hazards could become risks.

Reduce risks

Most accidents in the workplace could have been avoided if the proper **precautions** were taken. Health and safety is a joint responsibility between employers and employees and both must take measures to reduce risk.

Reducing risk

Methods to reduce risk include:

▭ following workplace policies/working practices: *these are in place for your own protection and that of others (see pages 158–161 for more details)*

▭ safe use of machinery, equipment and substances: *your employer will provide guidelines and training and you should also use your common sense (see page 163 for more details)*

▭ following manufacturers' instructions: *manufacturers spend a lot of time on testing their products and so know the best way to operate the machinery or use the product safely*

▭ correcting health and safety risks where possible: *even if you are not responsible for a health and safety risk, you should correct it if you can (e.g. mop up spillages, remove obstacles from gangways, etc.)*

▭ passing on suggestions about health and safety to the right people: *if you think there is a health and safety risk, you should tell your line manager or the health and safety representative, as you may have been the only person to notice it*

▭ maintaining personal presentation: *this includes being hygienic, wearing protective clothing where necessary, wearing the most appropriate clothing for the job and minimising accessories such as jewellery where these could cause problems.*

▲ **If you see a risky situation, tell your manager**

WHAT **if?**

... you spotted a potential risk in your workplace?

1 List the steps you would take to minimise the risk.
2 Who would you tell about the risk?
3 How would you tell them about it?

EVICENCE ACTIVITY

Reduce risks

For each of the hazards you described earlier (see page 165), describe what you could do to reduce the risk to health and safety.

END OF UNIT ASSIGNMENT

Task 1   P1 M1 D1

1 Choose a business where you work, have worked or have visited.

2 Choose one workplace policy from this business that would affect your work and workplace.

3 Write down the key points of the policy.

4 Describe what your responsibilities as an employee would be in this business.

5 Give examples of what your legal duties as an employee would be in this business.

6 Explain how these duties relate to the Health and Safety at Work Act 1974.

Task 2   P2 P3 P4 M2 D2

1 Choose a business where you work, have worked or have visited.

2 Identify **six** potential hazards that might be found in this business.

3 For each hazard, explain how it could be become a risk.

4 List all the risks that you know exist in this business or *could exist*. Explain how you would assess the level of each of these risks.

5 Explain what your responsibility as an employee would be in reporting these hazards and risks. Give examples of what could happen if these hazards are not reported quickly.

Task 3   P5 M3

1 For the risks you identified in **Question 4** of **Task 2**, give examples of different ways in which you, as an employee, could reduce these risks.

2 For the same risks, give examples of different ways in which the employer could reduce the risks.

3 Explain the basic steps you would take in the job role to keep health and safety risks to a minimum in this business.

unit 8

Communicating effectively at work

In this unit you will learn about communication and its importance within business. You will find out about different types of communication, both oral and written. You will also look at how to develop your own communication skills and the importance of integrity in business communication.

To complete this unit you must:

- ⊐ investigate different types of communication
- ⊐ be able to communicate well, both orally and in writing, within work situations
- ⊐ explore and understand the importance of integrity in business communication.

Types of communication

Communication is about sending and receiving information. Everyone communicates. For example, you communicate with your friends when you talk to them or send them text messages. When you write an essay you are communicating. In business, communication happens internally within departments and between departments and externally, with customers, distributors and suppliers.

▲ **Communication is vital to business**

Purpose of communication

Being able to communicate well involves knowing the **purpose** of the communication. Examples of the different purposes of communication include:

▱ *to find out information*

▱ *to give instructions*

▱ *to receive instructions*

▱ *to order goods*

▱ *to liaise with colleagues.*

● *Finding out information* ●

There are many different types of information that need to be used in a business.

Employees need information about how to do their jobs, for example, information about their **responsibilities** and about the products they sell or produce or about the service they provide. Employees need to be able to provide customers with information about products or services and special offers and discounts.

Financial managers and employees need information about sales figures and operating costs. Managers need information about employee **performance**. Everyone needs information about health and safety and other workplace procedures and guidelines.

Finding out information can involve looking it up in documents and books, asking colleagues or line managers and asking customers.

● *Giving/confirming instructions* ●

Giving and **confirming** instructions is a very important aspect of communication within business. Line managers and supervisors need to provide their staff with instructions on the tasks they need to do and their responsibilities. Employees need to understand these instructions and ask further questions when they do not.

Examples of instructions that might be given include:

- *work to be carried out*
- *method(s) to be used in undertaking the work*
- *use of equipment, machinery and materials*
- *standards to be met*
- *health and safety precautions to be observed*
- *reporting procedures.*

To avoid errors or misunderstandings, managers – including supervisors – should give clear instructions and support them with full explanations where necessary.

● *Ordering goods* ●

As well as internal communication, businesses need to communicate with suppliers to order goods. Businesses may use the Internet, telephone, letters or faxes to place orders with suppliers. They may also use special business documentation, such as purchase orders.

It is essential that all orders are clear and complete, so that the supplier will be able to provide the correct goods.

● *Liaising with colleagues* ●

Liaising with colleagues is an essential communication task for all employees. This includes liaising with colleagues in other departments as well as your own. It involves liaising with colleagues on the same level as you, as well as with your supervisor or line manager. Many employees work in teams, with each employee having responsibility for a specific task. In teamwork, communication and cooperation between colleagues is very important to ensure that the work gets done efficiently and well.

○○○ **THINK ABOUT IT**

Think of some situations in business, retail or administration where an employee needs to find out information, give instructions or liaise with colleagues.

Types of communication

There are various different types of communication that need to be used within business. Each of them has their own advantages and disadvantages. Types of communication include:

- *face to face*
- *letter*
- *telephone*
- *agendas*
- *minutes*
- *reports*
- *email*
- *Internet*
- *Intranet.*

● *Face-to-face communication* ●

Face-to-face communication is when you are talking to someone in person. It usually refers to a one-on-one meeting, but can also include, for example, talking in a meeting or giving a presentation. A large part of face-to-face communication is taken up by talking and listening, but it also includes elements of non-verbal communication such as eye contact, body language and tone of voice.

● *Letters* ●

Business letters are:

- *the most frequently used form of external communication between one business and another*
- *a written record that can be used to send almost any type of information*
- *usually on headed paper*
- *usually set out in fully blocked style*
- *written in a more formal language than personal letters.*

● *Telephone communication* ●

Telephone communication is a type of verbal communication. It also includes elements of non-verbal communication, such as tone of voice (though not as many as face-to-face communication).

Telephones are a quick and easy way to communicate with colleagues in the same building. Calls can easily be made between departments, for example, rather than going upstairs to talk to someone face to face.

More and more companies are increasing their use of the telephone in communicating with customers. Call centres and mail order are the fastest growing operational departments for UK organisations. In telephone communication, it is essential for all employees to represent their organisation in a professional and friendly way.

The increase in the availability of mobile phones means employees who are out of the office (e.g. salespeople visiting customers, managers going to meetings with clients) can quickly and easily contact the office.

GLOSSARY

An **agenda** is a list of items that are to be discussed in a meeting.

Minutes are a record of discussions and decisions made in a meeting.

▲ **Agendas help meetings run smoothly**

● *Agendas* ●

Agendas are documents put together for meetings. They set out the schedule for the meeting, with the topics for discussion and who will be introducing each topic. Agendas help meetings to run more smoothly and also to run to the time set aside for the meeting. Without an agenda a meeting can become very disorganised and the essential topics may not be discussed.

● *Minutes* ●

Minutes are the notes of what happened in a meeting, what was said and what decisions were made. It is usually the responsibility of one person in the meeting to take notes of these things and to then type up these notes after the meeting has finished. Minutes are then sent out to everyone who attended the meeting, and sometimes to other relevant managers as well. Minutes provide a written record of the outcomes of a meeting and are very important, as most of the people attending will not be able to remember everything that was said.

● *Reports* ●

There are lots of different types of **report** within business. Examples include financial reports, which summarise sales figures and profits;

GLOSSARY

A **report** is usually a multi-page document that deals with a specific issue or subject.

reports on customer service feedback; reports on testing new products; reports on overall employee performance.

A report is generally a document meant only for internal use within the organisation and is a means of providing detailed information to employees and managers where needed.

Reports are usually written in formal, and sometimes technical, language. They will be divided into sections in a similar way to a textbook and may include visual material such as graphs or diagrams.

• *Electronic communication* •

Email

These days email is widely used for internal communication between staff and has become the primary means for delivering short written messages within organisations that are networked. Email may also be used for marketing and to provide after-sales service or technical support to customers. Email between organisations (e.g. to suppliers, distributors and retailers) is also becoming more common and gradually taking the place of the fax.

Internet

The Internet provides businesses with the ability to make information widely available. For example, businesses can provide lists of the services they offer, portfolios of work done, brochures and catalogues, all on the Internet. A number of businesses also use the Internet to sell products or services, some selling exclusively on the Internet and some providing it as an extra service in addition to high-street shops.

Intranet

For internal communication, companies will often use an **Intranet**. This works in the same way as a website on the Internet, but is limited to internal use only. Many businesses put phone directories, product information, health and safety procedures, etc. on the Intranet for employees to access at the press of a button – or the click of a mouse!

> **GLOSSARY**
>
> An **Intranet** is a collection of web pages that are only accessible from within an organisation.

• *Advantages and disadvantages for each type of communication* •

All the types of communication described above have their own advantages and disadvantages. It is therefore important to choose the right type of communication for the intended purpose, rather than choosing the type of communication you are most comfortable with and only using that. Two advantages and two disadvantages for each type of communication are described in the table below, but you may well be able to think of more.

Table 8.1 Advantages and disadvantages of different types of communication

Type of communication	Advantages	Disadvantages
Face to face	Immediate More understanding through body language and tone of voice	No written record Not possible when long distances are involved
Letter	Provides written record Visual information can be included	Can take time to arrive Can be lost in the post
Telephone	Immediate Easy to use	No written record Can take up a lot of time
Agendas	Help meetings run on time Ensure everything is covered	Can hinder new ideas Use a lot of paper
Minutes	Provide written record of meetings Can help review employees' performance	Someone needs to take notes Staff need to spend time reading them after meeting
Reports	Explain complicated information Visual information can be included	Time-consuming to create May use a lot of paper
Email	Quick Cheap	Technical problems can mean emails get lost Requires a computer that is networked
Internet	Cheap Easy to update	Requires specialist staff May not reach all customers
Intranet	Cheap Easy to update	Requires specialist staff Information not available in case of electrical or technical problems

CASE STUDY – THE BOOKSHOP

Communication in our store

Staff at *The Bookshop* use the telephone to call customers and to call other branches to enquire about products. Staff use fax machines to send orders to suppliers. There is an intercom linked through all the phone lines. This is very effective as the managers and supervisors carry mobile phones, which are connected to the intercom. There is a phone in each department so there is always someone to answer calls.

Staff use telephones or fax machines to contact other businesses. Sometimes they also use email, for example, to send reports and orders. Application forms can be received by fax or email.

Questions

1 What types of communication are used at *The Bookshop*?

2 What are the advantages and disadvantages of these types of communication?

3 What other methods of communication not mentioned in the case study might be used in a bookshop?

4 Can you suggest any improvements to the types of communication used at *The Bookshop*?

◀ **Communication is important in** *The Bookshop*

EVIDENCE ACTIVITY

Types of communication

1 Explain what communication is used for in a business where you have worked or visited.

2 List the different types of communication which are used in a business where you have worked or visited.

Oral and written communication skills

Oral communication is made up of talking, listening and non-verbal communication (body language). Written communication includes letters, notes, memos, emails, etc. – anything that is written down.

All employees will need good oral communication skills and most will also need good written communication skills.

Oral communication

• *Verbal communication* •

Verbal communication is talking and listening. Conversations with colleagues are forms of verbal communication, as are meetings and presentations. Conversations and meetings with customers or suppliers also use verbal communication.

Verbal communication skills include:

- *using **appropriate** language (see page 177)*
- *being **accurate** (see page 178)*
- *using the right tone and level of voice (see page 178)*
- *being confident (see page 178)*
- *being welcoming (see page 179)*
- *using appropriate social conventions (see page 179)*
- *assisting (see page 179)*
- *questioning (see page 179)*
- *asking for **clarification** (see page 180).*

• *Non-verbal communication* •

Non-verbal communication includes body language and tone and level of voice (see page 178). Much information can come across through body language. For example, body language can show a person's mood, level of interest and level of confidence. Non-verbal communication skills involve paying attention to your own body language and also observing other people's body language. For example, if you sense that someone has lost interest, you can change what you are saying to get back their interest.

Smiling
Smiling is a simple act, but will show that you are happy to be in the conversation and may help to put nervous colleagues or customers at ease. Make sure you keep your smiles simple, though. If you grin widely, you may look sarcastic.

Making eye contact

Make sure you keep eye contact with the person you are speaking to. Keeping eye contact will ensure that they feel they have your full attention. If you look away or look at your feet you can appear nervous or bored.

Eye contact is also very important when giving a presentation. It shows that you are engaged with your audience and not just reciting a prepared speech. It can also help you feel more comfortable about speaking in front of a lot people. You should ensure that you move your eye contact around to different people, so that you are not just looking directly at one or two people.

Facial expression

Make sure your facial expression is welcoming. Do not frown or raise your eyebrows. If you think of yourself as calm and confident this will show in your facial expression. Watch other people's facial

▲ **Keep eye contact when you are addressing people**

expressions. If someone starts frowning, it may mean he or she does not understand what you are saying. **Simplify** your language or provide further details to help them and so that they do not have to ask first.

Gestures

You can use your **gestures** to show people that they have your full attention. Examples include nodding your head to show agreement (at the right point) and leaning forward to show interest. Be conscious of your own gestures and try not to fiddle, as this can show boredom or nervousness. Try to keep hand movements to a minimum and use them only to emphasise points or provide a visual **demonstration**. Watch other people's gestures as well to get clues as to what they are thinking and feeling.

• *Appropriate language* •

It is important to tailor the language you use to the person you are speaking with. Technical language should be fine with immediate colleagues in the same department, but may not be appropriate when talking to someone in a different department. Try to avoid the use of slang, as not everyone will understand and it can make you seem unprofessional. Avoid using swear words as many people find them offensive.

GLOSSARY

To **simplify** is to make clearer or easier to understand.

Gestures are hand and body movements that have meaning (e.g. nodding your head or waving).

Demonstration means showing how to do or use something.

• *Accuracy* •

Accuracy includes giving the right facts, as well as proper use of grammar. If you do not know something, then don't try to guess, as it will probably be obvious you are doing so. If you do not know something then apologise and either find the information, if you know where to look, or suggest someone else who will know.

• *Level and tone of voice* •

Your level and tone of voice show how you feel. For example, tone of voice can be sarcastic, patronising, frustrated, angry and so on. The level of voice needs to be carefully balanced. If it is too quiet the listener may find it difficult to hear you, or may assume you are nervous or lack confidence. If the level is too loud you can appear angry, frustrated or overexcited.

When speaking, you can change the meaning of sentences by putting stress on a particular word. You can make use of this technique to add extra meaning to your words. For example, if you read the following five sentences out loud, stressing the word in **bold**, you will see that there are five different meanings.

1 **Gerry** gave her the book.

2 Gerry **gave** her the book.

3 Gerry gave **her** the book.

4 Gerry gave her **the** book.

5 Gerry gave her the **book**.

Sentence (1) stresses who gave the book. Sentence (2) stresses that the book was given rather than lent or sold. Sentence (3) stresses who the book was given to. Sentence (4) puts a lot of importance on the book. Sentence (5) stresses that it was a book that was given, rather than something else.

Tone and level of voice are important in all oral communication, but they are particularly so in telephone conversations, where there are no other clues from body language.

• *Confidence* •

In conversations, meetings and presentations, it is important to be confident about yourself and about what you are saying. It is also important to show this confidence. If you know all the details you need to, then you should be confident. But you still might not feel it – especially if you get nervous talking to people you do not know well. Below are some tips that can help you feel confident, as well as look confident:

- *stand or sit up straight*
- *try to loosen the muscles in your neck, shoulders and jaw (rather than clenching them)*
- *take several slow, deep breaths, if there is time*
- *smile.*

● *Welcoming* ●

Be welcoming in your communications. If you show that you are happy to talk and listen, the person will be more willing to talk to you again and this will help to build a good working relationship. Turn away from your desk to face the speaker. Offer them a seat if there is one available. If there is not, then stand up so that you are both on the same level. Give the speaker your full attention.

● *Observing appropriate social conventions* ●

Be aware of social **conventions** when talking to people. While handshakes are widely acceptable in the UK, people from some other cultures and countries may find them offensive. Many gestures can also be **misinterpreted**, for example, in some countries nodding the head actually means 'no' rather than 'yes'.

> **GLOSSARY**
>
> A **convention** is a custom, habit or tradition.
>
> **Misinterpreted** means understood wrongly.

● *Assisting* ●

In conversations, you can help the other person or people if they are struggling. For example, if someone seems confused, you can simplify your language or use a different explanation. If the other person is nervous, you can help by showing **enthusiasm** for what he or she is saying and by questioning to provide the person with more time to think and more opportunity to put across his or her point.

> **GLOSSARY**
>
> **Enthusiasm** means interest, being keen and wanting to do something.

● *Questioning* ●

Use appropriate questions to get more information and to ask for clarification if you have trouble understanding. Good use of questions can also show that you are paying attention to the speaker. When giving instructions or reporting back to someone, you can use questions to confirm that the other person has understood you. For example, 'Do you agree?' or 'What do you think we should do?'. Questioning also involves the listener or listeners more, which will usually make them more interested in what you are saying.

⬭ THINK ABOUT IT

Think of some questions that you could ask a customer to find out what they are looking for. Think of some questions that you could ask your line manager if you need more information about a task you have to do.

• *Listening* •

Verbal communication is not just about speaking. Listening is an essential part of verbal communication. Make sure that you listen to and understand others' needs and points of view. Some tips to improve your listening skills include:

- *getting rid of any distractions (e.g. turn off your mobile phone, put your work to one side)*
- *not interrupting the other person in the middle of a sentence*
- *showing respect and asking questions*
- *not switching off half way through*
- *not hurrying the speaker*
- *trying to put yourself in the speaker's place (i.e. trying to understand their point of view).*

• *Asking for clarification* •

In verbal communication, it is very easy to mishear or misunderstand something. Many words have more than one meaning, so it may not always be clear which meaning the speaker has in mind. You should make a habit of asking for **clarification**. A good way to do this is to state what you understand the speaker's point to be, 'Let me see if I have understood. You are saying that. . .'. This enables the speaker to clarify what they have said without feeling offended that you did not understand them.

• *Telephone skills* •

When speaking or listening on the telephone, you do not have the advantage of body language to help you get across your point or to help you understand the other's point. It is therefore of extra importance to be very clear when speaking on the phone.

Pay attention to your tone and level of voice but also to the rate at which you are speaking. If you speak too slowly the other person may feel patronised; if you speak too quickly they may find it difficult to understand everything. Be pleasant and polite to the other person. Be prepared to ask and answer questions and to repeat or spell out information if necessary.

• *Taking/giving messages accurately* •

When taking messages for other people, it is vital to collect and write down all the relevant information. You need to make sure you have taken everything down correctly, so ask for clarification or for the caller to spell out names, if necessary. The following checklist will help you to make sure you haven't forgotten anything:

- *who the call is for*
- *the date and time of the call*
- *the name of caller (and the company, if relevant)*
- *the caller's telephone (and/or fax) number*
- *the reason for the call*
- *whether the call is urgent*
- *a convenient time to return the call*
- *your name*
- *details of anything you have agreed with the caller.*

Make sure you pass on all the information to the person the message is for as soon as possible.

● *Importance of timing* ●

Timing can be important in all verbal communication. Your colleagues and customers will probably be as busy as, or more busy than, you are. You should not spend too much time passing on a simple message, for example, but you do need to take enough time to ensure it is passed on accurately. If you are talking in a meeting, it is very important to keep to the time slot given you. If you go over, then the whole meeting will run on, which can cause knock-on effects for meetings later in the day, or for other people who need to use the meeting room. Likewise, when giving a presentation, keep to the allotted timeslot and make sure you allow time for questions. If you go on too long your audience may become bored.

Timing is also important within conversations. For example, you need to pick the right time to ask a question, rather than interrupting the speaker in the middle of a sentence. You need to pick the right time to nod or smile.

● *Oral communications in meetings and discussions* ●

Communicating during meetings and discussions can be quite difficult. Some people may **dominate** the time, while others do not get a chance to say anything. Good meetings will have a proper structure, in which everyone gets a chance to put their point across, to ask questions or to make suggestions.

> **GLOSSARY**
>
> To **dominate** is to take over or control.

Depending on the structure of the meeting or discussion, it may be appropriate to ask a question when a speaker has come to the end of a sentence or a specific topic. At other times, there may be a specific point in the meeting at which questions will be welcome.

▲ **Learn to recognise when your audience is bored**

If you have a question or suggestion to make, you will need to speak up (but do not shout) so that the other people know you want to say something. Try to keep any questions brief and to the point, so as not to make the meeting run over.

If it is your turn to talk, then keep your eye open for people who look like they have questions or something to add and call on them to speak. Watch for people looking bored or impatient. This may be a sign that you should wind up your speech.

Always show respect and politeness to the other people in the meeting. Listen to their viewpoints and do not criticise or mock them.

● *Using technical language* ●

When you have worked somewhere for a while, you will often find yourself using technical language without even thinking about it. You will learn the technical language necessary for the job gradually, but once you have it may seem quite natural to you. This makes it difficult to remember that not everyone will understand this technical language.

Colleagues in other departments will concentrate on different aspects of the business so may not be exposed to the same language. Customers and suppliers are also likely to be unfamiliar with it. It is very important, therefore, to only use technical language with the people who will understand it. When talking to other people, simplify the language or explain what you mean more thoroughly.

Written communication

Written communication is very common in business. Written communication includes such documents as letters, brochures, contracts, orders, faxes, invoices, safety guidelines and much more. For most job roles, skills in written communication are very important. These skills include:

⬤ *using appropriate language*

⬤ *accuracy*

⬤ *making notes*

⬤ *spelling and grammar.*

● *Appropriate language* ●

As with oral communication, appropriate language means targeting your language to your audience (see page 177). However, in written communication this language will generally be of a more formal and structured nature. It also requires close attention to using grammar correctly.

The purpose and type of communication will affect the language that needs to be used. For example, business emails may be less formal than business letters. In writing that is aimed to increase sales (e.g. brochures, leaflets, Internet sites), the language usually needs to be simple but enthusiastic and needs to clearly put across the point.

Slang should generally be avoided in any written business communication, even that between colleagues. For some business letters and documents, legal language may be needed.

If you are unsure of the appropriate language to use in a given situation, you will probably be able to find out by looking at examples of similar documents in the organisation. For example, if you need to write a letter to a customer, look in the files for another letter to see what language is used. If in doubt, you should ask a colleague or your line manager to read over your writing to make sure it does use the right language.

• *Accuracy* •

When writing, keep in mind that written communication can be more concrete than oral communication. Once a letter has been sent out, you cannot get it back. It is therefore very important to get the facts right. For example, if you are writing a letter to a customer to inform them when a product will be delivered, it is very important to get the date and time correct. In addition to accuracy of facts, you also need to make sure your spelling and grammar are correct.

Always read through your documents before printing them and after printing them to check for and correct any errors.

• *Recording and relaying messages* •

When making notes of phone calls or other messages, make sure that you write down all the relevant details and write neatly and clearly, so that the person the message is for will be able to read and understand it. (See page 79 for a checklist for taking messages.)

• *Importance of timing* •

Timing can be very important in written communication. For example, you may need to ensure that a letter is sent out in time to arrive the next day. In this case, it is important to know the last time for getting mail to the post room or to the post office and make sure the letter is finished well before this time.

Timing may also be important for getting sales documents or advertising copy out in time for publication deadlines. Some organisations send out special offers to customers at certain times of the year (e.g. Christmas, New Year, summer holidays, new school term, etc.), in which case it is important that documents are ready at the right time.

• *Reading and interpreting simple workplace communications* •

In the workplace it is very important to know how to read and interpret what a business document is saying. For example, you need to understand written instructions from colleagues or line managers. You need to understand written queries from customers. You need to be able to read these documents and work out what you need to do.

The person who wrote the document may not always be available to explain things further, so you need to understand as fully as possible yourself. If there are words you don't recognise or understand, then you can look them up in a dictionary. If in doubt, though, you can always ask your line manager or a colleague to try to clarify a point or a particular sentence that you are unsure about.

• *Making notes* •

Making notes is a very important skill to have in business. You use notes for different reasons, such as noting down a telephone message, making notes in a meeting or discussion and making notes of the steps involved to do a particular task.

Making notes does not mean writing down every single thing the person says, or writing an essay for every step of a task. Notes are summaries that will help you remember the full details. You need to record the key points, rather than every detail.

▲ **You don't need to write everything down**

• *Recording* •

A record is a written document that confirms something that has been discussed or a decision that has been made. Records can be in various forms, including memos, emails, forms and other documents. Records may be kept for legal reasons or to monitor performance. In the workplace, all accidents will need to be recorded in an accident book, for example. Records are kept of appraisals and of meetings.

When recording, as with note taking, it is usually the key points that are most important. In meetings these key points will include any agreed actions (e.g. who will take on a certain task).

If you are required to do a lot of recording as part of your job role, it is a good idea to look at samples of similar records to check how best to complete them. For example, look back in the accident record book, or look in the files for minutes of meetings. (Make sure you only look at documents that you are allowed to look at, though.)

GIVE IT A GO: recording

1 Choose a job role that you have worked in or would like to work in.

2 List the different forms that are used within the job role.

3 If possible get a blank copy of one of these forms. If this is not possible, then get or create a similar form.

4 Explain what information you need to put on the form.

• *Accuracy of punctuation* •

Punctuation is used to clarify meaning and to highlight structure. Punctuation makes writing easier to understand and can sometimes even change the meaning.

The simplest rule that you should always follow is to start sentences with a capital letter and finish them with a full stop (.). Questions should always end with a question mark (?). You should avoid the use of exclamation marks (!) in business communication and *never* use more than one.

You may have become used to text messages and emails between you and your friends that do not use capital letters or punctuation. While you may be able to understand these, this is because you know your friends and the way they think and someone else would find it difficult. In business, this would be very unprofessional.

You can find out more about punctuation in grammar books and some dictionaries. You might also have some old English textbooks from school that may have some useful tips.

• *Spelling and grammar* •

Some people find spelling very difficult. This could be because they never learnt it properly at school, or it could be because they are dyslexic. Spelling checks in word-processing software can provide a great deal of help and you should always make use of them. However, there are some words that a spelling check will not pick up. For example, 'to', 'two' and 'too' are all correctly spelt, but it is very easy to use the wrong one, especially if you are typing fast.

Grammar is something else that many people struggle with. If you find it difficult, it may be useful to buy a simple grammar book that provides good explanations. One of the most common grammar mistakes is using the wrong tense of a verb, or using a word that should be used for a different person. For example, 'I were late' is incorrect, 'I was late' is correct and so is 'They were late'.

It is important to proofread your work carefully and not just rely on the spelling check on the computer. If there are any words that you are unsure of, you should check them in a dictionary. If you are still unsure about anything, then you could check with a colleague or your line manager. It can be useful to have someone else proofread your work, if possible. A useful tip is to offer to proofread a colleague's documents and then have him or her return the favour.

• *Using technical language* •

Technical language should only be used when it is appropriate (i.e. when the audience will understand it). It is possible that you may work in a job role where you need to use or type up a lot of technical language. It is useful to keep a notebook with a list (preferably in alphabetical order – i.e. apple, bear, camera. . .) of technical words that you need to use. This will help you to ensure that you always spell them correctly. It may also help you to learn what the words mean and understand the documents you are typing better.

EVIDENCE ACTIVITY

Oral and written communication

1 Describe the skills which you use when communicating orally.

2 Describe the skills which you use when communicating in writing.

3 Identify any of these skills which you need to improve.

Integrity

Integrity is very important in business communication. Integrity includes:

▭ *being truthful*

▭ *being honest*

▭ *using discretion with confidential or sensitive information.*

Integrity

• *Importance of truthfulness* •

It is very important to be truthful in business. For one, you are very likely to be found out if you tell lies. It is also a lot easier to remember the truth than it is to remember a web of lies. Not being truthful can seriously harm the organisation's reputation. For example, if you tell a customer that a mobile phone offers a certain feature, then they buy it and discover it does not offer this feature, they may well return the phone. They are also unlikely to use your organisation again.

• *Honesty* •

Honesty means owning up to mistakes or to problems or flaws in products. For example, if you realise that you sent out a letter to a customer with a mistake in it, you can phone the customer to let them know and apologise. You should also tell your line manager. If a customer in a supermarket is looking for a wheat-free bread and you do not stock any, you need to tell them that, rather than saying that it will be in tomorrow. If a customer needs an item delivered tomorrow, but your delivery procedures are unable to do this, you need to tell them, rather than saying it will be there tomorrow, when it will take two days.

WHAT if?

... you were waiting for a delivery of a new computer?

1 What would you expect to be told about the time and date of the delivery?

2 If the delivery was delayed, how might this affect you?

3 What would you want the business to tell you about the delay?

4 If you discovered they had lied, would you still use the same company in the future?

GLOSSARY

Discretion means not sharing private information and not gossiping about others.

• *Discretion* •

Discretion is an important skill in business. It involves making sure that you do not release any confidential or sensitive information. It means not telling secrets (personal or business-related). It means not gossiping about the bonuses your bosses received. A good tip for being discreet is to think about how you would feel if someone gossiped about you, or told someone else a secret you had told them in confidence. Make sure you act towards others as you would like them to act toward you.

● *Building trust and reliability* ●

Good communication is grounded in trust. In order to have good communication within an organisation you need to ensure that you do what you say you are going to do. If you promise to finish a task by a certain time, make sure you do. If you promise to send a customer a catalogue make sure you do.

Trust and reliability are also built by being truthful, honest and discreet (see above) and lack of truthfulness, honesty and discretion in an employee can seriously harm the trust that customers have in the organisation.

● *Legal implications* ●

As well as being important to the reputation of the organisation, truthfulness, honesty and discretion can have legal implications. For example, organisations that say a product does something that it doesn't in sales literature can be prosecuted. If an organisation passes on information about a customer without his or her permission they can be prosecuted. Employees who leak sensitive company information (for example, information on new products or financial records) can be **dismissed** and could even go to jail.

> ### GLOSSARY
>
> To **dismiss** someone is to sack them from their job or to end their employment.

● *Importance of representing employers to external audiences* ●

When employees communicate with customers (e.g. to sell a product, provide a service or respond to queries) they are acting as representatives of the business and not just as individuals. It is therefore very important to keep this in mind in all external communication, to ensure that you come across as professional and helpful.

Retail customer service

If a sales assistant in your local supermarket is rude to you, this will affect your perception of the business and might put you off using the supermarket again. It is unlikely you will remember the person who was rude to you, but you *will* remember the shop in which it happened.

Call centre clients

More and more companies are increasing their use of the telephone in establishing and maintaining customer contacts. Call centres and mail order are the fastest growing operational departments for UK organisations.

▲ **Call centres keep contact with customers**

It is essential that all employees represent their organisation in a professional and friendly way. Clear and effective communication is essential to ensure that the business is not lost.

Call centre or telesales operators need to be:

- *confident at talking on the telephone in a clear, fluent way*

- *good at communicating and sometimes persuading*

- *able to deal efficiently and patiently with all customers.*

● *Discretion, confidentiality and sensitivity* ●

Many businesses rely on having information about customers and clients. This information is often stored on computers. It is very important to ensure that any confidential information is kept confidential. This means that only those people who need to and have permission to use it are allowed to see it.

In addition to confidential information about customers, some employees may have access to confidential information about other employees (e.g. human resources information, information about an alcohol problem or serious illness) or about the organisation (e.g. knowledge of an upcoming job restructuring or merger). It is important to keep this information secure and never pass it to anyone who does not have permission to see it.

Some employees may be told confidential personal information by customers (e.g. for completing a life insurance application or an application for a mortgage). The Data Protection Act 1998 restricts and sets down rules for the processing of sensitive information. The following are examples of sensitive personal information:

- *political opinions*
- *religious or other beliefs*
- *trade union membership*
- *physical or mental health*
- *criminal proceedings and convictions.*

Businesses that have to collect any personal information about their customers (including, for example, names, addresses and income) will have a privacy policy that sets out for customers what information will be kept and what, if any, will be passed on to outside organisations.

EVIDENCE ACTIVITY

Integrity

1 Choose a business where you have worked or visited.

2 Give an example of the use of:
   a truthfulness
   b honesty
   c discretion
   d building trust and reliability
   e keeping confidentiality
   f respecting the sensitivity of information.

END OF UNIT ASSIGNMENT

Task 1

1 Choose an organisation where you have worked or visited.

2 List **five** different types of communication used in this business.

3 Describe the advantages and disadvantages of each of these types of communication.

4 For each type of communication, give **two** examples of a situation when it would be appropriate to use it.

5 Select and use an appropriate method of communication in the following situations (give reasons for your answers):
   a telling a customer a delivery has been delayed
   b deciding which team members need to carry out which tasks
   c enquiring about the features of a mobile phone
   d a manager instructing an administrative assistant to prepare a letter for a supplier
   e an employer telling employees about a pay rise.

Task 2

1 In your own words, describe the purpose of communication.

2 Demonstrate good use of your oral and written communication skills in the workplace, for example, in your part-time job or during your work experience.

3 In your own words, explain why good communication skills are important in business, retail or administration.

Task 3

1 Identify examples of the use of integrity in a business where you have worked or visited.

2 For each example, describe how integrity was used.

3 For each example, explain why it was important to show integrity.

unit 9

● ●

Introduction to retail

This unit will introduce you to the basics of working in the retail environment. You will learn to develop your knowledge of customer needs and the skills required to respond to them and will find out about different payment methods. You will also explore various areas of stock handling, including lifting, carrying and stacking different types of stock, stock control and how to deal with damaged stock. You will find out about different security measures used within retail, including security staff and procedures, opening and closing procedures and procedures for handling cash.

This unit provides some of the theory behind retail. However, in order to complete the unit for your qualification you will need to practise a lot of the tasks described here and provide evidence of your skills. Ideally, this should be done in your own workplace, but your teacher or tutor may be able to provide you with facilities to practise at school or college.

To complete this unit you must:

▭ be able to respond to customer needs in a retail environment
▭ explore methods of stock handling in retail outlets
▭ understand security measures used to support retail outlets.

Customer needs

Customers have needs and wants which they satisfy by buying goods and services. All customers are different and will satisfy their needs and wants in different ways. Customer needs can be split into the following three categories:

▭ *products or services*   ▭ *skills of staff*
▭ *payment processing facilities.*

Products/services

The most obvious need of any customer is the product or service they are looking for. To be successful, a business needs to offer the right product at the right price and offer it when and where the customer wants it. Product and service needs include:

▭ *purchases*

▭ *information*

▭ *additional services.*

● *Purchases* ●

Most customers who come into a retail outlet are looking to buy something. For example, you go to the supermarket to buy food and grocery items. You go to a clothes shop to buy clothes. You go to a mobile phone shop to buy a mobile phone, or accessories for your mobile phone. When you work in the retail sector, you need to do as much as you can to help customers make the purchases they want to make. For example, this could include making sure that the products are on the shelf or helping customers get to goods they cannot reach (e.g. on high shelves).

● *Information* ●

For many **purchases**, customers want information about the product before they buy it. Some customers come into retail outlets to find out more about, and compare, products before they decide to buy.

▶ **Retail outlets have a wide variety of shops**

The amount of information customers need will usually depend on the nature of the product. For example, customers do not usually need detailed information about cartons of milk or other basic food products; however, a customer buying a new computer would need a lot of information.

Examples of information customers may need include cost, location, availability, accessories, value for money and guarantee/warranty.

Cost

Customers want to know how much a product costs. They might also want to know how much different versions of the same product cost for comparison.

Location

Customers may want to know where to find a certain product in the store. They might also want to know the location of other branches of the retail outlet.

Availability

Customers need to know whether a certain product is in stock and, if it is not, when it will be arriving. Timing can be crucial for some purchases. For example, a customer who needs a certain ingredient for a dinner party that evening will go somewhere else if the ingredient will not be in store until the next day. For other larger products, such as cars, customers may be happy to wait a few days for the product they really want to be available.

Accessories

Customers may want to know what extras they can buy for a product. For example, if they were buying a mobile phone, they might want to know if they could get a hands-free set or an in-car charger. Customers will also need to know if they will have to buy any extras. For example, many printers do not come with a printer cable to connect them to the computer, so a customer will need to know if they have to buy this as an extra.

Value for money

Customers need to know if what they are buying provides value for money. Value for money does not always come down to the product itself, it can include things like after-sales service and guarantees (see page 196). Customers will often want to know how the price of a particular product compares to similar products from other brands or outlets. If the costs are fairly similar, it may come down to the extras that are provided for that cost.

Guarantee/warranty

For electrical items and large expensive items, customers will usually expect a guarantee or warranty. They may want to know how long the guarantee/warranty lasts, how much it costs to extend the warranty and what is covered by the guarantee/warranty (e.g. refund, repair, replacement).

● *Additional services* ●

In addition to purchases and information, customers may also be looking for additional services or facilities. Many retailers (especially larger ones, such as supermarkets and DIY stores) provide these facilities to save customers time and make their experience in the retail outlet more pleasurable and comfortable. Examples of such facilities include cash machines, toilets and cafés.

Cash machines

Many retail outlets now provide cash machines outside or inside the store, meaning customers can easily get out a little extra cash if they decide to buy more than they intended, for example. In addition, in high-street stores, customers may want to know where the nearest cash machine is, so it is a good idea for sales staff to know this.

Toilets

Many large stores and shopping centres have toilets for customers to use. Customers may also want to know where they can change their baby's nappy, for example. Sales assistants should be able to direct customers to the store's own facilities or tell them how to get to the closest external public toilet.

Café

Many supermarkets and department stores have a café on site. Customers may want to sit down and have a coffee while they wait for someone to collect them, or they might just like to relax a little after spending a long time on their feet. Some customers may even come to the store specifically for its café, in which case they might also be persuaded to buy something on their way through. While the café can provide extra income for the business, it also gives the customers an extra incentive to shop there instead of somewhere else.

⌒ THINK ABOUT IT

Think about the additional services that are provided by the large supermarkets in your local area. Are there any more facilities other than those listed above? Can you think of any additional facilities that customers might find useful?

Skills

Customers need and expect sales staff to have certain skills. These include good communication, personal presentation and knowledge of products and services. If these skills are lacking in a salesperson, customers may decide to go elsewhere.

● *Communication skills* ●

Customers expect retail staff to be friendly and polite. They expect salespeople to welcome them and to be happy to serve them. They also want the staff to be able to explain things clearly to them and show confidence and **enthusiasm** for the products or services.

● *Personal presentation* ●

In the retail sector, customers will have certain expectations about the presentation of staff. As a minimum, they will expect good personal hygiene standards, which includes regular washing, clean and brushed or styled hair, clean hands and nails and clean and brushed teeth.

Dress expectations will vary according to the outlet. Some shops provide uniforms for staff. This does make it easier for employees, but they still need to make sure the uniform is clean, ironed and correctly worn. Customers in clothing shops expect staff to be dressed in clothes from that shop. If this is the case, then employees are usually given an allowance to buy this clothing. In most outlets a smart appearance (e.g. suit and tie, skirt and blouse, trouser suit) is required.

In shops where name tags/badges are required, they need to be worn so that they are easy for customers to see.

● *Knowledge of products and services* ●

Customers expect staff to know about the products and services that the retail outlet sells. The amount of knowledge that customers expect will usually depend on the actual product. For example, a customer probably would not expect a sales assistant in a supermarket to know all about the ingredients in a ready meal; but they would expect them to know where to find that ready meal. A customer in an electrical goods store, however, would expect the salespeople to be able to answer technical questions about the products on sale. A customer in a car salesroom will need staff to know about, for example, the features of various models, information about warranties, the meaning of manufacturers' descriptions and the financing options available.

Examples of the types of information customers need salespeople to know include:

- *facts about the products and services and the basics of how they work*
- *technical and reference information, as well as back-up data such as statistics*
- *details about pricing structures, discount limits and circumstances*
- *details about delivery*
- *set-up and installation*
- *maintenance.*

CASE STUDY – NIRUPA SHALWA

Personal profile of a car parts salesperson

Nirupa sells car parts for a car sales and service business. Her job involves packing and sending out parts, telephoning customers and taking calls from customers, preparing quotes and building up her knowledge about the cars and parts the business sells. Nirupa says, 'You need to know a bit about how motor vehicles work, so that you know what role the parts you're dealing with have.'

Providing good customer service is an important part of Nirupa's job. She says, 'We need to give our customers good service because people can shop around and go elsewhere to get the same parts. I spend about a quarter of my day dealing with customers over the phone or in the shop, helping them with their parts enquiries. It can be tough trying to sell some parts, especially the more expensive ones, so it's great when I make a sale.'

Questions

1 What are the key skills that a car parts salesperson needs?

2 Describe why communication skills are so important in Nirupa's job role.

▲ **Nirupa is pleased when she makes a sale**

Payments

When a customer comes to a retail outlet to buy something, they need to be able to pay for it. Most customers will expect a variety of payment processes to be available (e.g. cash, cheques, cards). They will expect standard procedures to have been set up for making these payments, so that the process is quick and error-free. They will also expect staff to be able to answer questions about payments and, in some cases (e.g. supermarkets, clothes shops), will want a loyalty card to be available to give them discounts for using the shop a lot.

● *Processes* ●

The most common forms of payment are:

- ▭ *cash*
- ▭ *cheque*
- ▭ *credit or debit card*
- ▭ *account payment*
- ▭ *voucher.*

Cash

Despite the popularity of debit and credit cards, people still like to pay cash for certain purchases – especially small ones, such as buying a newspaper or packet of mints. There are also people who make most of their purchases using cash, as they find it helps them keep track of their spending (e.g. only getting out a certain amount of cash each week can help to ensure you don't overspend).

Retail outlets need to provide the facility for customers to pay in cash. This means that the till will need to have a **float** that will enable cashiers to give customers the correct change. While some customers may hand over the exact amount for their purchases, the majority will have a larger amount (e.g. a £10 note, £2 coin, etc.) and will therefore need to get change back.

> **GLOSSARY**
>
> A **float** is cash in a till (in different notes and coins) that allows cashiers to give customers change.

In some retail outlets, staff will need to work out how much change to give a customer themselves. However, most modern tills can do this, if the cashier enters the amount they are handing over and the amount they have to pay. It is still necessary, though, for staff to work out for themselves how to best make up that change from the different coins and notes in the till.

It is also necessary for cashiers to check that they have been given enough money to pay for the purchases. So anyone working as a cashier will need to have good **numeracy skills**, in particular, the ability to do simple sums in their heads. Cashiers may also need to check bank notes for forgery and there will probably be a procedure for this.

> **GLOSSARY**
>
> **Numeracy skills** are skills with numbers (e.g. adding, subtracting, etc.).

GIVE IT A GO: making change

In your till you have £20, £10 and £5 notes and £2, £1, 50p, 20p, 10p, 5p, 2p and 1p coins. For each of the transactions below, state how much change you need to give the customer and how you would make this change up using the notes and coins in the till.

1 The goods cost £5.36; the customer gives you £10.

2 The goods cost £11.05; the customer gives you £21.05.

3 The goods cost 52p; the customer gives you £1.

4 The goods cost £52.78; the customer gives you £60.

5 The goods cost £100.24; the customer gives you £110.

Cheques

While payment by cheque in most retail outlets is becoming less common these days, there are still a lot of people who prefer to pay by cheque. In fact, there are almost two billion cheques written every year in the UK.

Most retail outlets require a customer to have a cheque guarantee card, if they wish to pay by cheque. This guarantees that the business will receive the amount written on the cheque, even if the customer does not have enough funds in his or her account.

Cheque guarantee cards come in different amounts, for example, some will guarantee cheques up to £50 and some up to £100. Most shops will not accept payment by cheque for amounts over the guarantee figure, as there is a chance that they will not receive the money. It is therefore important for cashiers to check these figures before allowing a customer to pay by cheque.

In addition, cashiers will need to check the customer's signature matches the one on the guarantee card. If it does not, then the guarantee is likely to be invalid.

Many modern tills offer the ability to print a cheque for the customer. This will save them time and also ensure that the details (e.g. name of the business, amount to be paid and date) are correct. Some customers still prefer to write their cheques by hand, though, so it is important to offer them the choice. If a customer does write the cheque by hand then the cashier will need to check it carefully to make sure that all the details are correct.

Credit/debit cards

Credit and debit cards are probably the most popular method of payment for most customers, particularly for medium to large purchases, such as weekly shops or new clothes.

For businesses, credit and debit cards work in a similar way, in that the business will usually receive the money more quickly than they would with a cheque (though not as quickly as with cash). Most businesses are charged a small fee by their bank for processing card payments. Some businesses charge a fee to customers to cover this fee, while others provide the facility to customers as a free option.

Making payment by debit card

When making a payment by debit card, a customer may be offered the option of getting **cashback**. Not all retail outlets offer this facility, but it is quite common in supermarkets. For the customer, this is similar to using a cash machine, but saves them the trouble of finding one. Businesses provide this facility as an additional customer service, because it does not make them any money. Where the facility is available, cashiers should ask the customer if they want cashback, before processing the payment. Some modern tills provide cashiers with a prompt to ask this, so that they do not forget.

> ### GLOSSARY
>
> **Cashback** means getting cash from a cashier when you pay for a purchase using a debit card (like using a cash machine).

Most retail outlets will have special machines for processing card payments. Sometimes this is built into the till and sometimes it is separate. The cashier will usually have to swipe the card and enter the amount that needs to be taken from it. The machine will then contact the customer's bank or credit card company to ensure that they have enough money (or credit) to cover that amount.

The customer will then either need to sign a payment slip or key in the pin number for the card (this process is known as 'chip and pin'). These processes are there to ensure that someone is not using a stolen debit card. The cashier will need to check that the signature matches the one on the card. If chip and pin is used, then the machine will contact the bank or credit card company to make sure that the correct pin number has been entered and will then approve (or decline) the purchase.

What if payment is declined?

If a customer's payment has been declined, the customer will need to find another method to pay for the purchase, or they will not be able to make the purchase. In some cases, a card may be declined for security reasons, such as a stolen card. In such cases, the retail outlet will probably have procedures to follow, which may involve contacting the police. It is important, therefore, for cashiers to be aware of the correct security procedures in the outlet where they work.

▲ **Chip and pin machines help avoid credit card fraud**

Account payments

Account payments are common in retail outlets that sell mostly to other businesses. Examples include builders' merchants, office suppliers and cash and carries (which are like large supermarkets for the catering industry). Business customers set up accounts with the retailer and provide details of which members of staff are allowed to make purchases. These staff then come in and pick the goods and then provide a card or sign a form to record the purchase they have made. The business customer then pays for all the purchases at the end of the month (or sometimes every three months).

When taking payments from account customers, it is essential to check the identity of the customer. Where the customer has an account card, this will usually just involve checking the signature; however, in other cases it may be necessary to check ID such as a driving licence or passport.

Account payments can also refer to customers making purchases on credit. For example, a customer buying a car can often put down a deposit and sign a finance agreement to pay for the car in monthly payments. This is a form of credit and, for the customer, works in a similar way to credit cards or personal loans.

For all types of account payments there will be specific procedures to follow and customers will expect these to be smooth and easy. Staff will need to know all the tasks involved in following these procedures, so that customers do not need to wait unnecessarily.

Vouchers

Many retailers sell gift vouchers. These can be used as presents for birthdays or any occasion. Gift vouchers are usually available in varying amounts (e.g. £1, £5, £10, £50) and can be used to purchase goods or services (or as part payments). Some retailers give their customers vouchers when they make large purchases and some businesses give their employees vouchers as bonuses.

Some vouchers are specific to one retailer, while others may be usable in a wide variety of outlets. For example, book tokens can usually be used in any bookshop.

Customers may want to buy gift vouchers and usually they expect to get a card and envelope along with the voucher (usually these come as a free extra, so in a sense the customer is getting a birthday card for free). There will be certain procedures set up for taking payment in gift vouchers. Some retailers will not give change from vouchers, so customers need to use the whole amount of the voucher in their purchase. Other retailers may give change only in other vouchers. For example, if a customer buys a book that costs £7.99 with a £10 book token, he or she might get two £1 book tokens as change and so lose a penny. Some retailers are happy to give full change or even exchange a voucher for cash.

Some vouchers have expiry dates, which means they cannot be used as payment after a certain date. Staff taking payment in vouchers need to check that they are still valid.

It is important for staff to know the procedures that need to be followed both for buying gift vouchers and for using them as payment.

● *Procedures* ●

All retail outlets will have procedures for taking payment. This will include the correct procedures to follow for each different payment method. For example, there may be a procedure on whether to ask customers if they want cashback when they use their debit card or to wait for them to ask themselves. There might be special procedures to follow for customers paying by cheque. There will be special procedures for any account payments. There may be procedures for checking bank notes for forgery, or for not accepting certain larger bank notes (e.g. £50 notes). It is also probable that there will be procedures for when cards are declined or a customer's signature does not match that on the card. It is important for all staff to know what these procedures are and to follow them clearly.

● *Queries* ●

It is important for staff to know the answers to common queries that customers might have. For example, these could include:

- ▭ *How can I pay?*
- ▭ *Do you accept Visa/MasterCard/American Express/etc.?*
- ▭ *Can you print cheques?*
- ▭ *Can I charge this to my account?*
- ▭ *Do you give cashback?*
- ▭ *Can I have a receipt?*
- ▭ *Can I have a VAT receipt?*
- ▭ *Can I split the payment over these two cards?*
- ▭ *Can I pay for these items separately?*

▲ Loyalty cards help businesses to track customers' buying habits

● *Loyalty cards* ●

Loyalty cards give regular customers of a retail chain or outlet vouchers, discounts or special offers. The more money you spend in the outlet or chain, the more bonuses you will receive. Loyalty cards are common with supermarket chains, but there are many other retailers who offer them as well. They are especially useful for people who do a lot of shopping in the same outlet and some customers might even be persuaded to choose one shop over another on the basis of the loyalty card bonuses.

Loyalty cards are useful to businesses because they can track customers' buying habits. This helps businesses keep the right items in stock. They are also able to provide customers with targeted vouchers or offers. For example, if someone buys a lot of dog food in a supermarket, they might get special vouchers for discounts on dog food; while someone else who never bought dog food but bought a lot of fruit juice might get special offers on fruit juice.

EVIDENCE ACTIVITY

Customer needs

1 Choose a retail business where you have worked or where you would like to work. (If you have not worked there, you will need to visit the business to do some research.)

2 List and describe **five** products or services that business sells.

3 List and describe **five** pieces of extra information that customers might need in this business.

Stock handling

Many jobs in the retail sector involve handling stock. This might include, for example, picking stock, unpacking stock and stacking shelves. Staff who deal with stock need to know how to handle it properly and they need to know about the procedures for stock control and damaged stock.

Handling

When handling stock, you need to take care to use correct techniques and procedures, so that you do not cause yourself injury and so that you do not cause **hazards** or **risks** to other people. Examples of possible hazards in stock handling include:

- *someone falling when climbing on shelving*
- *stock blocking fire exit routes*
- *build up of used packaging*
- *poor storage causing increased manual-handling risks (e.g. bulky items above head height)*
- *spillages of goods causing environmental damage or increasing the potential for slips and trips occurring*
- *goods falling from shelving or racking.*

● *Techniques for lifting* ●

Stock replacement is a daily activity in most retail stores. It can involve lifting and carrying **merchandise**. To avoid injuring yourself, it is important to use the correct manual handling techniques when lifting and carrying. Below are some tips for safe lifting, but your employer should give you training and instructions in lifting techniques if it forms part of your job.

Tips for lifting

- *Think before you do anything.*
- *Stand as close to the load as possible.*
- *Never lift anything that is too heavy.*
- *Keep your feet apart, bend your knees (do **not** bend your waist) and lift with your back as straight as possible.*
- *Keep the load as close to you as possible.*
- *Avoid twisting your body.*
- *Use gloves if the load has sharp edges.*

> **GLOSSARY**
>
> A **hazard** is something that could cause harm.
>
> A **risk** is something that is likely to cause harm.

> **GLOSSARY**
>
> **Merchandise** means things for sale.

> Use a table or bench as a half way resting point.

> Use a wheelie or trolley when transporting even relatively small, but heavy, loads.

... you had to lift a large pane of glass?

1 Would you need help?

2 What steps would you take to lift the pane of glass?

• Carrying and stacking •

When carrying items, it is important to reduce the risk of injury to yourself and others. Below are some tips for carrying, but your employer should give you instructions and training for carrying loads, if you need to do it as part of your job.

Tips for carrying

> *Hold the load tight against your body.*

> *Support the load on your shoulder.*

> *If you are carrying an item in each hand, try to make sure they are of similar weight, so that the load is balanced.*

> *Don't carry objects in a bent over, stooped position.*

> *Make sure that you can see where you are going.*

> *If the load is too large for you to see properly, you should use a mechanical aid (e.g. trolley) or ask for help.*

> *If you need to carry a load with another person, one of you should act as the leader and should face forward, not walk backward.*

When you are shelving stock – in the shop itself or in the stock room – you need to ensure that you do not cause any hazards. Your employer will probably have guidelines or procedures set out for how to stack goods. You should follow these carefully, to ensure you are doing your job correctly and safely.

• Using mechanical aids •

If your stock handling requires lifting or moving heavy or unwieldy items, your employer should provide mechanical handling equipment to help. This equipment could include conveyors, lifts, trolleys, trucks, carts, dollies, barrows, slides, stackers and forklift trucks. It is essential to ensure that you make full use of the equipment provided, as it is provided to prevent injuries to you or others.

▲ **Mechanical aids must be used correctly**

It is also very important to follow instructions, guidelines and procedures for the use of these mechanical aids, including manufacturers' instructions where appropriate. Incorrect use of mechanical aids could provide as much of a risk as not using them.

Tips for using trolleys

- *Do not overload the trolley.*

- *Make sure you can see where you are going.*

- *Take particular care at corners.*

- *Do not run with the trolley.*

- *Make sure the load is stacked correctly and secured in place.*

• *Handling heavy/bulky items* •

If handling heavy or bulky items is a regular part of your job, your employer should provide you with mechanical aids (see page 206). If there are none available you should ask for help from a colleague or supervisor. Make sure that you take care to use correct lifting and carrying techniques (see page 206).

• *Sharp edges* •

Any sharp edges should be covered to avoid risk of injury. If you have to handle broken glass or other items with sharp edges regularly, your employer should provide you with protective gloves.

• *Disposal of waste/litter* •

It is important to follow guidelines and procedures for the disposal of waste or litter.

All businesses have a duty of care to store and correctly manage the waste they create. Businesses must store waste in suitable sacks, containers or skips, making sure it doesn't harm the environment.

All waste materials must be stored and **transferred** safely and securely in suitable containers such as skips or labelled drums. The only exceptions to this would be loose material or liquid that is loaded into a suitable vehicle.

Waste must only be **transported** in suitable containers and vehicles (such as tankers) that are secure and will prevent spillage of waste during transit.

Stock control

Stock control is about how much stock you have at any one time, and how you keep track of it. In retail, it applies to all the items you have for sale, whether they are out on the shelves or in storerooms or warehouses. Stock control is very important in the retail business, because the products need to be there for the customers to buy. Efficient stock control means having the right amount of stock in the right place at the right time.

Working in stock control can include:

- *picking stock*
- *checking/replenishing items on display*
- *rotating stock*
- *checking 'best before' and 'use by' dates*
- *keeping track of stock deterioration*
- *counting stock.*

● *Picking stock* ●

In some retail outlets, customers do not just take the product from the shelf and then to the cashier. Instead, there may be display items or catalogues for customers to browse. When they decide what they want to buy, someone has to get the product from the store room and bring it to the customer. For large items it is common for stock to be kept in warehouses rather than at the shop and these items then need to be picked and delivered to the customer.

If it is your role to pick stock, you will need to make sure that you pick the correct item or items. You will also need to ensure that the goods are complete and are not damaged in any way. The procedures for stock picking will vary from business to business. For example, there might be a computerised system, where you get a list of items to pick and where they are to go. You might get a handwritten or printed list of items to pick or you might just be told by a sales assistant that a customer needs a certain product.

It is important to follow the procedures in your work place carefully, as this will ensure that the stock is managed efficiently. For example, there might be a procedure for recording what stock has left the warehouse or storeroom, to ensure that new items are ordered when necessary. There might also be a list of things that you need to check for certain items, such as all the necessary accessories being included in the box.

● *Checking/replenishing items on display* ●

In retail outlets, it is essential to keep the products for sale in a place where customers can see them and access them. This means keeping an eye on the shelves to make sure that there are always enough of any one item.

The number of items that need to be on display will depend both on the type of retail outlet and the item itself. Larger numbers of popular products will be needed than of products that get bought less often. In a supermarket or grocery shop, for example, there will be more items such as milk and bread on display than items such as expensive boxes of chocolate or luxury cheeses.

◀ **Restocking shelves before they are empty is important**

Items should be replenished when they are getting low, rather than waiting until there are none left. The retail outlet may have specific guidelines as to the amounts of each item that need to be on display. If so, the checking/replenishing role will involve counting the items and adding more when necessary. In other outlets you may need to use your own judgement and take note of any items that seem to be selling fast.

GIVE IT A GO: items on display

1 Visit a local retailer.

2 Ask a member of staff for permission to do some research.

3 Choose one shelf and count how many of each item is on the shelf.

4 Suggest which items need replenishing.

GLOSSARY

Stock rotation usually means displaying older stock before newer stock.

Perishable means that it may rot or go off (e.g. fruit and vegetables).

● *Stock rotation* ●

Stock rotation usually means that older stock is displayed for sale before the newer stock. This is sometimes known as 'first in, first out' (FIFO) and ensures that old stock does not end up being left on the shelves until it is unusable.

In some stores (for example, where products are not **perishable** food items), there may be a policy (for certain items) of displaying newer stock in front of older stock. This is sometimes known as 'last in, first out' (LIFO) and can give the store a fresher and brighter appearance.

● *Best before/use by dates* ●

In some retail outlets (e.g. shops that sell food or certain cosmetics) it is necessary to check the dates on the packaging. Dates that may need checking include:

▱ sell by date: *this is the last date by which an item must be sold; after a customer has bought it there are usually a few days or weeks in which it can be eaten (or used) after the sell by date*

▱ use by (or expires by) date: *this is the date by which the item must be eaten (or used); if it is eaten or used after this date it could cause serious illness*

▱ closed (or coded) dates: *these are packing numbers used by manufacturers to track their products; the codes help the manufacturer to rotate stock and locate products if there is a recall.*

● *Stock deterioration* ●

Stock deterioration refers to how stock can become less usable/buyable as time goes on. It is used, for example, to refer to food such as fruit or vegetables going off over time. It can also be used about the deterioration of other products. For example, clothes can become bleached in the sun and metal can become rusty in the damp.

It is important to keep an eye on stock to look out for the level of deterioration. For some products there will be a point at which the item is no longer sellable. Most outlets that sell products that are likely to deteriorate will have procedures and guidelines on when to remove an item of stock from display or dispose of it.

● *Stock counts* ●

Stock counts (often known as stocktaking) are a regular task in retail outlets. How often they need to be done will depend on the individual outlet. Many retail outlets have computerised stock management systems, which keep track of how much stock is available and will let stock managers know when items need to be reordered.

However, it is still necessary in most shops to do manual stock counts. This involves counting how many of each item are on the shelves (on display) and how many of each item are in the storeroom or warehouse. Even stores that have computerised systems will do manual stock counts, because there may have been errors in entering data into the system, or there may have been thefts from the store, which the computer will not know about.

Stock counting, whether manual or computerised, is essential to ensure that stock is at the right level – that is, low enough to allow for the space available and high enough to satisfy customer demand. The more an item sells, the higher its stock level will be.

There are many different methods of stock counting. For example, each employee might have responsibility for counting ten different items. They would then go round the shelves in the shop and in the storeroom noting down exactly how many of each item exists. Another method that could be used is with a barcode scanner to scan each item on a particular aisle in the shop (with each employee taking an aisle). The scans are than entered into a computer, which works out the number of each item in stock.

When doing a manual or a semi-automatic stock count, it is essential to ensure that you do not count any example of an item more than once. You need to keep a careful note of which shelves you have already counted, to make sure of this.

Damaged stock

In any retail business there is likely to be damage to stock. There are various different reasons why stock can become damaged, and different types of damage. The business will have procedures for how to deal with damaged stock, as will the suppliers.

● *Reason for damage* ●

There are many different reasons for stock becoming damaged, and these will vary from store to store, depending on the types of product that are sold and also on the condition of the premises. Examples include:

- *refrigeration or freezer failure*
- *power supply failure*
- *deterioration over time (especially food products)*
- *contamination (e.g. from chemicals or rotten food)*
- *fire damage*
- *incorrect storage (e.g. not following the guidelines/instructions)*
- *flood damage*
- *damage from accidental spills (e.g. of liquids or chemicals)*
- *damage in transit (e.g. on the journey from the suppliers or in transporting and unpacking the goods once they have arrived)*
- *sun damage.*

Businesses and their employees need to minimise the risk of damage to products by setting up and following guidelines for storage, transportation and general upkeep of the premises. Keeping stock levels to the minimum necessary to satisfy customer demand will also help reduce the potential for damage.

● *Type of damage* ●

Damage can be internal or external.

- *Internal damage happens when the actual material or product is damaged or broken during transportation or storage. Internal damage can often cause a fault in the product and make it totally unusable (and therefore mean it cannot be sold).*

- *External damage is damage to the packaging of the product. With external damage, the content itself may still be safe and intact and so often does not affect the usability of the product. However, external damage to packaging may make it harder to sell the product.*

● *Procedures for damaged goods* ●

Businesses will have procedures for how to deal with damaged goods. Suppliers will also have procedures for returning damaged goods to them (where this is available).

It is essential for employees to follow the business's procedures carefully. There may be different procedures for different types of goods. For example, perishable goods such as fruit and vegetables may just need to be disposed of correctly when damaged, whereas longer-term goods such as electrical equipment may need to be returned to the manufacturers for replacement or repair.

Returning stock

Different suppliers will have different guidelines on what can or cannot be returned. Usually anything that has been damaged in transportation from the supplier to the business can be returned for a full refund or replacement. Other suppliers may have a policy where they will take returns of items damaged after arrival at the business. For example, they might provide a partial refund in cases where they can reuse parts from the product.

It is essential to follow the supplier's procedures very carefully when returning stock, otherwise the refund may not be given. Procedures could include:

▭ *completing a returns form, which states the type of damage, when it occurred, etc.*

▭ *contacting the supplier as soon as the damage is noticed*

▭ *packing the return in its original packaging*

▭ *paying for delivery of the return or arranging collection with the supplier.*

◯ THINK ABOUT IT

Think about why goods might need to be returned. When do you think the retailer might get a refund from the supplier?

Packing for dispatch

Returns often need to be sent back in their original packaging. Where this is not available, it is essential to wrap the returns carefully to ensure that no further damage occurs in transportation to the supplier. Follow the supplier's guidelines on packaging returns very carefully to ensure that any refunds will not be refused or additional charges made.

EVIDENCE ACTIVITY

Stock handling

1 Describe how you would decide what stock needs to be replenished.

2 Describe the steps you would take to safely:
   a lift goods
   b carry goods
   c stack goods.

▲ You must know how to lift goods safely

Security measures

When working in the retail sector, there will be a number of security measures that need to be followed in order to ensure the safety of staff and customers. These include general security in the workplace, security when opening and closing the shop and also secure cash handling.

Workplace security

Workplace security is essential both for the safety of staff and that of customers, as well as ensuring stock, cash and premises are secure. It can include:

⮑ *the use of security staff*

⮑ *security attachments and equipment*

⮑ *procedures for security alerts*

⮑ *procedures for suspected theft*

⮑ *dealing with suspicious packages*

⮑ *general health and safety in the workplace.*

● *Uniformed/non-uniformed security staff* ●

The presence of uniformed security staff in a store, whatever the nature of the business, can act as a **deterrent** against thieves. While some thieves plan their crimes, the majority are opportunistic – that is to say they see an item that can easily be stolen and take it. Opportunist thieves will be put off if they see uniformed security guards, because the theft will no longer be seen as easy.

Uniformed security staff can also provide reassurance to customers and staff as they can make people feel safer. In addition, a uniformed member of security staff is someone that people (customers and staff) will be able to go to with any suspected security problems. For example, a member of staff might see a customer acting suspiciously or a customer might see an unattended package. If there is a uniformed security guard available it is easy to know who to tell about these problems.

> ### GLOSSARY
>
> A **deterrent** is something that puts someone off from doing something (e.g. security guards may be a deterrent to shoplifters).

◀ **Security staff are there to help customers**

Some retail stores also employ non-uniformed security staff (sometimes known as store detectives). These staff will usually act as though they are customers themselves, while they watch actual customers to check for shoplifting and other security alerts. A store detective's duties might include:

⬭ *patrolling the store to look out for shop thieves*

⬭ *following customers behaving suspiciously or who are known to have stolen from the store before*

⬭ *catching and holding suspected shoplifters*

⬭ *carrying out searches of suspects*

⬭ *dealing with customers suspected of credit card theft or fraud*

⬭ *calling the police, describing observations and attending while a suspect is being questioned*

⬭ *taking evidence from witnesses*

⬭ *writing a general report on an incident.*

• *Security attachments and equipment* •

Most retail outlets will have some form of security attachment or equipment, even if (or especially if) they do not employ any security staff. These could include:

⬭ *burglar alarms*

⬭ *fire alarms*

⬭ *safes*

⬭ *alarm buttons (e.g. in case of armed robbery)*

⬭ *special lighting (e.g. lights that turn on when someone is moving around).*

Employees may have responsibility for keeping this equipment in working order. This is a very important task as security equipment that is faulty can cause considerable loss of profits and also risk of serious injury to staff or customers.

• *Procedures in the event of a security alert* •

Businesses will usually have procedures to follow for specific types of security alert. These alerts could include:

⬭ *possible bombs*

⬭ *theft by customers or staff*

⬭ *use of stolen credit cards, debit cards or cheques*

- *armed robbery*
- *people coming into the store who have been banned (e.g. because they have stolen from store)*
- *threats toward members of staff.*

It is essential for all staff to know the correct procedures for any security alert. It is not just the security staff who will need to act in the case of a security alert. For example, a security alert could require staff to evacuate the store, which means helping customers to leave, as well as leaving themselves.

• *Procedures for suspected customer/staff theft* •

Most retail outlets are at risk of theft. Thefts can be carried out by customers, but also by members of staff. Some staff may think of taking goods as a bonus of their job. This is not the case and taking goods without permission and without paying for them is theft and is something that the employee can be **prosecuted** for. Giving discounts to friends and family without clear permission is also theft.

> **GLOSSARY**
>
> To be **prosecuted** is to be taken to court.

All retail outlets will have a procedure to follow when a member of staff suspects a customer or another member of staff of stealing. This will usually involve watching the suspected thief carefully to ensure that there is evidence of theft.

There will usually be specific people, such as security staff or managers, to whom employees should report any suspicions they have. Where a store detective is employed, he or she should usually be told of the suspicion.

There may be procedures and policies in place to reduce the potential for staff theft. These might include:

- *counting all cash at the start of a shift and signing the register tape*
- *giving customers a receipt for every transaction*
- *approval of any voids or errors at the cash desks by a supervisor*
- *only supervisors or managers being allowed to enter employee purchases*
- *immediate replacement of receipt tapes, so that no transactions are made without a record.*

Many shoplifters are not regular thieves, but are influenced by opportunities such as easily accessible display areas or goods left **unattended** on counters. Some shoplifters are regular thieves and will be less easy to catch. You might, for example, find that one of your oldest and most trusted customers has been stealing from the business for years.

> **GLOSSARY**
>
> **Unattended** means without anyone close by to keep an eye on it.

▲ Thieves may be tempted by easily accessible goods

It is important to follow the procedures that have been set down for suspected theft. If you do not do so, you could be putting yourself and others at risk.

Some tips for spotting suspicious behaviour include watching out for people:

- *constantly looking around and watching staff*
- *appearing nervous*
- *taking little notice of products*
- *wearing clothing that could be used to hide goods (especially if the clothing is not normal for the time of year or weather)*
- *carrying a large bag*
- *carrying a coat over their arm or shoulder*
- *repeatedly refusing offers of help*
- *appearing to have concealed an item*
- *spending a long time browsing.*

It is important to note that these are just possible indications of theft. Many of the above behaviours could be quite innocent. When you see quite a few of these behaviours together, however, it makes it more likely that you are dealing with an actual thief.

● *Suspicious packages* ●

Most retail outlets these days will have procedures for dealing with suspicious packages. Suspicious packages are those which might contain bombs or other purposely dangerous materials (e.g. chemicals). Some tips to follow in the case of a suspicious package include:

- *do not touch the package or move it to another location*
- *shut any windows and doors*
- *leave the room*
- *keep yourself separate from others and available for medical examination*
- *switch off any air conditioning system*
- *call 999.*

These are just tips and it is essential to follow the business's procedures for suspicious packages if there are any.

... you saw a suspicious package in a shop?

1 What steps would you take as a customer?
2 What steps would you take as an employee?

▶ **Be aware of unattended packages**

• *Health and safety in the workplace* •

It is essential for all employees to follow the business's health and safety procedures, policies and guidelines. This may include:

▭ *using equipment safely and correctly*

▭ *identifying and removing any hazards (e.g. boxes in the aisles, spillages of liquid on the floor)*

▭ *keeping good personal hygiene*

▭ *careful and correct disposal of any waste.*

Opening/closing a shop

Most retail outlets will have specific procedures for opening and closing the shop. This may just be down to unlocking and locking the doors and setting burglar alarms. However, it will usually include a number of other tasks and involve a number of policies. For example, employees who have responsibility for opening and/or closing a store may need to deal with the following issues/tasks:

▭ *location of security devices, such as locks and alarms*

▭ *location of public utilities, such as electricity, gas and water*

▭ *covering or uncovering stock*

▭ *end-of-day procedures and reports.*

• *Location of security devices* •

Any employee who is responsible for opening or closing the store must know where the security devices, such as locks and alarms, are located.

When opening the store, employees will need to disarm any burglar alarms and when closing up, they will need to set the alarms. To do this, they may need a key and/or a security code.

They will also need the correct key or keys for opening all the doors that need to be opened. This may just be one external door, through which all staff and customers enter, or there may be several **external** doors for customers and others for staff and deliveries. Some **internal** doors, such as those to a storeroom, may also need to be unlocked.

• *Location of public utilities* •

Employees responsible for opening and/or closing stores will need to know the location of public utilities, such as stopcocks for the water supply and gas supply and fuse boxes for electricity. It is essential that these are clear from any obstacles so that the emergency services can access them quickly and easily if necessary.

In addition, any manholes or other external access to public utilities need to be clear for the same reasons. This will usually mean checking any rubbish bags or bins that have been left out to ensure they are not covering any access to public utilities.

● *Covering/uncovering stock* ●

Another possible task for employees when opening or closing the store is to cover or uncover stock as necessary. For example, in supermarkets, open freezers are usually covered when the store is closed to further protect the goods. Perishable goods may be moved into a cool room while the store is closed. Computers and other electrical equipment may be covered during closed hours, to protect the parts from dust.

At the start of the day everything that is covered will need to be uncovered and at the end of the day everything that needs to be will have to be covered.

GIVE IT A GO: covering and uncovering stock

1 Visit five different retailers in your local area, either at opening time or closing time.
2 Observe the staff setting up or getting ready to close and identify what items they are covering or uncovering.
3 If possible, interview a member of staff to find out whether you identified all the items.

● *End-of-day administrative procedures and reports* ●

Most retail outlets will have specific end-of-day administrative procedures to complete, which may include producing certain reports. Examples of end-of-day procedures include:

▱ *cashing up (counting all the cash, cheques and card receipts in tills and comparing this to the till receipts)*

▱ *taking cash, cheques and card receipts to the bank*

▱ *producing daily sales reports*

▱ *producing daily cash receipt reports*

▱ *producing daily reports of any differences between sales and cash received.*

Cash handling

Most retail outlets will need to handle a considerable amount of cash. Cash can be a target for criminals – both customers and members of staff. In addition, cash is more at risk of staff errors than other forms of payment. For example, cashiers could give a customer too much change

or not count the cash they receive properly. Businesses will therefore
have specific procedures for handling cash in order to **minimise** the risk
of theft and losses due to staff error.

● *Floats at the beginning of the day* ●

Cashiers need to have a **float**, which is a certain amount of money (in
different notes and coins) that needs to be available for giving customers
change. Different businesses will have different limits for the float, but it
should always be kept to the minimum necessary to provide efficient
service. Floats that are too large can prove tempting to thieves.

At the start of the day, the floats for each till need to be set up. The full
amount of cash that is in the float at the start of the day needs to be
recorded. During the day, money may be taken from or added to the
float to ensure it remains at the necessary level and that there is not too
much cash in the till, in case of robbery.

● *Cashing up at the end of the day* ●

Retail outlets will have procedures for cashing up at the end of the day.
This could include:

➦ *counting the cash in each till*

➦ *counting the cash in the safe*

▲ **Cash may need to be delivered to a night safe**

🗩 *filling in paying-in slips*

🗩 *noting down the serial numbers of all bank notes.*

The cashing-up task may also include taking the cash to the bank and putting it in the night safe (or paying it in at the counter if the bank is open). It is essential that this task is carried out securely according to the business's guidelines, policies and procedures.

THINK ABOUT IT

Think about what possible problems could happen when cashing up. Can you think of any measures that could be taken to prevent or minimise these problems?

● *Reconciling cash with till reading* ●

The cashing-up process may include reconciling cash with till readings or this might be a separate procedure undertaken by a different member of staff. Most modern tills have the facility to print an end-of-day report which will include all **transactions** and a total amount received. Some machines will also be able to separate cash from other forms of payment such as cheque or credit card.

It may be necessary in some retail outlets to manually (usually using a calculator) add up all the transactions to calculate the total amount of cash that should be in the till.

It is usually necessary to record the calculations, for example, in a cashbook. Any differences should be reported to the correct person (according to the procedures of the business) and any very large differences will probably require investigation.

GLOSSARY

Transactions happen when money changes hands (e.g. in payment for goods or services).

EVICENCE ACTIVITY

Security measures

1 Choose a retail business where you have worked or where you would like to work. (If you have not worked there, you will need to visit the business to do some research.)

2 Describe the security measures that are used in the business.

3 Describe the procedures for:
   a opening the shop
   b closing the shop.

END OF UNIT ASSIGNMENT

Note: To complete this unit you need to provide evidence of practical experience in a number of retail tasks. If you already have a job in a retail business, you should be able to use your work to provide evidence. If you do not have a job in retail, then it would be useful to arrange a work-experience placement in a retail outlet. If this is not possible your teacher or tutor may be able to provide equipment and material for you to use to produce the evidence.

Task 1

1 Describe the products or services which your business sells.

2 Describe any additional information that you need to give to customers.

3 Provide evidence to show you have completed the payment process using different types of payment, for example, payment by cash, cheque or credit card.

4 Describe three situations where you have responded to customer needs in your business. (Provide evidence such as a witness statement from your supervisor.)

5 List the different skills that you use in your work in the business.

6 For each skill, describe a situation where you have used the skill on your own (without being prompted by a supervisor or tutor). (Provide evidence such as a witness statement from your supervisor.)

Task 2

1 Describe the procedures in your business for:
   a picking stock
   b checking stock
   c replenishing stock.

2 Provide evidence of following each of the above procedures.

3 Provide evidence of safely:
   a lifting goods
   b carrying goods
   c stacking goods.

4 Describe the procedures used in your business for controlling stock, including:
   a stock rotation
   b best before or use by dates
   c stock deterioration
   d stock counting.

Task 3 (P4) (P5)

1 Describe the use of security staff and security attachments or equipment in your business.

2 Describe the procedures in your business for:
   a security alerts
   b suspected theft by a customer
   c suspected theft by a member of staff
   d health and safety.

3 Describe the procedures in your business for:
   a opening the store
   b closing the store.

   Include details about:
   a the location of security devices
   b the location of public utilities
   c any stock that needs to be covered/uncovered
   d any end-of-day administration procedures or reports that are used.

▲ **Security is important to businesses**

Task 4 (M1)

Describe and provide evidence of a situation where you showed confidence and effective retail skills in the workplace without any support or prompting from your supervisor or colleagues.

unit 10

Introduction to administration

In this unit you will learn about some of the basic tasks in administration. You will find out about photocopying and typing a range of different business documents. You will also learn about sorting and dispatching internal and external mail for a department or organisation.

You will explore different paper-based filing systems and find out how to find, update and store files. You will find out the basics involved in entering and finding data, including both words and numbers.

This unit provides some of the theory behind administration. However, in order to complete the unit for your qualification you will need to practise a lot of the tasks described here and provide evidence of your skills. Ideally, this should be done in your own workplace, but your teacher or tutor may be able to provide you with facilities to practise at school or college.

▶ **Efficient administration helps a business run smoothly**

To complete this unit you must:

- prepare a range of business documents
- copy a range of business documents
- distribute mail
- dispatch mail
- use a paper-based filing system to find, update and store files
- use a computer to enter and find data.

Prepare and copy

A major part of a lot of administrative jobs is preparing and copying business documents, such as letters, faxes, memos, reports and flyers.

Preparing documents

The preparation of documents does not just involve typing up a handwritten letter. There are lots of elements that contribute to good document preparation, such as:

- *checking the original document*
- *using standard layouts*
- *checking input*
- *correcting mistakes*
- *making further changes*
- *storing the document safely*
- *keeping the original document*
- *completing the work on time*
- *dealing with problems.*

• *Checking the original document* •

As an administrator, you will generally be typing or amending documents written by other people, rather than writing them yourself. The original document could be handwritten or it could be a printout or photocopy with changes and additions handwritten on the paper.

Before you start typing up the document (or making amendments to an existing one), it is important to check that:

- *you have all the bits of paper you need*
- *you are clear on what parts need to be typed or changed*
- *you can read the handwriting.*

● *Using standard layouts* ●

Most businesses will have standard layouts to follow for different documents. Word-processing templates may be provided for documents such as faxes and memos. Business letters will usually be printed onto headed paper and will need to be set out in the way required by the organisation.

While you may be provided with templates and instructions on layout, not all businesses will give you such definite guidelines. A useful tip when starting at a new business is to look at a few examples of previously created documents of the same type. Look at how they are set out and follow the same layout.

● *Checking your input* ●

When you are typing up any documents, it is essential to thoroughly check your own input before printing. This checking process involves a number of tasks, including:

- *checking that your input matches the original document*

- *using the word processor's spellchecking facility to spot typing errors*

- *carefully proofreading the document to check for errors that the spellchecker would have missed (e.g. too/two/to; their/there/they're; it's/its; our/hour; here/hear)*

- *checking that no punctuation has been left out*

- *checking that the layout is correct.*

You should do as much of the checking as possible on-screen before printing out the document, so that you do not waste paper. However, it is also useful to give the document a final read after it has been printed to look for any errors you might have missed.

Using a dictionary

If you are uncertain about the spelling of a word then use a dictionary to check it. If you need to type up a lot of technical language, it may be useful to use a specialised dictionary as well as an ordinary one. For example, there are scientific dictionaries, legal dictionaries and medical dictionaries available.

It is a good idea to keep a notebook of spellings. When you have to look a word up for a particular document, write it in your notebook as well and include the meaning of the word, as you will find it easier to learn the spellings if you understand what the words mean.

Asking your line manager

If there is anything you are unsure of, such as spellings or layout, then you should ask your line manager. Part of your line manager's job is to help you learn how to do your job and improve your performance.

In addition, it can be useful to ask your line manager or a colleague to read through your work before you pass it on to the relevant person or before you send it out. Sometimes you may not spot errors you have made because you are too close to the document. Having another eye to look over it can help **minimise** any errors. Your line manager will also be able to give you guidance and tips for improving any common errors you make.

> **GLOSSARY**
>
> To **minimise** is to reduce or lessen.

● *Correcting mistakes* ●

When you have handed the document to the person who asked you to do the work (e.g. your line manager, a manager who you work for, another colleague), they may return it to you with errors that need fixing. You should be very careful when correcting these errors to ensure that you do not accidentally bring more errors in while making the changes.

In addition to correcting the errors, it is a good idea to keep a note of what these errors were. If you keep a record of the errors you make, you will then be able to use this information to find out what problems you have and develop ways to improve.

You could use your list of errors as a checklist when you are checking your own input. That way you should be able to considerably reduce the number of errors you make.

● *Making further changes* ●

In addition to correcting your own errors, you may also be asked to make further changes to the document. For example, the document originator may have realised that a new paragraph needs inserting or he or she might decide to delete some words or change the order to make it clearer.

Again, it is essential to be very careful when making these changes so that you can minimise the chance of further errors creeping in. When you have made the changes, you should check the document again thoroughly, paying particular attention to the parts that have been changed. Make sure that all the **requested** changes have been made and that you haven't missed anything out.

> **GLOSSARY**
>
> To **request** is to ask for.

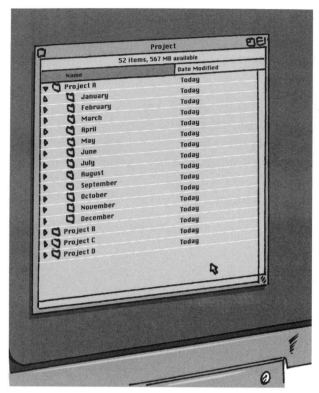

▲ **Any filing system must be managed**

• *Storing the document safely* •

Safe storage of the document will include storing the electronic file safely on the computer, as well as storing the printed document safely until you can pass it on to the person who requested it.

It is useful to manage your computer filing system as carefully as you manage a paper filing system. There are different ways you could organise your computer filing system, including:

▭ *creating separate folders for each project*

▭ *creating separate folders for each person you do work for*

▭ *creating separate folders for each customer*

▭ *creating separate folders for each day or week.*

You should choose the system that works best for you, taking into consideration the type of work which you do and the business where you work.

For certain documents, it may be necessary to password protect them, so that no-one can access them without permission. If you do not know how to password protect files on your business's system, it is useful to check with the IT department (or ask a colleague).

You also need to make sure that you store the printed page(s) safely. You need to be able to access them quickly when the time comes to pass them on to the relevant person. You will need to store them securely (e.g. in a locked drawer) if they contain **confidential** or **sensitive** information. You might want to set up a system of cardboard folders, in a similar way to those suggested above for an electronic filing system.

• *Keeping the original document* •

It may be necessary to keep the original document along with the one you typed. If so, you will need to have a filing system set up for this. Alternatively, the person who requested the document preparation might prefer to keep the original document themselves.

It is useful to keep the original document somewhere safe until the final document has been approved or sent out. This should be done even if you are not required to keep original documents. You can then dispose of it when the final document has been approved.

GLOSSARY

Confidential means private, secret or classified.

Sensitive means that it could cause problems if it is discovered.

• *Completing the work on time* •

Any document you are asked to prepare will have a deadline. For example, documents such as letters and faxes will usually need to be finalised in time to be sent out in the post on the same day. For reports and memos you may have a bit longer to work on them, however, they are also more likely to need further changes than a simple letter.

To be a good administrator you need to manage your time carefully, so that you can meet all the deadlines. If the person requesting the document preparation does not give you a specific deadline it is very important to ask.

It can be useful to keep 'to do' lists, with a note about when the tasks need to be completed. Keeping a short-term list, a medium-term list and a long-term list can help. Set aside specific amounts of time during the day to do some work on the medium- and long-term tasks, but prioritise those that are urgent.

• *Dealing with problems* •

It is important for an administrator to be able to deal with as many problems as possible him or herself. However, sometimes it may be necessary to go to your line manager for help or advice if you cannot sort the problem out yourself. Examples of some problems that could occur when preparing documents include:

▭ *difficulty reading handwriting*

▭ *original document has gone missing*

▭ *electronic file has become corrupted*

▭ *printer is not working*

▭ *someone else has requested a more urgent task be done.*

⬭⬭◠ THINK ABOUT IT

Think of as many problems as you can that might occur when you are preparing a document. What do you need to do to deal with each of the problems?

Copying documents

Although many businesses now distribute documents electronically rather than on paper, photocopiers are still used a lot. Administrators are frequently required to make copies of various documents from single-page letters and memos to multi-page reports.

● *Using a photocopier* ●

Most photocopiers have similar functions and facilities, although there are many different types and sizes of machine throughout the business world. When you start work in a new organisation, you should be shown how to use the photocopier (it is part of your job role). If no-one shows you then ask your line manager or a colleague if they can give you a quick **demonstration**. Make sure you take notes as it may take a while to remember everything.

▶ **Photocopiers are important pieces of equipment**

Some useful tips for using a photocopier include:

- *make sure the machine is turned on and ready to use*

- *if necessary, place your copy card in the correct place or key in your ID code*

- *press the* Cancel *key to ensure that any previous settings are cleared*

- *if using a paper feeder, make sure that the paper is straight and aligned to prevent paper jams*

- *if placing a document on the glass (e.g. with stapled pages or books), make sure that it is placed square to the guidelines so that nothing is cut off*

- *select the required options (e.g. number of copies, contrast quality, paper size, reduction or enlargement)*

- *when everything is ready press the* Start *or* Copy *button to start the photocopying*

- *when the copying is finished, collect the copy and check it*

- *if the copy is satisfactory, collect the original*

- *if necessary, take out your copy card or cancel your ID code.*

• *Following manufacturer's instructions* •

It is essential to follow the manufacturer's guidelines when using a photocopier (or any other equipment). Ideally, the handbook should be kept close to the photocopier so that it can be referred to when needed. If this is not the case you should ask your line manager where it is stored. You may be able to download a copy from the manufacturer's website, if the handbook has been lost.

• *Producing the correct number of copies* •

When you are asked to photocopy a document (or documents) you should be told how many copies are needed. If you are not told then make sure you ask. Be careful to select the correct number of copies. Most copiers will have a key pad on which to key in the number and a small screen that tells you what you have selected. Double-check that you chosen correctly before you press the *Start* or *Copy* button.

• *Checking the quality of the copies* •

If you are making a large number of copies it is a good idea to make one copy first and check the quality of the copy. For example, you might need to make changes to the contrast setting if the copy is too light or too dark. You might need to make slight enlargements or reductions to ensure that everything fits neatly on the page.

Once the copying has finished you should also do a quick check of the quality of each copy and, if necessary, make some new copies to replace those that were of poor quality.

• *Reducing paper wastage* •

Doing a simple test copy (as described above) should considerably minimise paper wastage. If it is acceptable for the document you are copying, you could copy double-sided. Many photocopiers have this facility. Make sure you are very careful when choosing the number of copies you need. For example, if you need 10 copies and accidentally put an extra 0 on the end (100) you will have wasted 90 sheets of paper (or many more if it is a multi-page document).

▶ **Try not to waste paper**

• *Sorting/fastening the photocopies securely and in the correct order* •

Many large photocopiers have a facility for sorting and stapling multi-page documents. When using this facility it is very important to make sure that the original document is in the correct order before putting it in the paper feeder. It is useful to do a test copy before starting a multi-copy run. Make sure you choose the correct settings (e.g. *Sort* or *Collate and Staple*).

If the photocopier you are using does not have a sort and staple facility, you will need to do this **manually**. Without a sort facility, all copies of each page will come out together. You will find it useful to use a large desk, if one is available, or you might have a special sorting tower, that can be used instead. Whether you sort manually or **automatically** (but especially manually), you will need to check the collated documents carefully to ensure that none of them has pages missing or pages upside down.

GLOSSARY

Manually means using your hands (or not using any equipment).

Automatic means using a computer or other piece of equipment.

• *Completing the work on time* •

As with all administration work, it is essential to complete the photocopying by the deadline. If you are not given a deadline make sure you ask for one. You can use the strategies outlined before (see page 231) to help you manage your time and workload. If necessary, for example for an urgent job, you may be able to ask a colleague or your line manager to give you some help to get the job completed on time.

WHAT if?

... *you were very busy?*

It is 9 am and you have just arrived at work. You have three photocopying jobs to get finished before lunchtime and three letters to type before 3 pm. One of the manager asks you to urgently make 100 copies of a 50-page document and collate and staple the copies. She needs the copies by 10 am.

1 What would you do?

2 How would your decision affect the rest of your work?

3 What strategies could you use to make sure all your work gets done on time?

• *Dealing with routine photocopier problems* •

There are a number of routine photocopier problems that you should be able to deal with yourself. These include replacing paper or toner cartridges and clearing paper jams. Anything more serious that you cannot deal with yourself needs to be reported to the relevant person, such as the maintenance supervisor or your line manager.

Replacing paper or toner

Most photocopiers will show a warning light or a message when the machine is low on paper or toner. You should check the manufacturer's handbook to make sure that you know how to replace these – the steps will be different for different machines.

Some toner cartridges require you to wear protective gloves when handling them. There should be a procedure for what you need to do with the toner cartridge that you have removed. For example, some businesses will have a toner recycling bin near the photocopier. Make sure you are aware of these procedures when you start working in a new business, as they may be different in different organisations.

It is a good idea to check the level of the paper trays after you have done a large copying job and refill them if necessary. This is a common **courtesy** to your colleagues, ensuring that the machine is ready for use for the next person.

Clearing paper jams

Many photocopiers will provide a message that tells you where the paper jam is. Be very careful when opening up the photocopier as the parts can be extremely hot. Most photocopiers have plastic parts that are usually coloured green. This indicates that they are safe to touch and are usually the parts that you have to pull, push or move to get to a paper jam. You may need to check the manufacturer's handbook if you have problems finding the paper jam. If you still cannot find it then ask your line manager or a colleague.

> **GLOSSARY**
>
> **Courtesy** means politeness (e.g. saying 'please' and 'thank you' and showing respect and fairness to others).

EVISENCE ACTIVITY  P1

Prepare and copy

1 Describe the steps you would take to prepare a letter from handwritten copy.

2 Describe the steps you would take to photocopy, collate and staple 10 copies of a 10-page document.

Distribute and dispatch mail

Many administrators are required to deal with mail (also known as post), either for their own department or, in smaller organisations, for everyone in the building. Dealing with mail includes **distributing** (taking to the right person) incoming mail and **dispatching** (sending out) outgoing mail.

> **GLOSSARY**
>
> To **distribute** is to send out to everyone who needs to receive the item.
>
> To **dispatch** is to send out.

Distributing mail

If you need to distribute mail as part of your job role, this may involve:

▭ *receiving and sorting incoming mail (both internal and external)*

▭ *dealing with damaged or suspicious items*

▭ *ensuring the mail is correctly distributed*

▭ *dealing with delays*

▭ *dealing with couriers.*

● *Receiving/sorting incoming mail* ●

Large organisations will usually have a specialised mailroom, which receives and distributes incoming mail to the different departments, so administrators will deal only with mail for their department. In smaller organisations a single administrator may be responsible for the whole organisation's mail.

▲ **The mailroom is the hub of any big business**

The procedures for receiving and sorting mail will vary from organisation to organisation. You may need to collect the mail yourself from the mailroom or post office or it may be delivered to your desk. In some organisations you will be required to open the mail and decide who it should go to. In others you may need to distribute it unopened to the right person.

You must never open mail that says *Private* or *Confidential* on the envelope. This should always be distributed directly to the **addressee**. Mail marked *Urgent* should be delivered or opened and dealt with immediately, as appropriate.

Where it is your responsibility to open mail, you may need to unfold documents and date stamp them, so that it is clearly recorded when they arrived. Ensure the date stamp is on a blank place on the page and does not hide any important text.

In some businesses, it may be necessary to fill in a post book with details of all mail received. This might include details of who the sender was, who the **recipient** was and the date and time it arrived.

Parcels may need to be unpacked and items distributed or stored appropriately. If in any doubt about what to do with the contents of a parcel you should check with your line manager. If a parcel is heavy, you may need to use a trolley to take it to the recipient.

> **GLOSSARY**
>
> The **addressee** is the person to whom a piece of mail is being sent.

> **GLOSSARY**
>
> The **recipient** is the person receiving an item of mail.

GIVE IT A GO: incoming mail

1 Visit a large business in your local area.
2 Find out what the procedures are for sorting and distributing incoming mail:
   a in the mailroom
   b within one of the departments.

● *Damaged or suspicious items* ●

You will need to look out for suspicious packages. Any package or mail item that looks suspicious should not be opened and you should contact the relevant person (e.g. security manager, line manager) immediately to inform them of your suspicions. Things to look out for include:

- *too much postage*

- *wires or aluminium foil sticking out*

- *handwritten or poorly typed addresses*

- *strange return address or no return address*

▱ *incorrect titles or title without a name*

▱ *not addressed to a specific person*

▱ *unusual labelling*

▱ *marked with restrictions (e.g. Personal, Confidential or Do not X-ray)*

▱ *lopsided or uneven envelope*

▱ *threatening language*

▱ *misspellings of common words*

▱ *postmarked from a place that does not match the return address*

▱ *powdery substance felt through or appearing on the package or envelope*

▱ *oily stains*

▱ *lots of packaging material (e.g. masking tape, string, etc.)*

▱ *ticking sound.*

Some of the above may not on their own mean that the package is likely to be dangerous, but a number of them combined could be cause for suspicion. If in any doubt at all, make sure you tell someone.

• *Correct distribution* •

It is important that mail is correctly distributed according to the organisation's procedures. Some departments may have pigeon holes or file folders for each member of the department. It is important to put the right items of mail in the right pigeon hole or folder. In other departments you may need to take mail directly to people's desks. There may be an in-box on the desk where the mail should go. If not, the mail should be placed in the correct place according to procedure, such as on the chair or on the desk or handing it directly to the recipient.

• *Delays* •

As an administrator, it may be your responsibility to chase up mail that has not arrived on time. For example, this could include calling the mailroom or area sorting office to find out whether anything arrived after the mail was delivered. If there are any tracking numbers (e.g. for special delivery or courier services) it can involve calling a phone line or using the Internet to check where the package or letter is.

• *Dealing with couriers* •

Couriers are private businesses that deliver letters and packages, usually for other businesses, rather than individual members of the public. Some courier services are next-day, like ordinary post, while others may be same-day services for urgent deliveries.

◄ **Couriered items must be signed for**

Most courier services require a signature to **confirm** delivery. Before you sign for a delivery you should check that it has come to the right place. It might also be necessary to check that the contents are not damaged.

With same-day courier deliveries, the contents will normally be very urgent so it is essential to take the letter or package directly to the addressee.

GLOSSARY

To **confirm** is to show you understand.

Dispatching mail

Dispatching mail means getting it ready to be sent out and sending it out. If you need to dispatch mail as part of your job role, this may involve:

- *following correct procedures*
- *sealing and securing mail*
- *protecting contents from accidental damage*
- *addressing mail or checking it is correctly addressed*
- *stamping mail or using a franking machine*
- *making sure mail is sent out when it needs to be*
- *reporting any problems to the correct person.*

● *Correct procedures* ●

It is important to follow the organisation's procedures for dispatching mail. For example, this could include filling in a post book detailing items that have been dispatched (e.g. sender's name, recipient's name, time and date sent). It could include using specific envelopes or packaging for certain items. It could include specific delivery types for different items, for example:

▭ *first class for urgent items*

▭ *second class for non-urgent items*

▭ *special delivery or next-day courier for items that absolutely must arrive the next day*

▭ *same-day courier for very urgent items.*

If dispatching mail is part of your job role, you must make sure that you understand all the procedures in place.

● *Sealing/securing mail* ●

It is important to ensure that all envelopes and packages are properly sealed. It may be necessary to add extra tape to ensure that the packaging will not come open during delivery. Staples should be avoided as they can jam up franking machines. It you need to use staples, you should cover them with a layer or two of tape.

In some organisations it may be necessary to use a rubber stamp over the seal so that the recipient can easily see if the package has been tampered with.

● *Protecting contents from accidental damage* ●

Some documents, such as transparencies or certificates, need to be kept flat and not get bent in the post. These should be packaged in a stiff envelope and marked *Do not bend.*

Some packages will contain breakable products. These should be well wrapped, using bubble wrap, shredded paper or scrunched up waste paper before being boxed. The external packaging should be marked *Fragile: Handle with care.*

Some items may need to be placed in a Jiffy bag or other specialist packaging (e.g. there are special envelopes available for CDs and videos).

● *Addressing mail* ●

As an administrator it may be your responsibility to address outgoing mail. If it is not, you should still check that it is correctly addressed. This should include:

⇨ *name*

⇨ *title*

⇨ *organisation*

⇨ *building name or number*

⇨ *street name*

⇨ *postal town or city*

⇨ *county*

⇨ *full postcode*

⇨ *country (if appropriate).*

If you do not have all the information, you should check in your files, with your line manager or with the person sending out the mail.

Your organisation may have specific requirements for addressing mail, both external and internal. It is important to follow these requirements carefully.

● *Stamping mail* ●

In smaller organisations it may be the administrator's job to put stamps on outgoing mail, while in other larger organisations it is usually the role of the employees who work in the mailroom.

In order to place the correct stamps on mail, you will need to weigh each item and you will also need to know whether it is to be sent first or second class. Some organisations will have special electronic scales which tell you the exact amount that needs to be put on. Others will just have ordinary scales and you will need to check the different postal rates for the weight of the item yourself. You will need to use some basic numeracy skills for packages that require more than the minimum first or second class postage and place stamps to cover the full cost.

For some mail you may also need to add stickers, such as air mail or special delivery. You may also need to complete special delivery, recorded delivery and other forms for certain items.

● *Franking machines* ●

Many organisations use franking machines instead of using stamps. These make it much easier and quicker to 'stamp' large amounts of mail. You will need to key in or set the amount for the postage and then either push the item through or push a special franking label through (which you then stick on the packaging).

When franking a lot of mail it can be useful to do all items of a certain postage amount in one go. This saves you from resetting the amount too much.

● *Meeting time requirements for dispatching mail* ●

In many organisations there is a cut-off point for getting mail to the mailroom. As an administrator it is important for you to set aside enough time to get all mail ready for dispatching in time. In smaller organisations, where you may need to take mail to the post office yourself, you will need to ensure that you get there before it closes or before the last collection. For special postage services, such as special delivery, the post office may need to receive the items by a specific time.

▲ **Make sure your outgoing mail is ready on time**

Large organisations will have special procedures for dispatching mail and these can include cut off points for different types of delivery. For example, same-day delivery might not be possible after 12 noon. Next-day courier deliveries might need to be ready earlier than other types of mail.

⬭◯ THINK ABOUT IT

Think about the possible problems that could happen if you miss deadlines for dispatching mail. What could you do to prevent these problems from happening in the first place? What could you do to sort the problems out if they do happen?

• *Reporting problems* •

It is important to report any problems to the correct person. This might be your line manager, the person sending the mail or someone in the mailroom, for example.

Problems with dispatching mail could include:

- *addresses not complete or not following organisational requirements*
- *franking machines running out of money or breaking down*
- *other machine failure, such as electronic scales*
- *people getting mail to you too late for dispatch.*

EVIDENCE ACTIVITY  P2

Distribute and dispatch mail

Describe the techniques you would use to:
a   sort mail
b   distribute mail
c   dispatch mail.

Find, update and store files

As an administrator you will need to manage a filing system for your own work. You may also need to use a departmental filing system and possibly an organisation-wide filing system. Your own filing system will need to be clear, both to help you and also so that people can easily find files when you are on holiday or off sick.

In order to manage and use filing systems you need to understand:

- *different types of filing systems*
- *how to find files*
- *what procedures to follow in updating and storing files.*

Filing systems

There are different types of filing systems, including **alphabetical**, **numerical** and **chronological**. Large filing systems usually have indexing systems which you will need to understand and may need to update. You will also need to learn how to keep an effective, efficient and tidy system as well as knowing when to report problems and who to report them to.

• *Types of filing system* •

The three main types of filing system are alphabetical, numerical and chronological (date order). In addition files may be temporary (sometimes known as 'working') or permanent (sometimes known as 'archival'). Working files will usually be labelled for a specific purpose or function, such as 'Marketing' or 'Customer feedback'.

Alphabetical

Alphabetical filing systems are often used for customer or employee records. An alphabetical system runs from **A** through to **Z** in order. When filing using individual names, you use the surname first. For example:

- *Dobson, Michael*
- *Evans, Thomas*
- *Haynes, Anne*
- *Lalwani, Gayatri*
- *Martin, Jane*
- *Oliver, William*
- *Wang, Yi*

Where there is more than one person with the same surname, you then use the first name. For example:

- *Harrison, Elizabeth*
- *Harrison, John*
- *Harrison, Peter*
- *Harrison, William*

Occasionally, there may be identical first names and surnames. When this happens, file by second name (or initial if the full second name is not known). For example:

- *Brown, Carole F*
- *Brown, Carole Joanne*
- *Brown, Carole W*
- *Brown, Carole Z*

GIVE IT A GO: filing

1 Write the following names in the correct alphabetical order:
David Roberts
D Roberts
D B Roberts

2 Write the following names of hotels in the correct alphabetical order:
The Red Dragon Hotel, Oxford
The Red Dragon Hotel, Henley
The Red Dragon Hotel, Guildford
The Seven Lakes Hotel, Ipswich
The Seven Lakes Hotel, Brentwood
The Quality Hotel, Isle of Wight

3 Write the following names in the correct alphabetical order:
Paul Hull
Darren G Hand
Elizabeth V Hand
Susan Thomson
Patricia Mayo
Julie Allan
Jack Dixon

4 Which name would be filed first in the following pairs of names?

James Wood	James Woods
Thomas Jones	T P Jones
Mary Machin	Martin Machin
William Smith	William Smithe
Robert Smith	Robert Smithers

Numerical

Numerical filing might be used for employee or customer identification codes, for example:

- *1309*

- *1310*

- *1311*

- *1312*

Some numerical systems may be more complicated than this, using codes made up of different numbers, for example:

- *01-555-987*

- *01-567-012*

- *02-139-923*

- *10-098-398*

In this case you take the first number and file under that. If there is more than one file with the same first number, you then move to the second number and so on.

Where complicated filing systems are used, you should be provided with instructions and/or training in using the system. Make sure you keep notes on the system, so that you do not make mistakes.

Chronological (date order)

Chronological systems file in date order and are often used for financial documents such as invoices and receipts. In chronological files, the most recent documents are usually kept closest to the front. For example:

- 11 June 2005
- 3 June 2005
- 30 March 2005
- 3 February 2005
- 12 December 2004

• Indexes •

Large and complex filing systems, such as archives of older documents, will often have indexes. These indexes make it easy for files to be located without having to look through many boxes or cabinets. Indexes could be **computerised**, use index cards or be kept in folders. If you need to use or update complex filing systems as part of your job role you should receive instructions and/or training in how the index works.

• Effective, efficient and tidy systems •

It is very important for administrators to keep filing systems working well and to keep them tidy. Below are some tips on how to do this, but you will probably come up with your own strategies as you progress in your job role.

Tips for managing filing systems

- *Rough-sort your filing into orderly piles, according to which filing system they need to go in.*
- *Take a pile at a time and sort it according to the system. Start by splitting it into smaller piles, then sort each smaller pile into smaller piles, until you can easily file the documents.*
- *Make sure all documents or folders within a system are clearly labelled.*

● *When you take a folder out, make sure you put it back in the correct place. It can be useful to put a placeholder where the folder goes so that you can put it back quickly. It is also useful to say on the placeholder what the folder is and who has it, so that someone else looking for that folder will know where to go.*

● *Set aside specific times during the day to do your filing. This will help you keep on top of it and stop large piles of filing from building up on your desk.*

● *When you put new items into a folder, check older items to see if they are still needed. You might need to archive them, or you may be able to shred them or throw them out.*

● *Make sure that documents are placed neatly in their folders and are hole punched where necessary.*

● *Make sure labelling is clearly readable (e.g. you could use a word processor to create the labels).*

▲ **Filing systems must be well organised**

● *Potential problems* ●

It is important to deal with problems yourself wherever possible. If you cannot sort out the problem then discuss it with your line manager who should be able to help. Examples of filing problems that could occur include:

● *items that do not fit into any category or system*

● *folders becoming too full*

● *cabinets becoming too full*

● *items going missing*

● *items being filed in the wrong place.*

Finding files

You need to know the different filing systems you use very well in order to be able to quickly find a file you need or that has been requested. The process of finding files can include:

● *following the correct procedure to find and remove a file*

● *keeping files and their contents safe and intact*

⊃ *passing the file to the right person*

⊃ *meeting deadlines*

⊃ *keeping confidentiality.*

● *Using the correct procedure to find/remove a file* ●

Departmental and organisation-wide filing systems will usually have procedures set up for removing files from the system. There may also be procedures to follow for finding files, such as an index system (see page 246).

In many filing systems it is necessary to put a placeholder in to replace the file or folder that has been removed. This placeholder will need to say which file or folder has been removed, when it was removed, who it was removed by and where it can be found. There may be other procedures to follow and it is important to keep to these carefully.

● *Keeping the file and its contents safe and intact* ●

It is essential to keep files safe and intact when they are out of the filing system. This means, for example, keeping all documents within a folder inside the folder and not letting them get out of order. It is usually the administrator's responsibility to keep track of the file and it may be necessary to chase members of staff to return the file.

● *Passing the file to the correct person* ●

It is important to make sure that the right person gets the file. This is particularly important for files that contain confidential or sensitive information, but also for other files. It is useful to keep a notebook that records who has requested which files and when you retrieved them from the filing system. When you have given it to the correct person you should note this down and also make a note of when the file needs to be returned to the system.

● *Meeting deadlines for file handling* ●

As with all administrative tasks it is important to keep to deadlines for file handling. When you receive a request for a file, you should make sure you are told when the person needs it. As with other tasks, it is useful to keep a notebook of the deadlines for everything you need to do, splitting tasks up into short-term, medium-term and long-term. As well as retrieving files by the deadline it may also be necessary to ensure that they are returned by a deadline. This may involve chasing members of staff to give the file back to you.

• *Maintaining confidentiality* •

Maintaining confidentiality is essential in all administrative tasks, but especially so for filing. Some documents and files may contain confidential or sensitive data, such as personal information about employees or customers. Only authorised people will be allowed to see confidential or sensitive files and it is essential to ensure that no-one else sees these files.

Confidential and sensitive information will usually be kept locked away with limited numbers of people having keys. You should keep a list of who is authorised to see confidential files and check this list every time you receive a request for one of them.

If confidential or sensitive documents are no longer needed it is important to shred them, so that the information cannot be found, either accidentally or on purpose, by **unauthorised** personnel or people outside the organisation.

▲ **Sensitive information should be kept confidential**

WHAT if?

... *someone gossiped about you?*

1 How would you feel if your best friend told another friend a secret you had told him or her?
2 How would you feel if a colleague told another colleague about a disciplinary action that was being taken against you?
3 How would you feel if the receptionist at your GP surgery told your mother about a confidential medical matter?
4 How would you feel if a business sold your personal data to another business without your permission?

Updating files

In order for records to be useful, they must be up to date and accurate. Updating files includes:

▱ *carefully following instructions and guidelines*

▱ *adding new items*

GLOSSARY

Unauthorised means without permission.

- *making sure files and their contents are complete*
- *keeping confidentiality*
- *meeting deadlines for file handling.*

• *Following instructions* •

It is important to follow procedures, instructions and guidelines when updating files. This will ensure that everyone can find the files they need when they need to. Instructions could include:

- *the correct filing system to use*
- *when records need to be **purged** (removed and archived or destroyed)*
- *how records should be stored.*

• *Adding new items* •

When adding new items you may need to:

- *add an entry to the file index*
- *remove older entries to keep the folder or cabinet from getting too full*
- *start a new folder.*

Make sure that you keep to any procedures or guidelines when adding new items to a filing system.

• *Making sure the file and its contents are complete* •

When you add new items, remove items at someone's request or replace items that have been removed you need to check that the file and the contents of the file are complete. If anything is missing you will need to chase up the last person who used the file for the missing contents. If you are unable to find the missing item, you will need to report this to the appropriate person, for example, your line manager.

You should also check that everything within the file is in the correct order and is not damaged in any way.

◯ THINK ABOUT IT

Think about the problems that could occur if documents went missing. What could you do to prevent these problems happening in the first place? What would you do to deal with problems if they did occur?

• *Maintaining confidentiality* •

When updating files it is essential to make sure that documents are kept confidential where necessary (see page 249). Make sure that you understand all the procedures for **maintaining** confidentiality in your organisation and that you follow them carefully. If in any doubt, ask your line manager for advice.

• *Meeting deadlines for file handling* •

As with all administrative tasks, you need to ensure you meet deadlines for updating files. See pages 231 and 234 for tips on how to manage your time and your workload to ensure that you are able to meet deadlines.

Storing files

When working with filing systems it is important to pay attention to how files are stored. This could include:

⏩ *storing files safely*

⏩ *following correct procedures*

⏩ *maintaining confidentiality*

⏩ *meeting deadlines for file handling.*

• *Safe storage* •

Files need to be stored safely, so that they do not get damaged. Files are often kept in strong metal filing cabinets that would keep the files protected in cases of fire or flooding. Some tips for safe storage include:

⏩ *keep file handling to a minimum*

⏩ *do not store files in direct sunlight*

⏩ *files that are not kept in cabinets should be stored off the floor in case of flooding*

⏩ *when files are not being stored keep them on desks or drawers and not on the floor.*

• *Correct procedures* •

As with other filing tasks, it is important to follow the organisation's procedures for storage of files. There may be different procedures for each filing system, or for different types of document or item. For example, transparencies and photographs will need to be stored in special protective containers or folders. As with other procedures, make sure that you fully understand them and ask your line manager if you are unsure of anything.

> **GLOSSARY**
>
> **Maintaining** means keeping, or keeping in good repair.

GIVE IT A GO: storing files

1 Visit a business in your local area.
2 Find out what the procedures are for storing files.
3 Are there different procedures for different types of file?

• *Maintaining confidentiality* •

Procedures for storing confidential and sensitive information will usually be different for the storage of other files. It is essential to follow these very carefully.

Confidential files should be stored in a secure place, such as a locked filing cabinet or a safe. Only **authorised** personnel should have keys to these storage facilities. (See pages 249 and 251 for more information about confidentiality in relation to handling files.)

• *Meeting deadlines for file handling* •

As with all administrative tasks, you need to ensure you meet deadlines for updating files. See pages 231 and 234 for tips on how to manage your time and your workload to ensure that you are able to meet deadlines. When storing confidential and sensitive files, there may be specific limits to how long a file can be out of storage. It is essential to keep to these deadlines. In some organisations security measures may come into place if a file has been out of secure storage for longer than the set amount of time. This could mean that you or the person who requested the file could be disciplined.

EVIDENCE ACTIVITY   P3

Find, update and store files

Describe the techniques you would use to:
a find files in a paper-based filing system
b update files in a paper-based filing system
c store files in a paper-based filing system.

Enter and find data

Many job roles within administration involve entering and finding data. This usually refers to entering and finding data (e.g. text and numbers) in databases or spreadsheets, although technically document preparation could also be considered as data entry.

Enter data

If your job role includes data entry this may involve:

87854659	Part A		
78583628	Part B		
83466266	Part C		
17289273	Part D		

▲ **Data entry is an administrative role**

- ▱ *knowing and understanding the purpose for entering the data*
- ▱ *understanding the different types of data*
- ▱ *following clear instructions*
- ▱ *making sure the data is entered accurately*
- ▱ *identifying and correcting errors*
- ▱ *seeking help where necessary*
- ▱ *understanding and using reference codes*
- ▱ *deleting and amending existing data*
- ▱ *making sure the work is finished*
- ▱ *keeping to deadlines and schedules.*

● *Purpose of entering data* ●

There are many different reasons for entering data. Some examples include entering sales figures, entering information into medical records or employee records. Although it is possible to enter data without knowing the purpose, you will find it much easier and will make fewer mistakes if you do understand the data and the reason it needs to be entered.

Your line manager may be able to give you more information about the purpose of entering the data or you could ask the person who has given you the task. It is not necessary to understand it in great detail – for example, if you are entering medical information, you do not need to be a doctor. However, it is useful to have some background information.

• *Types of data* •

There are different types of data that may need to be entered and these will be either words or numbers – or a combination of the two.

Words

There are many different types of **text** (words) data that may need entering. Examples include:

- *names*
- *addresses*
- *product names*
- *accessory names*
- *job titles.*

Numbers

There is much data that can be represented in **numerical** (number) form. Examples include:

- *age*
- *shoe size*
- *number of brothers and sisters*
- *number of rooms in a building*
- *number of students in a class or school*
- *prices of products.*

Combinations of text and numbers

Some data will be a combination of text and numbers, especially codes (see page 257), for example:

- *product codes*
- *employment codes*
- *customer identification codes*
- *tax codes.*

The type of data will affect how you choose to enter the data. Most of the time you will be using a keyboard to enter data, although sometimes it may involve, for example, scanning documents into a computer. For numerical data it is usually best to use the keypad on the right-hand side of the keyboard. For text data you will need to use the main keyboard. For combined text and numbers it may be best to use the main keyboard (and use the numbers on this keyboard); however for some data it might be possible to use a combination of the main keyboard and the keypad.

● *Following clear instructions* ●

As with all administrative tasks it is important to follow any instructions, guidelines and training that you are given. When you start in a data entry role, you should be given thorough training in how to use the relevant software.

In addition, for each new data entry task you are asked to do, you should be provided with clear instructions on what needs to be done. For example, any codes should be explained to you as well as how the paper-based documents you are taking the data from relate to the fields in the software. Sometimes you may need to refer to a number of documents. For example, you could be entering data from supplier invoices and need to look up the supplier's code, purchase order codes and authorisation codes which are not on the invoice itself.

It is a good idea to take notes of any training or instructions you are given. You will then be able to check your notes whenever you are unsure of anything.

● *Accuracy* ●

It is very important to ensure that you are accurate in your data entry. This may mean spending a bit more time on the tasks, but in the long run it will save time, because there will be fewer mistakes to correct. Correcting mistakes is more time-consuming than getting it right in the first place. In some data tasks errors could have serious effects. For example, errors in data entry for a finance department could mean employees get paid the wrong amount of money. Errors in medical data entry could mean someone becomes seriously ill, or even dies.

● *Identifying/correcting errors* ●

As the person doing the data entry, it will be your responsibility to identify any mistakes you have made and correct them. Many databases are set up so that only valid data can be entered. For example, in a field where you enter a code, it may be impossible to enter one that does not fit the specific structure of the code. However, it is important not to rely entirely on the software to check for you (in the same way you cannot rely entirely on the spellchecker when preparing documents). For example, in entering the following code:

PD-89-01-FH-76

you might get some of the numbers the wrong way round:

PD-98-01-FH-67

This would probably still be a valid code, but it would be the wrong one.

A lot of software offers the opportunity to check the data you have entered before you submit it. It is important to take full advantage of this. For each record you enter check each piece of data (or field) immediately after entering it; check each record when you have completed it and before submitting it. After completing the data entry task (or after entering a certain number of records), if possible, go through and check all the data you entered.

GIVE IT A GO: identifying errors

Look at each of the records below to see if any errors have been made in the data entry.

1 *Original:*
National Insurance number: WM-22-29-01-Z
Name: Horatio Hartzenburg
Case number: 56-270
Entered data:
National Insurance number: WM-22-20-91-2
Name: Horatio Horatio Hartzenburg
Case number: 56-270

2 *Original:*
National Insurance number: BF-36-85-90-L
Name: Rossevelt Greer
Case number: 44-376
Entered data:
National Insurance number: BF-36-89-50-L
Name: Rossevelt Green
Case number: 44-367

3 *Original:*
National Insurance number: TD-44-34-12-C
Name: Rosemary
Case number: 33-876
Entered data:
National Insurance number: TD-44-43-12-C
Name: Rosemarie
Case number: 33-876

• *Seeking assistance where necessary* •

In some cases, you may find a mistake after you have submitted it and may not have permission to change the data. It is important, in this situation, to tell your line manager (or the database manager) where and what the mistake is, so that it can be corrected.

Whenever you are unsure of anything, check your notes first. Then check any guidelines or other printed instructions you have been given. If you cannot find the information you need, then you should ask your line manager or the person who gave you the task. Never guess as this could cause serious problems if you guess wrong.

◀ **Don't be afraid to ask for advice**

• *Reference codes* •

Codes are used for lots of different things within businesses. For example:

- *product codes*
- *supplier codes*
- *tax codes*
- *customer codes*
- *purchase order codes*
- *invoice codes.*

Codes are used to identify records (or pieces of data). They are particularly useful where there are a number of people or companies with the same or similar names. Having a **unique** code can help with finding data.

> **GLOSSARY**
>
> **Unique** means one of a kind.

It is very likely that you will need to enter some codes as part of your data entry tasks. It is important to know and understand the format of the codes. If you understand them, you will find it much easier to enter them without making mistakes.

● *Deleting/amending existing data* ●

It may be part of your data entry role to delete entries in a database or make amendments. For example, you might need to delete customers' details when they die or amend them when they move house.

It is essential to be very careful when deleting or amending data. You need to make sure that you have correctly identified the record that needs to be altered or deleted. If you were to delete or change the wrong record, this could have serious effects. For example, if you were to delete the wrong employee's record they might not get paid. If the instructions you have been given are not clear, then you need to check with the person who gave you the task. Never guess when deleting or amending data.

● *Completing data entry* ●

It is essential to make sure that you complete all your data entry tasks. This involves:

▭ *making sure you enter each piece of data (or field) for each record*

▭ *making sure you enter every record you have been given*

▭ *making sure you submit the data when you have finished entering it (where relevant)*

▭ *making sure you save the file (where relevant).*

● *Agreed timescales for data entry* ●

As with all administrative tasks, it is important to keep to the deadlines that you have been given. Many data entry tasks will be time-sensitive. For example, entering records of invoices from suppliers will need to be done in time for them to be paid by the correct date. Changing address information as soon as possible is important to reduce the risk of mail not reaching the people it is for. (See pages 231 and 234 for some tips on managing your time and workload.)

Finding data

As well as entering data, your role may include finding data. To do so well you will need to:

▭ *understand why the data is needed*

▭ *follow the instructions correctly*

▭ *understand and make use of different search methods, according to the task*

▭ *keep to deadlines*

▭ *seek assistance when necessary*

▭ *print records or data reports.*

• *Purpose of finding data* •

There are many reasons why a business may need to find data, for example:

▭ *for market research (e.g. to see what types of customers buy which products and how often; to understand customer needs)*

▭ *to analyse financial information (e.g. to forecast future sales and profits)*

▭ *to conduct marketing activities (e.g. address details for specific customers so that leaflets or brochures can be sent out)*

▭ *to find all details on a specific client (e.g. for a manager who is meeting with this client).*

Although it may be possible to find data without knowing the purpose, it will be a lot easier to do so if you know what the data is for. The person who gave you the task should have given you this information, but you can ask for more explanation if necessary. Alternatively you can ask your line manager to give you background on the different types of data-finding tasks you may need to do in your job role.

• *Following clear instructions* •

When you start working in a role that involves finding data, you should be given training in how to use the relevant software. Make sure that you keep detailed notes of the different features of the software, including different methods that can be used for searching for data.

It is also important to make notes on any instructions you are given about the data you need to look for. If you do not understand any of the instructions it is important to ask for more information. For example, you might be asked to find all customers between the age of 25 and 30. You would probably want to check whether this should include people aged 25 and aged 30, or whether it should just include people aged 26, 27, 28 and 29.

• *Efficient/effective search methods* •

Different pieces of software will have different search facilities. For example, there may be a *Find* facility which allows you to search for any record containing a specific word. Well set up databases will have a thorough search facility that allows you to look for specific text or numbers in specific fields as well as performing complex searches. These search facilities allow you to perform **automatic searches**.

GLOSSARY

Automatic searches are searches for text or numbers carried out by the computer.

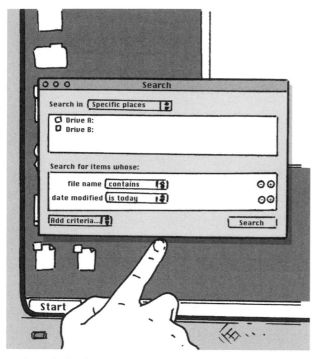

▲ **Search facilities are very useful**

GLOSSARY

Manual searches require you to do the search yourself (e.g. by hand).

Search criteria are conditions, elements or characteristics of data (e.g. all customers aged over 50 and who live in Scotland).

When you start work in a job role that involves finding data, you should be provided with training in the different search facilities available in the software you will be using. As with all training and instructions you are given you should make sure that you keep detailed notes to refer back to when necessary.

You may sometimes need to perform **manual searches**, for example, when the search facility does not allow you to enter details specific enough to the data you need to find. To perform a manual search, you need to browse through the records in the system and look at each record to see if it is relevant to the search.

Manual searches will usually take longer than automatic ones and it is possible you may miss some records or accidentally extract ones that do not fit the purpose. Manual searches may be relevant in cases where there are very few records to browse through, though. For example, it might take longer to key in the **search criteria** than browse through the records yourself.

CASE STUDY – NADEEN AND JONES ESTATE AGENTS

Our filing system

We use filing cabinets to hold information about the properties for sale (e.g. number of bedrooms, garden size, price, etc.). Each property has a file with all the details in it on different forms and pieces of paper. The files are organised by area. Staff sometimes find it difficult to find houses for people who specify criteria other than area (e.g. price, number of rooms, age of house, etc.). Some staff keep lists of houses that have a certain

number of bedrooms, that are within a certain price range and so on. But not all staff do this.

Questions

1 Identify the problems with *Nadeen and Jones Estate Agents'* information system.

2 Can you make any suggestions for improving the system and making it easier to find and update information?

● *Agreed timescales for finding data* ●

As with other administrative tasks you will need to keep to agreed schedules or deadlines when finding data. For example, managers may ask you to find data immediately for a client phone call they are making or they might need data for a meeting later that day or the next day. It is essential to ensure that you complete the tasks on time.

As you progress in your role, you will come to know which search methods are better for different types of data-finding tasks. Keeping detailed notes about the different methods will help you to perform your tasks more quickly. (See pages 231 and 234 for some general tips on managing your time and workload.)

● *Seeking assistance where necessary* ●

Whenever you are unsure about a task, you should first check your own notes. If these do not help then check any manuals or guidelines you have been given. If you cannot find the information you need or if time is very tight, then you should ask a colleague or your line manager for help. Do not be embarrassed about asking for help. Everyone needs to ask for help at some time and it is better to do so than to waste time and end up extracting the wrong data.

● *Printing data* ●

When finding data, you will often need to print this out for the person who requested it. Many databases allow you to print data in different ways and you will need to select the most appropriate method, for example:

▷ *print out each record in its entirety (more relevant when a few records are needed – e.g. a manager needs the records of two suppliers to decide which one to order from)*

▷ *print out a report of the selected records (more relevant when details of many records are needed – e.g. a manager needs the addresses of all customers who have bought more than five products – this method allows you to print only certain information for each record)*

▷ *print out a graph or chart of data (this can be relevant for financial data – e.g. for a sales manager to show increases or decreases in sales at a sales conference).*

Once you have selected the data you are going to print and what method you will use, you need to make sure that you select the correct printer and that there is enough paper and toner to complete the whole printout. Where printers are shared with other colleagues and you are printing a large number of pages, it is a good idea to check that no-one has anything more urgent to print. For example, if it is nearing the end of the day, your colleagues may be printing out urgent letters that need to get in the mail. You might be able to leave your printing until the morning, when the printer should be less busy. Of course, you should only do so if it will not cause you to miss the deadline.

When the printing is finished you should check to ensure all the records have been printed out and that there are no errors before you pass it on to the person who requested the data.

EVIDENCE ACTIVITY

Enter and find data

Note: To complete this unit you need to provide evidence of practical experience in a number of administration tasks. If you already have a job in administration, you should be able to use your work to provide evidence. If you do not have a job in administration, then it would be useful to arrange a work-experience placement in an office. If this is not possible your teacher or tutor may be able to provide equipment and material for you to use to produce the evidence.

Describe the techniques you would use to:
a enter data in a computerised system
b find data in a computerised system.

END OF UNIT ASSIGNMENT

Task 1 P1

1 Provide evidence of preparing a simple document according to instructions (e.g. a business letter, fax or memo). Explain the steps you took to carry out the task.

2 Provide evidence of photocopying a simple document according to instructions. Explain the steps you took to carry out the task.

Task 2 P2

1 Provide evidence of sorting mail. Explain the steps you took to carry out the task.

2 Provide evidence of distributing mail. Explain the steps you took to carry out the task.

3 Provide evidence of dispatching mail. Explain the steps you took to carry out the task.

Task 3 P3

1 Provide evidence of finding paper-based files in a filing system. Explain the steps you took to carry out the task.

2 Provide evidence of updating paper-based files in a filing system. Explain the steps you took to carry out the task.

3 Provide evidence of storing paper-based files in a filing system. Explain the steps you took to carry out the task.

Task 4 P4

1 Provide evidence of entering data into a computerised system. Explain the steps you took to carry out the task.

2 Provide evidence of finding data in a computerised system. Explain the steps you took to carry out the task.

Task 5 M1 M2 D1

1 Describe a situation in the workplace where you have shown confidence in your work and worked on your own (without help from a supervisor or colleague) to fulfil a major task. Provide evidence such as a witness statement.

2 Using your own words explain the importance of keeping documents, mail, files and computer data safe and secure at all times.

3 List the different skills which you use in your administration work.

4 For each skill, describe a situation where you have used the skill on your own (without being prompted by a supervisor or tutor). (Provide evidence such as a witness statement from your supervisor.)

Glossary

accounting dealing with a business's finances and book-keeping

accurate correct

acknowledge admit, accept

acquaintances people you know and who know you

addressee person to whom a piece of mail is being sent

administration general tasks involved in running an office

agenda list of items that are to be discussed in a meeting

aim plan, goal, desire, target

alphabetical in order of the alphabet (a to z)

alternative different

analysis looking at or studying something

appearance what something or someone looks like

appraisal meeting with a line manager to discuss performance and goals

appropriate fit for the purpose or situation

assertiveness standing up for oneself

assistance help

authorised with permission

automatic using a computer or other piece of equipment

automatic searches searches for text or numbers carried out by the computer

BACS method of paying individuals and businesses electronically

basic pay pay before overtime or bonuses

beneficial helpful, of use

benefits additional services on top of pay (employment); money from the government for people who do not have enough money to survive (unemployment)

bereavement when a family member or close friend has died

biodegradable will rot and become part of the earth

body language non-verbal language such as smiling, nodding and gesturing

bonuses extra money received on top of pay

budget amount of money available for a task or project (business); to look at how much money you have coming in and decide what you can afford to pay for different things (personal)

cashback getting cash from a cashier when you pay for a purchase using a debit card (like using a cash machine)

chronological in date order

clarify explain, make clearer, simplify

colleagues people you work with

commitment promise, duty or obligation

commuting travelling to work (especially over long distances)

compulsory necessary, must be done

computerised using a computer system

conclusion what you decide about something

confidential private, secret, classified

confirm show you understand

consequences results of an action

conserving saving

consistent the same throughout (e.g. consistent service is providing the same level of service to everyone)

constructed built

consumer the person who uses a product or service (not always the person who buys it – e.g. children are consumers of toys, but their parents probably buy them)

contractor someone brought in to an organisation to do a specific task and who will no longer work there when the task is finished

convenient fitting, suitable

convention custom, habit, tradition

core function main thing that an organisation does (e.g. the core function of a car manufacturer is to make cars)

courtesy politeness (e.g. saying 'please' and 'thank you' and showing respect and fairness to others)

criteria conditions, elements or characteristics of data

customer service department which deals with customers, providing information and advice

deductions money taken off pay (e.g. tax, National Insurance, pension)

demonstration showing how to do or use something

deterioration gradual lessening of quality

deterrent something that puts someone off from doing something (e.g. security guards may be a deterrent to shoplifters)

disciplinary and grievance procedures procedures for dealing with unwanted or dangerous behaviour

discretion not sharing private information, not gossiping about others

dismiss to sack someone from their job, end their employment

dispatch send out

dispose of throw away (or put in recycling bin, etc.)

distribute send out to everyone who needs to receive the item

distribution department that deals with getting products to customers

documentation pieces of paper (e.g. with guidelines or procedures on)

domestic in the UK

dominate take over, control

donate give to (e.g. donating to charity)

dress code rules about how to dress

e-business business carried out electronically (e.g. using the Internet)

efficiency being able to get a job done well and on time

empower give power to

enthusiasm interest, being keen, wanting to do something

entitlement right, privilege (e.g. if you earn less than a certain amount of money you may be entitled to get money from the government)

evacuating emptying a building (or area)

expectation what is expected (e.g. your employer will expect you to come to work on time)

expenditure outgoings, spending

expenses outgoings, spending

exposure being close to something (e.g. exposure to some chemicals can cause illness or death)

external outside

face-to-face communication talking to someone in person

feature characteristic, element (e.g. features of a mobile phone might include a camera and polyphonic ring tones)

finance having to do with money; the department which deals with the organisation's spending and receipts

flexible able and willing to make changes

flexitime ability to start and finish work at different times (as long as agreed number of hours are worked)

float cash in a till (in different notes and coins) that allows cashiers to give customers change

franchise ready-made business that can be bought and where premises, goods and fittings may be provided on a regular basis

freelance self-employed person who does jobs for a number of different individuals or organisations (e.g. photographers, illustrators, web designers)

full-time working a full week (e.g. 9–5, Monday–Friday)

gestures hand and body movements that have meaning (e.g. nodding head, waving)

gross income money you earn before deductions (e.g. tax, National Insurance, pension)

hazard something that could cause harm

honesty being truthful and admitting to mistakes

human resources department that deals with employees (e.g. taking on new employees, training employees)

impression what you think of someone or something

income money coming in (e.g. earnings, interest from savings, state benefits)

induction training given to new employees when they start work in an organisation

inexhaustible without limit, endless

inheritance money or items left to you when someone dies

initiative working on your own (e.g. to solve problems, decide what work needs doing)

internal inside

internal customer colleagues and people in other departments

international worldwide

inter-personal skills skills for dealing with other people

intranet collection of web pages that are only accessible from within an organisation

job description details of the tasks and responsibilities involved in a job role

judgement what you think of something or someone

liaising dealing with, communicating with, talking to

limbs arms and legs

limited company company that has shareholders, a board of directors and employees

line manager the person to whom you report in your job role

location where something is

maintaining keeping, keeping in good repair

manageable possible to cope with (e.g. a manageable workload is where you can do all the tasks within the time available)

manual searches doing searches yourself (e.g. by hand)

manual skills skills that use your hands

manually using your hands (or not using any equipment)

manufacture make, create

marketing department that deals with publicity and finding out about customer needs

material pleasures items that you buy and that keep you happy (will be different for everyone, but could include televisions and stereos)

mentor someone who acts as a guide, teacher and advisor

merchandise things for sale

minimise reduce, lessen

minutes record of discussions and decisions made in a meeting

misinterpreted understood wrongly

mixed economy economy that includes private and public businesses

motivation wanting to do the job well and enjoying it

multi-national company a large business that operates in different parts of the world, for example, BP

negotiation discussing a problem or a sale until everyone agrees

net income money that you actually get after deductions (e.g. tax, National Insurance, pension)

non-routine needs needs that occur less often; unusual needs

numeracy skills skills with numbers (e.g. adding, subtracting, etc.)

numerical to do with numbers; in order of number (e.g. 1 to 1000)

objectives goals, plans, what you want or need to happen

observe watch something or someone

operative tasks involved with the core function of the business

oral communication spoken communication (includes listening)

overtime working extra hours on top of normal contracted hours

partnership two or more people running a business together

pension fund type of saving that will provide you with an income or lump sum after you retire

performance how good you are at doing your job

perishable may rot or go off (e.g. fruit and vegetables)

permanent no fixed time to end (e.g. permanent job)

personal audit studying the skills and qualifications you have and deciding where your strengths and weaknesses are

personal specifications description of characteristics, personality and skills needed for a job role

policy guidelines or rules

posture how you sit, stand or hold yourself

potential how far you could go in your career, what you could achieve

precautions strategies to guard against danger, risk, error

procedures steps that have been set out for specific tasks or situations (rules, guidelines)

production department which deals in making products

productive able to get lots of work done in the time available

profits money that is left over after a business has paid for materials, expenses, overheads and so on (i.e. money left over after everything has been paid for)

proprietor sole trader (the person who runs the business)

prosecuted taken to court

protective clothing clothing that protects against damage, harm or injury (e.g. gloves, safety glasses, hard hats)

proximity how near something is

punctuality being on time

purchases things that are being bought

purged cleared out

purpose reason for doing something; what something is used for

recipient the person receiving an item of mail

records written documents (or computerised data) that set down information (e.g. what has happened in an accident, details about an employee)

redundancy when a company needs to cut down on staff (often comes with a lump sum to make up for losing the job)

reimburse give money back; return payment

replenishing filling up (e.g. replenishing the kettle would be putting more water into it)

report usually a multi-page document that deals with a specific issue or subject

request ask for

resignation stating that you plan to leave your job

respond answer or fulfil a request

responsibility doing everything that you need to do and are expected to do

restructuring changing the structure or organisation (e.g. having fewer managers and more operatives)

risk something likely to cause harm

routine needs needs that occur often; common needs

rural set in the countryside or in a small village

salary amount of money you are paid each year (which is usually split into 12 monthly payments)

sales department which deals with selling products or services

schedule timetable

search criteria conditions, elements or characteristics of data (e.g. all customers aged over 50 and who live in Scotland)

sector distinct area of industry

self-employed someone who works for themselves, either running their own businesses or taking on a number of different jobs for different clients

sensitive could cause problems if it is discovered

shift-work working non-normal hours (e.g. 2pm to 10pm, 10pm to 6am); often involves working one shift for one week and then a different one the next week

simplify make clearer, easier to understand

skilled work work that requires some training and/or judgement

software a program on a computer (e.g. spreadsheet program, word-processing program, web browser)

sole trader single individual who owns and runs a business (e.g. small shops, plumbers)

statutory regulations rules and laws that have been set out by government

stock control keeping track of stock levels

stock rotation usually displaying older stock before newer stock

strategy plan, technique, method, way of doing something

superannuation pension

supervisor person who tells you what tasks you need to do and keeps an eye on you (and other staff) to make sure there are no problems

teamwork working with other people to complete a task or project

temporary work short-term work (e.g. over the summer holidays or for six months to cover maternity leave)

terms and conditions details of your rights and responsibilities within a contract

text words

time-management keeping on top of tasks; making sure you meet deadlines

transactions money changing hands (e.g. payment for goods or services)

transferable skills skills which can be used in all or most job roles (e.g. communication skills, IT skills, punctuality)

transferred moved from one place to another

transported moved from one place to another (usually refers to longer distances and moving goods using lorries or trains, for example)

tribunal a trial or hearing to find out if someone has done something wrong

unattended without anyone close by to keep an eye on it

unauthorised without permission

unique one of a kind

unskilled work work that involves little or no judgement and only simple tasks

urban in a town or city

verbal communication communication that uses language (usually refers to spoken communication and includes listening)

vocational to do with work (vocational skills are skills for work)

voluntary work working without pay (e.g. for a charity)

wages money you get for doing a job (usually paid weekly)

withdraw take out (e.g. money from bank account)

written communication communication that is put down on paper or in electronic format and uses words

Index

Page numbers in **bold** indicate a key term, page numbers in *italics* indicate illustrations and diagrams.